Hegemony and Power

Hegemony and Power

On the Relation between Gramsci and Machiavelli

Benedetto Fontana

University of Minnesota Press

Minneapolis

London

Published by the University of Minnesota Press
2037 University Avenue Southeast, Minneapolis, MN 55455-3092
Printed in the United States of America on acid-free paper

Library of Congress Cataloging-in-Publication Data

Fontana, Benedetto.
    Hegemony and power : on the relation between Gramsci and Machiavelli / Benedetto Fontana.
        p. cm.
    Includes bibliographical references and index.
    ISBN 0-8166-2135-7 (alk. paper).
    ISBN 0-8166-2136-5 (pbk. : alk. paper)
    1. Gramsci, Antonio, 1891-1937. 2. Machiavelli, Niccolò,
1469-1527—Influence. 3. Communism—Italy—History—20th
century. I. Title.
HX289.7.G73F66   1993
320.5'32'0945—dc20   93-10166
                                            CIP

Contents

Contents

Preface

Machiavelli is central to Antonio Gramsci's thought. When, after the Second World War, Felice Platone and Palmiro Togliatti published for the first time Gramsci's *Prison Notebooks* in a thematically organized edition of six volumes, one was entitled *Note sul Machiavelli, sulla politica e sullo Stato moderno*. Gramsci himself, of course, devoted two notebooks specifically to Machiavelli (notebooks 13 and 18 of Valentino Gerratana's critical edition of the *Quaderni del carcere*). In addition, a selection of Gramsci's writings first appeared in English translation in an edition titled *The Modern Prince*. Quite naturally, therefore, a great many scholars and students, beginning with the appearance of Platone's edition and extending up to quite recent times, have dealt with Gramsci's interpretation of Machiavelli and its relation to Gramsci's thought. Yet there have been few book-length works dedicated specifically or exclusively to Gramsci's relation to Machiavelli. None, moreover, are in English. I have written this study, therefore, as a modest attempt to remedy the situation.

Certainly, today's "new order" is as far removed from Gramsci's *ordine nuovo* as his politics are light years distant from Soviet and Stalinist politics. Yet I hope that this study, in an age when some are prophesying the "end of history" and others are talking about the "end of politics," will, in a small way, contribute to the discussion regarding the vitality and centrality of politics.

My intellectual debts are many, and I am very happy to acknowledge them. Since my undergraduate days, Professors Martin Fleisher and the late Richard A. Styskal have combined the roles of teacher, scholar, and friend, and this book is in large measure a reflection of my association with them. I would also like to acknowledge the influence of Professor Marshall Berman, whose scholarship and intellectual integrity have never failed to inspire me.

I am grateful to a most "worthy pioneer" in Gramscian studies in the United States, Professor John Cammett, who read the manuscript, and who made many helpful and penetrating suggestions, thereby making the book a better study than it would otherwise have been.

Thanks are also due to Professors Stanley Aronowitz and Joseph A. Buttigieg, who not only read the manuscript and supplied useful comments, but also encouraged me to pursue the project, and who thus helped to get the manuscript published. In addition, I am grateful for the commentary and criticism of Professor Pellegrino d'Acierno.

Finally, I am very pleased to acknowledge the support and encouragement provided me by the members of the Political Science department of Baruch College of the City University of New York. With their courtesy, collegiality, and scholarship, they have shown an intellectual sympathy and stimulation which, to me, have always seemed reminiscent of the humanistic ideals of the Italian Renaissance. Most especially, I would like to thank Professors Thomas Halper, Howard Lentner, Mitchell Cohen, and Douglas Muzzio.

In addition, I thank my editor at the University of Minnesota Press, Biodun Iginla, for having seen promising possibilities in the project. With his editorial expertise, patience, and dedication, he has guided the project to a successful conclusion. Ms. Kerry Sarnoski and Ms. Elizabeth Stomberg, Minnesota's editorial assistants, were very helpful, kind, and considerate.

I cannot end without expressing my deep and profound gratitude for the material and intellectual assistance of Ms. Doris Suarez, who graciously read and incisively commented on the manuscript, and who urged and helped me to pursue this project.

Chapter 1

Introduction
Gramsci and Machiavelli

The purpose of this book is twofold: it will argue that the Gramscian interpretation of Machiavelli as the "democratic philosopher" and the "Italian Luther" is the vehicle through which he elaborates a fundamental and radical critique of bourgeois and liberal thought as expressed in Italy by the idealist philosophy of Benedetto Croce; and, it will further argue that such an interpretation identifies Machiavellian thought as an "anticipation" or "prefiguration" of Gramsci's notion of hegemony.[1]

Interpreters of Gramsci have rightly noted that his political philosophy is fundamentally humanist—or rather, as he himself puts it, "neohumanist." Human beings, for Gramsci, are not "givens" whose nature is immutable and fixed: they are not "essences" whose existence is already determined. They are a "becoming," ineradicably rooted in the historical process. Indeed, human beings are history, both as actors who through their practical activities make history, and as thinkers who contemplate themselves in history.[2] Gramsci's political theory, therefore, is a discourse on the genesis and formation of the historical subject. It is precisely this view of "political agents" who posit themselves and create themselves in and through historical action that led Gramsci to reject contemporary interpretations of Marxism, which he criticized as mechanistic and deterministic.[3] In such a view of Marxism, he believed, the historical subject is suppressed, and is· no longer seen as an active agent, but rather as a passive object at the mercy of historical contingency and economic forces. In this respect, Gramsci attempted to rescue Marxism from the determinist and revisionist encrustations with which the Second International

2   had surrounded it.[4] Thus his theoretical and political positions were developed and formulated in reaction to a Marxism he perceived to have lost its revolutionary and critical core.[5]

Most of the literature on Gramsci subscribes to this view, and it attempts to discover and identify the theoretical, political, and historical conditions that may have influenced Gramsci in his project to reconstruct a revolutionary political theory from his critique of the Marxism of the Second International (noteworthy are the essays found in *Studi Gramsciani*, *Gramsci e la cultura contemporanea*, *La città futura*, as well as the works by Salvadori, Nardone, Cammett, and Piccone).[6] On the other hand, when it comes to the problem of specifically identifying the nature and sources of Gramsci's theoretical work—especially on the question of hegemony—agreement ceases and a veritable plethora of antagonistic interpretations prevails throughout the field of Gramscian studies. Moreover, as is the case with many other political thinkers whose works have had a profound influence that extends beyond the thought and life of their contemporaries, Gramsci's writings became the source through which the postwar politics of the Italian Communists could be theoretically justified and ideologically, legitimated. They have also become the political and ideological weapons used by disparate groups in and outside Italy in their struggle for power.

But whether the literature is critical, ideological, or simply historical, there seem to be as many views on Gramsci as there are interpreters. Batteries of quotations and references gleaned here and there from Gramsci's works have been amassed to support this or that interpretation: the Crocean or Hegelian Gramsci, the Leninist Gramsci, the Jacobin Gramsci, the democratic-spontaneist Gramsci, the voluntarist Gramsci, and so on ad nauseam.[7]

It is possible, however, to classify the literature on Gramscian thought into three major schools of interpretation. There is, first, an orthodox or Leninist school that views Gramsci as a Leninist who translates the Bolshevik experience in Russia into the different conditions obtaining in Italy. Here Gramsci is the Italian Bolshevik who amplified and deepened the theoretical work of Lenin and who enriched it with his knowledge of Italian culture and history. Such writers as Togliatti, Spriano, Macciocchi, Buci-Glucksman, Ottino, Anderson, and Cammett are representatives of this school.[8] In effect, they equate Gramsci's *egemonia* with Lenin's dictatorship of the proletariat. A second group of interpreters includes basically anti-Marxist writers (such as Nardone, H. S. Hughes, and Lichtheim) who see Gramsci (especially in his notion of hegemony as an all-encompassing conception of the world) as a typical Marxist totalitarian.[9] It is interesting to note that **3** both of these schools, though issuing from different intellectual traditions and having different theoretical concerns, nevertheless converge in their view that Gramsci is a Leninist. The third school occupies a middle position between the first two. These authors (such as Williams, Matteucci, Garin, Bobbio, Piccone, Davidson, and the contributors to *La città futura*) assert that Gramsci has made an original contribution to Marxist revolutionary thought, and deny that he represents a mere Italian version of Leninism. In general, this school stresses the moment of consent and moral-intellectual leadership (that is, hegemony) in Gramsci's thought, and at the same time deemphasizes or neglects the moment of force or domination (dictatorship).

Although many studies of Gramsci (representing all three schools of thought) have noted the role that Machiavelli assumes in Gramsci's project to formulate a Marxist revolutionary political theory, and although there is a voluminous literature on the relation between Gramsci and Machiavelli,[10] few have analyzed the Machiavellian writings as a source for some of the Gramscian concepts or compared the two thinkers in such a way as to bring to life the Machiavellian text in the context of Gramsci's major theoretical and political concerns found in his *Quaderni del carcere*.[11] All three schools of interpretation point out the importance of Machiavelli's notion of the "new prince" to Gramsci's concept of the revolutionary party: what determines the political and theoretical attitude of each school to Gramsci's transformation of the Machiavellian prince into the "modern prince" represented by the revolutionary communist party depends upon the position taken by each interpreter regarding the question of Gramsci's Leninism or totalitarianism.[12]

The liberal bourgeois interpretation presents a Gramsci who understands Machiavelli through the political and theoretical prisms constructed by the Leninist and Bolshevik experience of 1917 and the civil war in Russia. In this view it is asserted that Gramsci envisions Lenin as a modern Machiavelli who develops and brings to fruition a revolutionary theory founded upon the principles of realpolitik and force.[13] Their opposite number—the orthodox Marxists and Leninists—agree that Gramsci sees Machiavelli through the figure of Lenin, but of course conclude that the liberal bourgeois critique is spurious and self-serving, for the rejection of the Leninist party is equivalent to the rejection of revolution and the construction of a new society.[14] The third school—which in this case includes both left critics of the former Italian Communist party and various democratic

4   and social-democratic intellectuals—finds an unfortunate duality or am-
bivalence within the Gramscian political and theoretical enterprise: on the
one hand, he is admired for his notion of hegemony as a conception of the
world elaborated by organic intellectuals that are to emerge from within
the life of the lower classes; on the other hand, he is criticized for accepting
Croce's interpretation of Machiavelli as the discoverer of the "autonomy of
politics," which to this school represents the reversal of the Marxian assertion of the supremacy of the "social" and "material" life of man over the
merely "political" and "ideological."[15]

What is crucial to each of these interpretations is that they are all
based on a negative or positive orientation toward the Leninist version of
revolution and revolutionary transformation, such that the relation between
Gramsci and Machiavelli is mediated by the figure of Lenin and by the Soviet revolutionary experience. Thus, all three schools of thought take the
Gramsci-Machiavelli relation outside of the Italian historical and cultural
context; it is assumed that Gramsci, in attempting to construct an interpretation of Machiavelli that could be employed toward the development of a
revolutionary theory of action, necessarily and blindly accepted the revolutionary problematic that confronted Lenin in Russia. In effect, analyses
and discussions of the nature and role of Machiavellian thought within the
Gramscian political and theoretical enterprise have failed to turn—or to
return—to the original sources. What needs to be done is to present
Gramsci's writings in relation to those of Machiavelli in order to discover
whether Gramsci is himself faithful to the direction and substance of Machiavelli's works. Such a procedure, however, does not assume that each
text exists in a "pure" or unadulterated state; both the Gramscian and Machiavellian texts are permeated by the sociocultural and sociopolitical en-
vironments to which they reacted and from which they emerged. But precisely because the text is immersed within the social and cultural life of
the respective historical periods, an analysis of the relation between
Gramsci and Machiavelli requires that account be taken of Italian cultural,
political, and ideological developments that shaped the thought of both
Gramsci and Machiavelli.

In fact, few works on Gramsci (especially in the English-speaking
world) have attempted a textual comparison of the major Machiavellian
ideas—such as *virtù/fortuna*, the nature of political knowledge, the new principality, the concept of a people, the relation between thought and action,
force and consent (Chiron the centaur), the relation between republic and
principality, and so on—what the literature considers to be Gramsci's orig-

inal and most significant contribution to Marxist political theory, namely, his concept of hegemony and the notion of moral and intellectual reform.[16] The overwhelming majority of the literature concentrates on the Leninist problematic regarding the nature and role of the political party. Whether one accepts or rejects the Bolshevik perspective, these debates reveal a reductionist tendency that transforms the political and theoretical question regarding the creation of a revolutionary subject and a revolutionary theory into a technical and instrumental problem revolving around various notions of organization—which merely translates into Marxist terminology the capitalist and modernist preoccupation with technique and the liberal reduction of politics to economic utility.

My aim is to understand the relation between Gramsci and Machiavelli in a novel and more fruitful way. Instead of looking at the Gramsci-Machiavelli relation in terms of the traditional and accepted perspective (which locates Gramsci's reading of Machiavelli within a problematic circumscribed by the well-known and well-argued discussions centered on the nature of the political party—debates that tend to reproduce, and thus never escape, the liberal and bourgeois assumptions that underlie the relation between those who rule and those who are ruled, and between "those who know" and "those who do not know"), what this study proposes is to redirect the analysis of Gramsci and Machiavelli into an inquiry into the relation between Machiavelli's political thought and Gramsci's concept of hegemony as the unity of knowledge and action, ethics and politics, where such a unity, through its proliferation and concretization throughout society, becomes the way of life and the practice of the popular masses. I hope to avoid a study that parallels a scholastic exercise where the Gramsci-Machiavelli relation is conflated into the Marxist-Leninist equivalent of the *sic et non.*

Whatever the differences that exist among the various schools of Gramscian interpretation, there is general agreement on the overall political and theoretical thrust of Gramsci's thought: Gramsci set out to formulate and elaborate a theory of political action that is at once a radical and uncompromising critique of the preexisting structures of Italian life and history (both as thought and as practice) and, concurrently, that would identify a political and historical subject, located within this established reality, that would be the carrier of this political theory.[17] The Gramscian enterprise is an attempt to uncover the cultural and political conditions that will either retard or contribute to the creation and development of an actor who, though existing as a subordinate entity within the existing so-

6 ciopolitical reality, nevertheless possesses within itself the seeds or potential that will enable it to move beyond the given reality. The formulation of a revolutionary political theory to Gramsci constitutes two simultaneous, mutually related, activities: the uncovering of the ideological, cultural, and moral structures of the established system, and the development of a political subject whose consciousness is itself the new political theory whose embodiment and concretization within the subject is also the uncovering and undermining of the established social structure.

What such a project requires is that there exist within the existing reality elements whose uncovering and critique will lead to a transformation of accepted reality. Such a transformation demands that the new political theory emerge from within the very system that this theory is attempting to negate and overcome. The Gramscian revolutionary theory, as the negation of the established and prevailing system of thought and practice, must be given, and presupposed, by what it seeks to contradict, and eventually to destroy. The opposition between revolutionary theory and the established system of thought and practice cannot be posited abstractly and mechanically, such that the relation between the two is merely formal and external. It must be one that occurs within the system to be overcome, for such a transcendence can only be realized through the unfolding and movement of elements that—precisely because they arise from the tensions internal to the system—represent the logical and necessary fulfillment of the established reality but that at the same time negate and transform it.

It is for this reason that Gramsci, as he writes in one of his letters to Tatiana,[18] intends to undertake a study and critique of the cultural, moral, and philosophical bases of Italian life and society. In so doing, he hopes to identify the elements and factors that have contributed to what he believes to be the crisis of Italian politics and society. To Gramsci *il reale presente*—the established and given reality of Italian society—is represented by the towering figure of Benedetto Croce. The Crocean formulations regarding the nature of philosophy, politics, and history are taken by Gramsci to constitute the fullest expression of liberal and bourgeois thought in Italy.[19]

Whether such an evaluation of the status and merits of Croce's thought is valid, or whether Gramsci attributes to Croce such a status because he is merely making a parallel between his own position in relation to Croce and the reaction of Marx to Hegelian thought, is not relevant to the issue. The point is that Gramsci perceived Croce as the intellectual figure whose work summarized both the best and the worst of liberal thought and philosophy, a work that represented the culmination of liberal culture and politics. Such a belief is what brought Gramsci to attempt a thoroughgoing critique of liberal philosophy and liberal politics through the analysis and investigation of Crocean philosophy.[20] If this philosophy is the highest expression of bourgeois philosophy and culture in Italy, Gramsci reasoned, then any attempt to construct a radical theory in opposition to the prevailing forms of thought and culture necessarily demanded a simultaneous attempt to analyze and confront the figure of Croce. The overcoming and transcendence of liberal thought and politics as posited by Croce is thus the formulation and elaboration of a new and radical form of thought. The new political theory emerges as the logical and necessary continuation, though in a higher and more universal form, of the established system of thought.

Some authors, especially Piccone, Finocchiaro, Garin, and the contributors to *La città futura*, have discussed and analyzed the relation between Croce and Gramsci, a relation that is generally recognized to assume a significant role in Gramsci's thought. Such a relation is particularly emphasized by those writers who interpret Gramsci as an idealist and a Hegelian who attempted to escape the mechanistic and positivistic notions of science and philosophy that prevailed at the end of the nineteenth and the beginning of the twentieth centuries. My position on the relation between Croce and Gramsci agrees with that of these authors. It is not possible to arrive at a proper reading of Gramsci without locating him within the political, moral, and intellectual atmosphere of an Italian culture whose points of reference and whose terms of discourse were set by the idealist philosophy of Croce.[21]

My argument, however, will address itself to a much more specific and concrete area of inquiry—the issue of the Gramscian reading of Machiavelli—and it will attempt to elaborate and elucidate particular notions and concepts that flow from such a reading. But since the influence of Croce on Gramsci is crucial to the understanding of the Gramscian theoretical and political enterprise, and since this enterprise is formulated and developed both as a critique and as a transcendence of Crocean thought, Gramsci's interpretation of Machiavelli also emerges as a counterreading of the interpretation of Machiavelli put forth by Croce.[22] The Gramscian Machiavelli is a figure that stands in radical opposition to the Crocean Machiavelli. What this means is that to understand the Gramsci-Machiavelli relation it is also necessary to understand the Croce-Gramsci relation; and,

8   further, any discussion of Gramsci's interpretation of Machiavelli necessarily presupposes a discussion of Croce's reading of Machiavelli. Thus the relation between Gramsci and Machiavelli can only be understood when it is located within the Gramscian critique of Crocean thought and Italian culture. And the interpretation of Machiavelli developed by Gramsci is a reading that issues from, and which (at the same time) attempts to negate, the Crocean and liberal interpretation of Machiavellian thought.[23]

These two sets of relations—Gramsci-Croce and Gramsci-Machiavelli—embody what to Gramsci has become the fundamental problem that defines the politics and history of the modern world. The modern world—whose advent was anticipated in the thought of Machiavelli and whose birth historically was signaled by the American and French revolutions—is characterized by the emergence and development of the popular masses as a sociopolitical and sociocultural force.[24] Both Croce and Gramsci (though from different perspectives that lead to radically divergent conclusions) see Machiavelli as the thinker who first understood and first theorized the need for a politics that would recognize the presence of the "mass" as a new factor in the power equation. Machiavelli understood that the nature of rule must be redefined so that a new form of politics could be constructed, a politics that must now be founded upon the "people." Thus in Machiavelli, and in the world since the French Revolution, all forms of rule must now be based on "mass" politics, and power must now issue, or at least seem to issue, from the "people."

It is in this context that we are to understand the purpose and direction of Crocean thought. Croce's philosophy posits a total and radical break between politics and ethics, between thought and action, and between philosophy and ideology.[25] The emergence of the masses in history—indeed, the very presence of the masses as a significant factor in society—will transform philosophy into ideology, and "thinking" into "feeling," unless the distinction between politics and philosophy, and between the culture of those who think (philosophers and intellectuals) and the culture of the popular masses (the "simple people" who merely "feel") is maintained and preserved. Since politics in the modern and postfeudal world is necessarily involved with the life and activity of the people, the preservation of the integrity and purity of thought requires that political activity and philosophical activity be kept within separate domains. This is the basis and meaning underlying the Crocean interpretation of Machiavelli as the thinker who was the first to discover the "autonomy of politics" and who attempted to formulate a theory of politics independent of ethics and philosophy. To Croce, Machiavelli theorized a form of political knowledge that understood politics as pure power and technique, a knowledge that reduces itself to the elaboration of means and instruments by which power could be attained and maintained.[26] The autonomy of politics is thus a concept that posits an absolute disjunction between ethics and philosophy, on the one hand, and politics and power on the other. The latter are simply instrumentalities employed to pursue ends and goals posited by philosophy and ethics. In effect, if political knowledge—the knowledge of the Centaur who teaches the "methods and rules" of the lion and the fox—is a "value-free" methodology, and if politics is a mere instrument and technique that addresses the proper use of "pure" power, then the political is a subordinate form of knowledge, and politics is a utilitarian and particularistic form of activity, whose nature and function are given by the necessity to maintain the strict distinction between philosophy and ideology, and between thought and sociopolitical activity.

But what does it mean to assert that these distinctions must be maintained in order to preserve the purity of thought from the "contamination" of action and from the "vulgarization" of the popular masses? Further, what does it mean to assert that politics is autonomous—that is, that politics is utility? These are precisely the questions that Gramsci addressed in his critique of Croce's interpretation of Machiavelli—or, which is the same thing, Croce's notion of the political. The concept of knowledge as "pure" thought, when it is linked (as it must be, given its premises) to the notion of the political as pure power and pure utility, postulates a radical distinction between action and thought, between the concrete and the universal, such that what is given by philosophy can only be realized in thought, and what is given by politics can never attain the level of philosophical "truth." What this means is that the particular will always remain immersed within its own concrete and "factually" given objectivity, and the universal will always remain an abstract entity that exists only through its contemplation by philosophy. If politics is indeed utility, if political knowledge is reduced to a technique, then the notion of the political defined by a free association of equals—where the universal posited by ethics and philosophy is realized within the political community—becomes absurd and meaningless (or at best utopian), and society is reduced to a sphere dominated by the clash of particular interests and particular "utilities," a never-ending struggle for brute advantage, escape from which is possible only for those who can rise to the level of philosophy and to what Gramsci calls *alta cultura* (the culture of intellectuals and of the dominant groups).[27]

10   In Croce, the interpretation of Machiavellian thought as the "autonomy of politics"[28] reduces the political to the level of the particular and the level of the economic; what is more, the political can never escape this level—only philosophy and ethics can ascend to the level of the universal. But if this universality can be attained only through the preservation of the purity of thought, then this amounts to saying that the overwhelming majority of the people are condemned to the realm of the particular, subject to the clash and competition of economic and utilitarian necessity, while a select few—those groups defined by the *alta cultura* and whose rule Croce calls an "aristo-democracy"[29]—may enter the realm of the universal and of freedom.

Croce assumes a typical posture toward the nature and character of the popular masses—what he calls the "*volgo*."[30] Such an attitude exemplifies the liberal aversion to the emergence of the masses into history and into politics. The masses exist both as a weight and as a threat, and the political is seen as the method by which the "revolt of the masses" may be controlled and directed into channels that will not destroy the *alta cultura* of the ruling groups. The nature of the masses is such that they will never attain the level of moral and intellectual discourse necessary to transform them into a free and purposive subject whose activity in history will realize the universal realm of freedom given by ethics and philosophy. As a consequence, the purpose and function of the political is to render (or to keep) the masses passive and malleable; the political encompasses the means and methods through which the people are brought to accept the rule of the "aristo-democracy." Thus politics is the activity that maintains the distinction between those who rule and those who are ruled, an activity whose goal is to maintain the people in their subordinate condition as an amorphous collection of isolated individuals rooted within the realm of particular interests. And political knowledge, rather than teaching the people, and rather than uncovering the causes and conditions that maintain the distinction between ruler and ruled, *alta cultura* and *cultura popolare*, is an instrument employed to mask and to cover the reality of power and of domination.

It is within this liberal problematic—the Crocean frame of reference that posits an absolute antithesis between knowledge and the people, between the freedom of *chi sa* (those who know) and the necessity of *chi non sa* (those who do not know)—that we should insert the Gramscian reading of Machiavelli's thought. Gramsci attempts to create a form of discourse and a form of knowledge whose very existence and internal structure are based upon the emergence of the masses, not as a mere aggregation or *volgo*, but as a body capable of moving from the particular to the universal, from the

realm of private interests to that of universal interest. The figure of Machiavelli assumes extreme importance in this attempt. Gramsci begins with
the Crocean Machiavelli and retranslates him into the prototype of what he
calls the "democratic philosopher," a thinker and man of action who theorizes and formulates a new political knowledge and a theory of action
whose foundation and whose object is the people as a collective and coherent entity.[31] The conception of Machiavelli as the figure who creates a
knowledge whose very embodiment and realization is the people is a radical critique of Crocean and liberal thought. It is the negation of the Crocean Machiavelli, the "pure scientist" whose political knowledge is the science of a "pure politics" independent of all other spheres of thought and
action. In Gramsci, Machiavelli is not the "neutral" or "amoral" scientist,
without passion and commitment. Machiavelli is the *politico in atto*—the active man of politics—an actor who takes part in the struggle to create a new
people and a new politics. The knowledge of the Gramscian Machiavelli,
therefore, is a knowledge that cannot exist without the people; it is a
knowledge that is created and developed as it simultaneously creates and
develops the subject—the popular masses—to which it is addressed.

To Croce, Machiavelli expresses the separation between thought and
action, philosophy and politics, knowledge and people, while to Gramsci,
Machiavelli is the figure who embodies the unity of thought and action,
knowledge and people. It is precisely this synthesis between politics and
philosophy, I will argue, that characterizes the Gramscian conception of the
political as the activity that transcends the given reality—the divorce between *alta cultura* and *cultura popolare*, the people as the *volgo* who "do not
know" and the educated rulers "who know"—and transforms this given
into a new and superior reality. This conception of the political as the unity
of knowledge and people, which in their mutual interaction creates a conscious and free subject that will move from the particular to the universal,
is precisely what characterizes the notion of hegemony as a conception of
the world that has become the life and activity of the people.

In effect, by focusing on Machiavelli, Gramsci is focusing on the question regarding the nature of politics, the role it plays, and the scope and
boundaries that define it in the modern world. Gramsci's interpretation of
Machiavelli therefore serves a double purpose: by presenting his version
of Machiavelli, Gramsci is at the same time presenting a critique of opposing and contemporary interpretations of Machiavelli. Gramsci attempts to
fashion a revolutionary Machiavelli in opposition to the liberal one. Thus a
study of Machiavelli is also a critique of Italian politics and Italian history.

12   Gramsci is able to use Machiavelli in order to construct a political and theoretical discourse whose purpose is simultaneously to uncover the established liberal contemporary interpretations of the Florentine secretary as
rationalizations and justifications for the existing power structure, and to
recover through such a critique the radical and revolutionary kernel of Machiavellian thought as a means by which a new conception of politics, both
democratic and realistic (that is, humanly possible), might be formulated.
This project is carried forward through the presentation of a basically Crocean and liberal interpretation of Machiavelli whose critical elaboration
leads Gramsci to imagine the outlines of a counterinterpretation.

The argument between Croce's and Gramsci's interpretation of Machiavelli is also a discourse on the difficult and classical problem regarding
the theoretical and praxiological nature of politics. This problem may be
conceived in two ways.

One, what are the contours and boundaries of the activity called
politics—that is, how is one to formulate and construct a sociopolitical
space whose essential defining characteristics delineate it properly as
"political"? The question pivots on the relation between thinking and acting (or between the "word" and the "deed," as de Sanctis puts it): such a
space must not only be thought ("imagined," in Machiavelli's words), but
must also be effectively realized. But this is another way of stating the pe-
rennial problem regarding the relation between morality or ethics (the
"ought") and politics (the "is"), the consciousness of which distinction is
first seen in Plato, and whose consequences are addressed by thinkers
from Machiavelli to Marx to Croce and to Gramsci.

Thus, the problem of the political is one of constructing a space or
topos that is expressed by a particular way of thinking, a knowledge, and, at
the same time, a knowledge that is defined by a particular way of acting, a
praxis or a way of life. Simply put, is a politics possible without the polis—
that is, what is politics without a public space? And what is a public space
without public actors engaged in the world defined by this space? Consequently, is a political knowledge possible without such a politics? What
happens to political practice and political knowledge when an open and
public *topos* undergoes change—contracts, expands, or indeed disinte-
grates? Croce and others, such as Strauss, Berlin, and Wolin, see the disintegration and collapse of the public-political space with the rise of the
modern world—that is, with the emergence of a world first shaped by the
sociopolitical and theoretical consequences of the American and French
revolutions.

Which brings me to the second way that the nature and problem of the political may be conceptualized. Whether one agrees with Leo Strauss that Machiavelli is a "teacher of evil" who signals the beginning of modernity, or with Sheldon Wolin that Machiavelli discovered the "mass" as a force in politics, or, finally, whether one believes along with Croce and Berlin that Machiavelli established the "autonomy of politics," there can be no doubt that he represents a radical and revolutionary rupture in the history of Western political thought and practice. The central importance of Machiavelli for Gramsci lies in the former's profound sense that all traditional and accepted forms of political activity and social relations are disintegrating, and in the consequent search for a new and ever-elusive *topos* upon which to reconstitute a meaningful cultural and political order. It is this juxtaposition of disintegrating sociopolitical structures and institutions, and of an emerging "mass" or people as a new and powerful force in history, that forms the organizing center of the theoretical, ideological, and sociopolitical struggles of modern society in general, and of post-Risorgimento Italy in particular. This very juxtaposition—the simultaneous decay of traditional power structures (both European feudal and Italian city-state) and the rise of the "masses" as a force that must be addressed—provided the spark or catalyst that led Machiavelli to reconstruct a politics derived from classical and republican Roman sources. The attempt to recover republican political *virtù* and make it the central arch of his new political edifice is what enabled him to imagine a politics whose boundaries or space are now defined by the activity (or the manipulation) of the people. Whether the "mass" is a passive object condemned to the manipulation of intellectuals, or whether it is an active subject engaged in the world, is precisely the question addressed by Machiavelli in his polemics against the humanists, and by Gramsci in his attacks on Crocean-liberal culture and practice. In addition, the rise of the people was a threat to the stability and integrity of liberal culture and society, a threat that Gramsci saw in Machiavellian terms as an opportunity to redefine and expand the boundaries of political thought and practice.

In effect, in the same way that Machiavelli used Livy, Cicero, Sallust, Polybius, et al., and Roman republican thought and practice, in order to reconstitute a politics (that is, precisely by deconstituting and criticizing his sources), Gramsci uses a critique of Crocean and liberal interpretations of Machiavellian politics and thought to reconstruct an opposing and radical conception of politics.

Chapter 2

Croce and Gramsci
From Philosophy to Politics

Croce represents to Gramsci both the apex and the summation of liberal and bourgeois thought in Italy. Such thought posits a radical and total opposition between philosophy and action, "thinking" and "feeling," culture and politics—an opposition that is translated within sociopolitical reality and within history into the opposition between the culture of those who rule (*alta cultura*) and the culture of those who are ruled (*cultura popolare*).[1] In Croce these distinctions are expressed and elaborated by means of a speculative and metaphysical system that posits philosophy as the universal realm of "truth" whose "purity" and integrity would be violated and compromised were such a realm of pure thought to come into a close and intimate contact with the world of action and sociopolitical struggle. Gramsci sees Croce as the organizer and proliferator of a highly elaborate and complex philosophical system whose political and social expression assumes a thoroughgoing antipathy toward political action on the part of the popular masses, and whose cultural and intellectual basis reveals a profound antipathy toward the *cultura popolare* of the masses. In both instances, Crocean thought posits the necessity for the exclusion of the people—that is, the lower classes—from the cultural and political life of the society. To Croce, and to most liberals of the late nineteenth and early-to-middle twentieth centuries, the subordination and passivity of the masses are both necessary and desirable.[2]

What to Gramsci is the central reality of history and politics of modern Italy—the emergence of the masses and their exclusion from the life of the nation such that a "national-popular"[3] culture and politics failed to emerge—is seen by Croce as a nonproblem that "true" philosophy and

14

"high" culture cannot possibly recognize, let alone address. Gramsci, however, points out that the very fact that Crocean thought defines the people out of existence is in itself a telling indication that such a system is both cause and product of the liberal-bourgeois distinction between knowledge and practice, culture and people. The attempt to deny the masses, and their role in politics and history, is itself a revelation that the masses cannot any longer be denied. The denial itself is an affirmation that in the modern world—especially after the French and American revolutions—the popular masses emerged as a social and political factor whose presence must be addressed. This affirmation of the importance of the masses, and the necessity for their participation in history and in politics, are implicit in the very distinction that Croce makes between *alta cultura* and *cultura popolare*, and between philosophy and practical action in society. This system would be rendered meaningless, and its construction would not have been attempted, without the recognition of the role the masses have come to assume.

The assertion that the masses are not able to attain the level of philosophy and thought achieved by the creators of culture and knowledge (intellectuals), and the notion that any connection of philosophy to the people will transform the former into "opinion" and "error," are transposed by Gramsci into a critical inquiry into the nature of philosophical thought, where he attempts to describe the social origins and the social character that such assertions presuppose.[4] If popular thought and mass culture are inherently "political" and ideological, then the thought of the intellectuals and the culture of the "educated" are similarly political and ideological— indeed, doubly so, for the latter deny to themselves such a character while attributing it to the thought and culture of the people. The distinction between theory and practice, thought and action, that is presupposed and required by Crocean philosophy is a political and ideological position, one that tends toward the maintenance and preservation of the real and concrete contradiction between the subordinate popular masses and the dominant groups.

Croce's position on the relation between knowledge and action, philosophy and politics, culture and people, is concisely summarized in a review he wrote on *Il Risorgimento*, a selection of Gramsci's prison notes published twelve years after Gramsci's death. In this review Croce says:

> It is both wearisome and annoying to listen to infinite restatements of the formula of the young Marx, one of several rash formulas both bizarre and

adventurous that were improvised during the years 1840 and 1848, a period
that saw the burning out {estinguisce} of the great philosophical blaze that for
about a century or so brought from Germany light and heat to the human
mind, and that was followed by the corrupt philosophy characterized by a
practical, political, and instrumental orientation {la corrotta filosofia di uso pratico e
politico}, a philosophy accepted and welcomed by amateurs but that disgusts
and repulses all those who respect the dignity of thought.[5]

Here we see the specifically Crocean attitude to Marx and his enterprise,
one closely related to his concepts of philosophy and culture. Croce continues in the same review with a more specific reference to Gramsci and to
his notion of hegemony as the elaboration within the popular masses of a
coherent and autonomous structure of thought: "Gramsci, consistent with
the premises from which he started, confused and mistook for philosophy
and for culture the project he had long worked for: the formation in Italy of
a party for which he already felt himself responsible as leader." And
Croce—"consistent with his own premises," which lead him to posit an antinomy between politics and philosophy, politics and culture—concludes
his review with a formulation that identifies and focuses to a sharp point
the major difference between liberal thought and the Marxian thought of
Gramsci: "Gramsci, therefore, is *totus politicus*, and not *philosophus*: such was
his real and effective ideal—an ideal which was given the 'bourgeois' name
of 'philosophy' and 'culture.' "[6]

    Croce identifies "the formula of the young Marx" with the "corrupt
philosophy" that asserts the necessity of praxis, that from his standpoint
asserts the primacy of action over thought. The date 1840-48 is significant.
For the rise of such a philosophy is paralleled in Croce's mind by the fall of
German philosophy (Kantian and Hegelian idealism) during a period of intense revolutionary and mass activity. The fall of German philosophy is
linked to the rise of popular and mass movements that occurred throughout the European continent: from the Kingdom of the Two Sicilies to Milan
to Paris to the German states.[7] The term *improvviste* ("improvised") is revealing, for it suggests that such a "corrupt philosophy" emerged not full-blown
from Zeus's head, like Athena, but rather from the ongoing, practical struggles that Europe experienced during that time—struggles and conflicts
that gave birth to a form of thought and a conception of the world that of-
fend the "dignity of thought." The "great blaze" of German philosophy was
extinguished by the irruption and intervention of the masses into the sociopolitical arena, an intervention that to Croce is fundamentally and in-

herently destructive of all thought and philosophy. This review of Gramsci's *Risorgimento*, rather than attempting to debate and rebut the Gramscian analysis of the Risorgimento as a liberal and bourgeois movement that excluded the workers and peasants and that rejected their participation in the social and political life of the newly created state, accepts the underlying position of such a critique by restating the thesis that posits a radical and irreconcilable opposition between philosophy and culture on the one hand, and politics and practical activity on the other. Croce reiterates his fundamental antipathy toward any kind of democratic mass movement: the ideas and concepts that emerge from this movement and that give it form and direction are, to Croce, mere "corruptions" from which philosophy, and those who respect it, will maintain a safe and antiseptic distance. Politics is "passion" and "feeling," not thought and philosophy, and the masses are naturally and intrinsically unable to arrive at the kind of cultural and philosophical activity necessary for thinking.[8]

It is important to point out that Croce is reversing the Marxian formulation that the victory of the proletariat is simultaneously the realization and concretization of classical German philosophy.[9] What Hegel had achieved in thought, Marx asserted, could only be achieved socially and materially through an understanding of social forces in history and through the political and ideological organization made possible by such an understanding. Such a consciousness of society and history is but the practical and concrete expression of a historical subject whose social and political condition gave rise to that very consciousness: thus the subject that is rooted materially within the structure of society and the consciousness that is the thought and memory of this subject together form a unity where objective conditions and subjective actor are inextricably interwoven in such a way that the internal movement between object and subject creates new forms of consciousness, new forms of thought; the opposition between object and subject is resolved through praxis and through critical activity. To Marx, philosophy is realized when the conditions that give rise to the subject whose consciousness is both the product and the negation of these conditions are transcended by the political and practical activity that the very consciousness of this subject reveals.[10] The proletariat is such a subject, which contains within its practical life the seeds of a genuine universality, where the development of the proletariat as a universal class becomes equivalent to the development of reason and philosophy. The victory of the proletariat—that is, the proletarian revolution—is the realization of philosophy in action, and not merely in thought.

18   Croce attacks this formulation and asserts that the development of the proletariat—or of the masses in general—represents the fall and the "corruption" of philosophy, not its realization. What Gramsci identifies as the period of the birth of the "philosophy of praxis"—that is, Marxian theory—the philosophy that is linked to the emergence of the masses as a political force, is identified by Croce as the period that marks the beginning of the degeneration of philosophy, the death of thought and of the dignity of thought—the rise of ideology, which is the corrupt philosophy. Yet Croce fails to notice the influence and effect that the French Revolution and Napoleon wielded on German philosophy, an influence that both the young Hegel and Marx recognized.[11]

Croce accuses Gramsci of confusing philosophy and culture with politics, with the practical and concrete activity that goes into the founding of a political party or a political organization.[12] The Gramscian enterprise, which is the formation and development of a mass social movement, and the creation of a concrete historical subject capable of expressing and representing the philosophy of praxis in practice, is viewed by Croce as antiphilosophy and anticulture. What to Croce signaled the death of philosophy, to Gramsci represented the beginning of the realization of philosophy. Thus Croce in a review of Gramsci's *Gli intellettuali e l'organizzazione della cultura* in 1949:

> It is a cause of wonderment that a man of such gravity and nobility as Gramsci let himself be lured by sophisms to such an extent that he concealed |*velare*| to himself the evidence |of the truth| that his mind and experience must have discerned. Because in the striving toward a truth, there is within the very nature of this act a necessary detachment from all other human interests, so that only the interest for the truth itself remains the dominant and ruling consideration of the mind. Even the smallest truth is the natural outcome of this detachment and overcoming. And if another and different interest prevails, either mediately or immediately, thought—do you know what happens to it |*sapete che cosa fa*|?—it does not think.[13]

Here we find Croce's response to the Gramscian formulation that the relation between intellectuals and culture is not an immediate, but rather a mediated one[14]—that is, intellectual and cultural activity is not socially and politically autonomous. Intellectuals are a social group that organize and elaborate culture in its widest sense, and the function of intellectuals is precisely to formulate and proliferate a culture and a system of thinking and valuing throughout society.

Croce believes that "the interest for the truth" presupposes and de-   **19**
mands a "detachment and separation [distacco] from all other human
interests"—by which he means social, economic, and political interests.
Such a *distacco* is necessary to the very act of thinking, for without it there is
no thought, no thinking, and no *verità*. But the problem with such a way of
posing the question, as Gramsci points out,[15] is that the subject that
thinks, that performs the "act of thinking," is "thought" itself: "Il pensiero
pensa"—not human beings or social persons rooted within space and
time. Thus what Croce creates is a disembodied subject abstracted and
reduced to *pensiero* and to the activity of the individual philosopher isolated and divorced from "all other interests." The *verità* that Croce believes
is the object of thought requires the *distacco* from social and historical reality; yet to Gramsci such a *verità* is the product and object of a thought that
emerges from the very social reality that it expresses and attempts to
grasp. It is this dialectic between social reality and thought that to Croce
has led to the rise of "la corrotta filosofia di uso pratico e politico."

It is interesting to note that both Gramsci and Croce accuse one another of engaging in a process of *velare* (to mask or to conceal). Gramsci is
attempting to construct a political and social knowledge that will *svelare*
(uncover or reveal) the ideological and political character of the ideal activity of *pensiero*. On the other hand, Croce says that Gramsci has become
ensnared by "sophisms"—that is, the "corrupt philosophy"—"to such an
extent that he has concealed within himself the evidence" that shows
thought must be autonomous from the social and the political. The difference in each accusation lies in the fact that Gramsci criticizes Crocean
thought because it sees itself as "true philosophy" while it functions to
mask sociopolitical interests: the *velare* refers to social and historical reality.
Croce identifies Gramsci's error within Gramsci himself, such that this self-
deception is one that is completely isolated from external reality, and the
"veiling" occurs within Gramsci's own mind. Thus the critiques that each
launches against the other are faithful to their respective methods: the first
to discover ways by which the *distacco* between intellectuals and masses
may be overcome, the second to preserve the integrity and the "dignity" of
thought, which in practice requires the subordination of the masses to the
intellectuals.[16]

This distinction in the identification of precisely what is being veiled
and how it is being veiled—the method is also a means of evaluating the
distance between the two thinkers, for *velare* to Gramsci is the separation of
pensiero from reality, while in Croce *velare* means the interpenetration of the

20   two—corresponds to the differences the two have regarding their notions of "reality" and "truth." Gramsci often employs the term *realtà effettiva* to emphasize the transformative effects of human action on sociopolitical and historical reality, a term that is closely related to Machiavelli's notion of *verità effettuale*, a term that describes a constantly changing reality perceived as the product of political action (of the "uomini virtuosi").[17] Both Gramsci and Machiavelli use their respective terms as critical theoretical tools to unmask and uncover a "truth" and a "reality" that are not simpy in "error," but rather are products of a belief system and a moral-intellectual construction whose function within this *verità effettuale* is to veil this very reality, so that the accepted and perceived reality becomes a function of these systems of thought. We should recall what Croce said of Gramsci, that he "mistook for philosophy and culture the |otherwise political| work" ("confondeva con la filosofia e con la cultura l'opera") to establish in Italy "a party of which he already felt himself to be responsible as leader" ("un partito del quale già si sentiva capo e responsabile"). Gramsci's self-delusion lies in the fact that he attempted to create within history and society a social and political movement whose activity and practice would change the existing structure of society. As a political actor in contact with the workers and peasants, therefore, Gramsci and his movement could not attain the realm where "thought thinks" and "truth" dwells. Such an engagement, this very immersion in the material world of the "flesh," cannot but be the degeneration of thought and culture. It would seem that to Croce the "word" cannot become flesh and simultaneously retain its integrity as the *logos*. Nor, for that matter, can the Spirit recognize itself in the world, let alone incarnate itself in a man on horseback. Croce's *creator spiritus* is an intellectual and mental entity, whose "march" in history takes place within the heads of intellectuals,[18] and the *veritas* to which it aspires and attains is simply the *spiritus* regarding its own reflection as in a mirror. It is the self-contemplation of the mind thinking as pure thought.[19] But to Gramsci such a position substitutes the ideal and "disinterested" category of Truth for the material and historical *realtà effettiva* and *verità effettuale*.

Thus Croce on Gramsci: *totus politicus*, and not *philosophus*, an antinomy that Gramsci rejects and synthesizes into the concept of *egemonia*. Hegemony is the formulation and elaboration of a conception of the world that has been transformed into the accepted and "normal" ensemble of ideas and beliefs that interpret and define the world. Such a process is immediately political, for such a transformation cannot be accomplished without the people viewed as a social force. Hegemony is thus, in a very real and

concrete sense, the moment of philosophy as politics, and the moment of
politics as philosophy. In Gramsci's words,

> Ideologies ... are the "true" philosophy, because they are those
> philosophical "vulgarizations" that bring the masses to concrete action and
> to the transformation of reality. That is, they are the mass and popular aspect
> of every philosophical conception, which in a "philosopher" assumes the
> character of a universal abstraction outside of time and space, a character
> specifically literary and antihistorical in origin.[20]

And if this is the case, if hegemony is constituted by the unity of politics
and philosophy, then it must also follow that hegemony implies the unity
of philosophy and history, for "concrete action" and the "transformation of
reality" (which are the object of politics) presuppose a social reality and a
conception of the world that are anchored within "time and space." But
whereas to Croce history is the history of philosophy (the ethico-political),
to Gramsci history is the history of *egemonia*—that is, the history of the
unity of philosophy and politics, thought and action.

The unity of philosophy and history (or what Gramsci calls "absolute
historicism")[21] is made concrete *hic et nunc* through political action, where
"political" is understood in its "integral" (and classical) sense of the unity
of theory and practice.[22] The Crocean *totus politicus*, therefore, is retranslated
into the Gramscian political subject constituted as the totality of memory,
philosophy, and action. The Gramscian *totus politicus* may be compared to
the notion of the *politikos* in ancient Greek politics, where the distinction
between philosopher and statesman had not yet attained prevalence, nor
was it desired as a positive result. The classical *politikos* represents the philosopher-actor that elaborates the sociopolitical institutions and the
moral-intellectual practices of the *polis*, where he incarnates the moral and
political knowledge of the conditions necessary not just for life, but for the
good life.[23] It is this *politicus* that Gramsci has in mind in his critique of
Croce and his idealist philosophy. As Gramsci often points out, the foundation of a state is in itself a form of philosophical activity.[24] For if, as Croce
would have it, the state should be seen as an ethico-political entity, then
the "work" necessary for its coming to be is not simply "practical," nor is it
entirely the result of the activity of the Spirit, but is rather the result of the
formation and elaboration of a conception of the world that has become
"life," that has become the "practice" of the people, so that this life and
this practice are the concrete, specific expression of the moral and intellectual totality that it incarnates.[25]

To Gramsci *il politico* is an actor who "philosophizes" to the extent that he organizes and forms the disparate impressions of reality into a unified and stable totality—this totality understood as being in a dynamic and active relation to the world. In the most fundamental sense *il politico* is the actor whose reality is being created constantly in the very process of acting, where this acting is itself a unity of thought and practice.[26] Thus *politicus* + *philosophus* = the political subject, which in its active engagement with the world founds and creates a *realtà effettiva*, where this reality is constituted not by discrete elements of thought and action, philosophy and politics, mechanically related to each other, but by the active movement of thought and action, so that reality is constitutive of thought, and thought is inherent in the action that constitutes reality. Hegemony thus addresses the problem posed by the relation between politics and philosophy, a relation necessary to the formation and development of a historical and political subject. Moreover, to address such a problem is at the same time to address the antinomies that obtain between culture/intellectuals and the people.[27] This is the sense of the proposition that the German proletariat is heir to classical German philosophy;[28] and this, too, is the problem (both political and philosophical) that is raised by the Eleventh Thesis on Feuerbach—that philosophers have only interpreted the world differently, but the point is to change it.[29] The interpretation of the world—which is a function of the prevailing conception of the world—and the transformation of the world presuppose each other and in their mutual interaction resolve themselves into historical praxis, into political action "in space and time." What this means is that the transformation of reality is a historical process that engages the political subject.

    Therefore, *il politico* is necessarily "a historian . . . not only in the sense that he makes history |*fa la storia*|, but also in the sense that he interprets the past by acting in the present |*operando nel presente*|" so that "the historian" is also "a political actor |*un politico*| and in this sense . . . history is always contemporary history—that is, politics." Such a formulation identifies history with politics and therefore ideology with philosophy, whose combined elements, of course, constitute a conception of the world as a totality.[30] If the *politico* (the historical subject) "*fa la storia*," then he is also *filosofo* for "by acting in the present he interprets the past." The interpretation of the past (as well as the present) and the acting in the present, though it is always possible to differentiate them analytically and abstractly, are necessary moments or aspects of one and the same "event" or phenomenon. These two moments together constitute the event as a total and concrete

"act," which is in itself an aspect of the *realtà effettiva*. *Fare la storia* is *operando*   **23**
nel presente, and this *operando* is simultaneously *interpretando il passato* (interpreting the past)—all of which converge to create the Gramscian *politica*.
History and philosophy, politics and history, philosophy and politics, acting and interpreting: Gramsci stresses the profound and unbreakable relation between these apparently opposite moments of one concrete and unified totality.[31] In effect, *fare la storia* is the transformation of the world, an activity that assumes the existence of a historical subject possessed of a conscious and purposive political will, which in its consciousness acts in the world, and which in its activity is conscious of itself in the world. As Gramsci writes,

> The active man of politics [*politico in atto*] is a creator, an innovator [*suscitatore*]. But he neither creates from nothing nor does he move in the turbid void of his own particular desires and dreams. He bases himself on the effective reality, but what is this effective reality? Is it something static and immobile, or is it not rather a relation of forces in continuous movement and change of equilibrium? To apply one's will to the creation of a new equilibrium among the forces that really exist and are operative ... one moves within the terrain of effective reality ... in order to dominate and transcend it.[32]

This is a task that requires a new subject and a new notion of politics. *Politica* is *storia in atto* and *filosofia in atto*.[33] Such a notion represents in real and concrete terms the essential and defining characteristics of what Gramsci calls the philosophy of praxis. The philosophy of praxis is "absolute historicism" in the sense above of the unity of acting in the present and of interpreting the past.[34] The formulation posits an absolute and total identity between acting and interpreting: thus philosophy = history = politics. As a consequence, *"tutto è politica"* (everything is politics),[35] where politics is now understood as the action that springs from the unity of theory and practice in order to "dominate and transcend" the *realtà effettuale*. And, since this reality is in "continuous movement," politics is the activity by which reality is continually created and re-created. The Gramscian concept of the political implies an innovative, activist, and "prefigurative" orientation toward the world and toward history.[36] To the extent that action is purposive and directed toward an end that is anticipated but not yet in existence, such action presupposes and embodies *"in concretezza"* philosophy and thought. Furthermore, to the extent that what is anticipated and made purposive by thought and philosophy is not yet a reality—to the extent that what ought to be has not yet been transformed into what is—then philos-

24   ophy, in order to become *realtà effettuale*, in order to *"creare il reale"* ("create reality")[37] must translate itself into action and become *politica*. The political in Gramsci therefore assumes a purposive and prefigurative character (which is related to the notion of *egemonia*). And to the extent that such a prefiguration necessitates the engagement of the conscious will within a world-in-becoming, the political is an innovating and creative form of activity. (All this, however, does not deny the "restorative" and "conserving" forms of historical action: the point is that *politica* assumes within its praxis the dyads history/philosophy, philosophy/politics, and politics/history; what is not *politica* Gramsci calls *diplomazia*, a form of political action that leads to the preservation, as opposed to the transformation, of the historical structure of forces.)[38]

"To apply one's will" "to forces really existing and that are operative" is to "operate and act in the present," which is simultaneously "to interpret the past"—all of which is concretely embodied in the *fare la storia*. Thus the equation: *politico in atto = politicus + philosophus*. The transformation of the world is in itself a philosophical and moral act in that it presupposes a coherent and rational prefiguration of an "ought to be" rooted within a material and concrete "is" of the present and the past. Moreover, to interpret the world differently—that is, to present a conception and view of the world in opposition to the prevailing and established ones—is to discover *in nuce* within the existing reality the germs and seeds, "forze realmente esistenti ed operanti," whose growth and development will lead to the overcoming of the present, and to the creation of a new structure of forces and a new reality.

The Gramscian concept of *politica* brings us back full swing to the problem posed by the emergence in history of the people. Gramsci poses this problem in terms of his concept of *riforma morale e intellettuale* (moral and intellectual reform).[39] *Riforma* is directly related to *egemonia* and to the political viewed in the dual sense discussed earlier: as moral and intellectual activity (philosophy), and as practical and concrete engagement in society and in history (politics). The philosophy of praxis—Marxism—is envisioned in terms of a modern and popular reform of the totality of sociocultural and sociopolitical relations. More particularly, the philosophy of praxis is the conception of the world that expresses the life and experience of the subordinate groups in society. The subordination of the workers and peasants is due to their inability to develop a type of intellectual and a type of culture independent from those of the ruling groups. Intellectual and moral reform is the movement of the popular masses toward the creation of such an intellectual and such a culture. Such a development is necessary if the masses are to achieve a conception of the world that is not a mere reflection of the ideas and values of the dominant groups.

Riforma is thus the concrete process that connects politics and culture, alta cultura and cultura popolare, people and intellectuals. It is the concrete, practical mediation that transforms the opposition between politics and philosophy, history and thought, into a sociopolitical and sociocultural subject materially and historically embodied in a mass movement guided and possessed by a collective moral-intellectual will. The philosophy of praxis is the animating and directing conception of the world that gives the emergence of the masses political and moral force. Philosophy and movement together are seen by Gramsci as the cumulative result of a lengthy and difficult process of reform, both in theory and in practice. The origins of such a reforming process Gramsci locates in the Machiavellian enterprise in Italy and in the Lutheran Reformation in Germany, and he sees it progress through the religious Reformation throughout northern Europe, the later Enlightenment and revolution in France, up through classical German philosophy, and finally reaching its theoretical and practical synthesis in Marx.[40]

As Gramsci writes,

> The philosophy of praxis presupposes all of this cultural past—the Renaissance and the Reformation, German philosophy and the French Revolution, Calvinism and English classical economics, laic liberalism and the historicism that is the base of the entire modern conception of life.[41]

It is the "fulfillment" of this process of cultural, moral, and intellectual reform, which it perceives and embodies dialectically in the relation and in the opposition between cultura popolare and alta cultura.[42] Thus the philosophy of praxis is the thought of the popular masses. As such it is a cultural and moral movement directed toward the achievement and realization of two related ends: to launch a critical attack on the established modern conception of the world—that is, on those ideologies and thought systems "più raffinate"[43] that express the most sophisticated and complex interpretations and representations of the modern world (in fact, on the liberal-bourgeois alta cultura, of which, as we have seen, Gramsci sees Croce as the most important and acute philosopher). Such a critique is necessary in order to lay the groundwork for the task of constructing and developing a group of intellectuals that are independent both of the established system of thought and values and of the established power structure around

26 which the "reigning" and "magisterial" intellectuals of the Crocean type revolve and receive their gravitational balance.[44] Simultaneously with the critique of modern thought and the unveiling of the social and political bases of the "pure intellectuals,"[45] the philosophy of praxis is to assume the political and cultural education of the masses. Both of these projects presuppose and imply each other. To the extent that the masses are educated, they will create an independent culture and an independent view of the world in opposition to the existing ones and thus be able eventually to replace the *alta cultura* of the established intellectuals by a new and different one. To the extent that the people are educated—to the extent that the *cultura popolare* assumes an autonomous and self-directing character—to that extent will they elaborate and organize a type of intellectual internal to themselves, and an intellectual and cultural apparatus whose sociopolitical activity is the continual and ongoing elaboration and transformation of the culture and thought of a subordinate group into a system of thought and a conception of the world that become increasingly ruling and hegemonic. The process by which a subject and derivative system of thought possessed by a subordinate group becomes autonomous and innovating is precisely the process by which such a system is transformed into a hegemonic conception of the world, a system of thinking and interpretation that permeates all areas of social, economic, and political life.

What this means is that the *"andare al popolo"* (going to the people)[46] is viewed by Gramsci as a pedogogic and educational relation between the philosophy of praxis and the *cultura popolare* of the peasants and workers. Such a relationship, however, should not be conceived in terms of what Gramsci calls an abstract and "strictly scholastic" posture.[47] The relationship "between teacher and student is an active relation, reciprocal, and thus every teacher is *always a student and every student is always a teacher"* (emphasis added).[48] This formulation is a commentary on the Marxian thesis in "Feuerbach," where Marx says that the educator himself must be educated.[49] Such an orientation suggests that the relation between the popular masses and the philosophy of praxis—between the intellectual who arises and is individuated from within the social and cultural matrix that locates the masses in time and in space, and the masses whose thought and culture the intellectual expresses and reflects—is inherently a hegemonic, and consequently, political relationship. "Every relationship of 'hegemony' is necessarily an educational relationship," and "every educational relationship is a political relationship."[50] The relationship is political and hegemonic not simply because the teacher-student relationship is reciprocal and mutually interacting, but also because each emerges from, and gives rise to, the other, and because each is informed by the interests and culture of the other. The environment (constituted by the life and activity of the masses) is the teacher of the educator-philosopher.[51] Gramsci envisions a new type of intellectual and a new type of philosopher: a " 'democratic philosopher'—that is, a philosopher who is convinced that his personality is not limited to himself as a physical individual, but is rather an active social relationship of modification of the cultural environment."[52]

The "democratic philosopher" is equivalent to the "organic intellectual." The latter term is more familiar and more widely known than the former. Yet the former more adequately captures the substance of the teacher-student relation that forms the core of the Gramscian concept of *egemonia*. The organic intellectual is precisely that intellectual who is in close and intimate contact with the people, a type defined by a relationship between the two that is reciprocal and dialectical, where intellectual and people mutually define each other and where the relationship is precisely pedagogic, hegemonic, and political in the sense described earlier.[53] The organic intellectual or the democratic philosopher is the teacher and educator whose knowledge and activity are constantly modifying, and being modified by, the "environment"—especially the people—such that the educator and the people become engaged in a process of self-definition and self-overcoming. The notion of the democratic philosopher is precisely a notion of a type of intellectual that Croce would look upon as a self-contradiction, a philosophical and theoretical absurdity. For the relation in Croce between thought and society, as we have seen, is one of a categorical *distacco*, where thought is given an independent role such that the teacher-student relation that Gramsci ascribes to the intellectual-masses relation is always frozen and mechanical. In Croce, the student— the people—has nothing to teach the educator-philosopher; and the educator has nothing to learn from the student. The philosopher issues not from the student but from other philosophers, and thought issues not from the environment but from thought.

The Gramscian intellectual-philosopher is thus diametrically opposed to that envisioned and represented by Croce. What Gramsci calls the "traditional intellectual"[54] is that philosopher who posits an independence and autonomy from the environment and the people. The traditional intellectual describes a particular social structure and sociocultural relations where (1) intellectuals represent a conception of the world and a

28 way of life whose proliferation and acceptance as "truth" and as "science" are a function of the intellectual and moral activity of intellectuals organized into a social group or category, where as a result of such activity the conception has come to be perceived as "universal" and has thus become political and hegemonic; (2) the independence of thought from social and political practice is asserted; (3) the traditional and customarily accepted distinction between the *colti* and the *semplici* is not simply taken as a given, but is also socially and culturally reproduced; and (4) consequently, the traditional philosopher or intellectual legitimates and masks the contradictions and anomalies within society by means of the generation and reproduction of the values and the way of life of the dominant and ruling groups. The traditional intellectual not only is not able to "create an ideological unity between the bottom and the top, and between the 'simple people' |*semplici*| and the intellectuals" but also generalizes and freezes the distinction into an ahistorical principle, such that the thought of the intellectuals is perceived as "philosophy," whereas the thought of the *semplici* is seen as "common sense" and "prejudice." But to accept such a distinction is "to maintain the 'simple people' within their primitive philosophy founded upon common sense."[55]

On the other hand, the democratic philosopher-organic intellectual describes a social relation and a political-cultural orientation where philosophy and knowledge are envisioned as the ever-changing product of an ongoing practical interaction between people and philosopher. Such an interaction is the motive force that propels into movement the moral and intellectual reform necessary to the development of hegemony. The new type of intellectual uncovers and reveals the power and social bases of thought and knowledge, while at the same time this process of uncovering creates a critical type of knowledge. The philosophy of praxis reveals that "tutti sono filosofi" (all people are philosophers),[56] that all people engage in a philosophical activity that is not merely literary, but social and material. As such, the philosophy of praxis recognizes the necessity to forge close links between the intellectual and the *semplici* in order not to "restrict scientific activity and preserve unity at the low level of the masses, but precisely in order to construct an intellectual-moral bloc that will make politically possible the intellectual progress of the mass, and not only that of small and restricted intellectual groups."[57]

Gramsci employs the politics and thought of the Catholic Church to exemplify and to emphasize the differences between the traditional and organic intellectuals. He points out that the church has always attempted to maintain a link between its priests (intellectuals) and the "faithful." Historically, it has striven to achieve "the doctrinal unity of the entire mass of the 'faithful' " to insure that "higher intellectual strata do not become separated from the lower." For "the Roman church has always been the most vigorous in the struggle to prevent the 'official' establishment of two religions, one of the 'intellectuals' and the other of the 'simple people.' "[58] The clerical intellectual functions to integrate the intellectually sophisticated and complex theology of the church with the beliefs and rituals of the common people in order to prevent the emergence of a "popular religion" in opposition to the official doctrine of the hierarchy. The integration of these popular beliefs and practices into the Catholic theological and educational systems is what accounts for the continuity and stability of the church as a political and social entity: the power of the church is derived from the intellectual and moral force it can generate by means of its "union" with the ordinary people of the faith. Thus the church is the embodiment of a unitary polarity between the hierarchy and the faithful, and this unity is maintained by the religious intellectual who adapts to each other the faith of the people and the theology of the hierarchy. By means of such a moral and intellectual adaptation, the latter is able to assert and maintain its hegemonic supremacy over the "community of the faithful."[59] But such a hegemony, Gramsci points out, is achieved not by developing within the people a new form of knowledge and by raising them to the level of the church intellectual, but rather by preserving the difference between the consciousness of the faithful and that of the cleric. This is precisely what the traditional intellectual does in the secular world, and what the new organic intellectual attempts to uncover and overcome. The popular beliefs, the traditions, the customs, and the past usages that together form the "common sense" of the masses, and that tend to preserve the supremacy of the ruling groups, are to be transcended into a new philosophy and a new knowledge defined by a critical self-consciousness, a "comprensione critica di se stessi."[60]

The organic intellectual, as the product of the teacher-student relation, represents the unity of theory and practice, and as such is the embodiment of the interactive process that obtains between politics and culture. This process sparks within the masses the self-awareness and self-consciousness that is the philosophy of praxis. The self-consciousness is a critical and active orientation toward the totality of what is given, which in turn makes possible a cultural, moral, and intellectual reform, "which moves to replace common sense and the traditional conceptions of the

30 world,"[61] and which acts to "elevate intellectually ever-larger strata of the popular masses—in other words, to give a personality to the amorphous mass element. What this means is to work toward the generation [*suscitare*] of *elites* of intellectuals of a new type who arise directly from within the masses, and who will remain in contact with them to become, to use a metaphor, the whalebone in the corset." It is important to note that the new intellectual springs "directly" from the people in the same way that the teacher springs directly from the student. Gramsci continues: "The adhesion or nonadhesion of the masses to an ideology is the real critical test [*critica reale*] of the rationality and historicity of ways of thinking [*modi di pensare*]."[62] Such a "real critique" can only be undertaken and realized through the "*andare al popolo*," through the real participation and active involvement of the masses—all of which is but another way of saying that the philosophy of praxis realizes itself concretely in and through the masses, which realization is itself the "critica reale dei modi di pensare" and of the ways of acting. To the extent, therefore, that the philosophy of praxis develops organic intellectuals who emerge from within the popular masses, who are constantly in contact with them, and from whom the former derive their meaning, goals, and inspiration, to that extent does it concretize and realize itself. Moreover, to the extent that the *modi di pensare* are simultaneously products and carriers of the activity and experience of the masses, to that extent have they become "rational" and necessary, and not mere results of individual whims and desires. The criterion or "mode" by which the historical and sociopolitical import of a way of thinking and perceiving is evaluated is through its ideological and political—that is, hegemonic—character. The *modi di pensare* must be such that they encompass the life and experience of an entire people; thus these *modi* are nothing if not the totality of the social and cultural practice of the people.

Such a notion is related to Vico's famous formula: *verum factum est*—that is, reality is that which is created and made by human beings, or knowledge can only comprehend that which it itself has created. Gramsci compares this statement to his conception of the realization of "rationality" in history. The *modi di pensare* are rational and historically necessary when they embody and express the concrete activity of the people; conversely, the consciousness of the people engaged in action is the *modi di pensare*. The "historicity" and the "rationality" of the "ways of thinking" may be seen as Gramsci's retranslation of the Vichian formulation into Hegelian language.[63] Vico's *factum* is not the posited and empirical given of the existing reality, but is rather what is constantly becoming, a reality conceived as the product of social activity. The philosophy of praxis, and the organic intellectuals located within the popular masses, are the conscious and individuated self-reflection of such an activity—a becoming that springs from the mutual and reciprocal interaction between the *modi di pensare* and mass action, where the movement between organic intellectuals and popular masses generates the critical consciousness of the people as a collective and social force. In a sense, the *factum* is this very reciprocity and mutuality between theory and practice, and between *cultura* and *politica*. Therefore, "what is" is the historical product of social action, and it is constantly produced and created by the active intervention of a particular subject whose activity, and whose consciousness of such activity, together form the *verum*. The democratic philosopher is the new type of intellectual, who is central to the emergence and development of a people as a collective and moral force that fulfills itself in history and that creates its own reality and its own "truth"—that is, its own *factum*. The unity between the democratic philosopher and the people is precisely the philosophy of praxis as it seeks to realize itself as *factum* through its concrete activity within history. The intervention of the popular masses into history and politics, and the generation by the people of its own particular social *facta*, are equivalent to the *critica reale* of the established and prevailing *modi di pensare*. This intervention is signaled by the formation of the democratic philosopher within the collectivity that is the people. The masses, once "amorphous" and undifferentiated, initiate the long and arduous process of coming to know themselves as a political and moral subject, and as a determinate and purposive actor, able and competent to *"operare nel presente"* and to *"interpretare il passato"* in order to *"creare il reale."*

The democratic philosopher is a popular intellectual who does not exist in solitary isolation, one who recognizes that thought becomes real and historical when linked to the people (and thus becomes politics). The democratic philosopher is an innovator, who attempts to modify the social reality through the organization and proliferation of a new type of knowledge and a new type of culture.[64] The latter are the products of the philosophy of praxis, which in turn is the expression and consciousness of the dyad democratic philosopher/popular masses. In a very real sense, the democratic philosopher is the *hegemon* of the people, the teacher and guide who leads the people to a new way of life and a new practice. The characteristic element that defines hegemony is this quality of moral and intellectual *direzione* (leadership).[65] The "organization of culture" and the "organization of permanent consent" are the products of the hegemonic

32 activity of the democratic philosopher.[66] The process by which the subordinate groups become hegemonic and ruling is a process that, as the coming-to-be of the people as a self-directing and self-determining subject, presupposes the generation within and among the masses of the new type of intellectual. Such a process means that the people, as a hegemonic force and a moral and intellectual entity that exercises leadership, is itself transformed into the democratic philosopher, a collective and national-popular philosopher.[67]

> Critical understanding of self takes place therefore through a struggle of political 'hegemonies' of opposing directions, first in the ethical field and then in that of politics, in order to arrive at the creation and elaboration at a higher and superior level of one's own conception of reality.[68]

This elaboration of a new view of reality is the creation and "modification" of social *facta* through the moral and intellectual conflicts of opposing conceptions. In this process the democratic philosopher attempts to elaborate a new social reality by educating and instilling within the people a new conception of the world derived from the praxis and life activity of the people from whom the philosopher springs: "The consciousness of being a part of a determinate hegemonic force (that is to say, political consciousness) is the first stage toward a further and progressive self-consciousness in which theory and practice will finally unite."[69] Political consciousness is the self-consciousness of being in an active and purposive engagement with society and with history—an engagement that is both the product of such consciousness and the ground that gives rise to it. Philosophy becomes "real" when it develops into a "determinate hegemonic force," that is, when it has become the consciousness of the people who as a consequence feel and perceive themselves as a determinate force. The realization of philosophy, the consciousness of being a political force, is the transformation of a subordinate, particularistic mass of disaggregated individuals into a leading and hegemonic subject whose thought and values have become the prevailing conception of the world.

Thus the generation of the democratic philosopher, and the coming-to-be of a subaltern group into a popular hegemonic force, demand the "political development of the concept of hegemony," which is equivalent—in opposition to the Crocean notion of the "corrupt philosophy"—to "a great philosophical advance as well as a political-practical one. For it necessarily presupposes and involves an intellectual unity and an ethic in conformity with a conception of reality that has moved be-

yond and overcome the common sense |of the established *modi di pensare*| **33**
and that has become, if only within narrow limits, critical thought."[70] This
developmental process whereby a group assumes a hegemonic and leading role in society is one that requires the emergence of an organic intellectual within the masses themselves such that the relation intellectual-
people adumbrates and summarizes the meaning of the democratic
philosopher.[71] The relation intellectual-people is given by the teacher-
student paradigm where the unity resulting from the interaction of the two
entities is transformed, and resolves itself, into the unity of the two mo-
ments theory/practice, or philosophy/politics: thus *"filosofico oltre che* |as well
as| *politico-pratico."* It is this totality constituted by the interacting moments
of thought and action, philosophy and politics, that describes the Gramscian concept of hegemony. This totality implies the "absolute historicism"
and the "absolute laicism"[72] of the philosophy of praxis, an orientation
aptly and concisely summarized in Marx's "Theses on Feuerbach."

The relations of hegemony created by the intellectual/people dyad
spark a movement that aims at ever-higher and ever-wider cultural, moral,
and intellectual spheres of action, where the people's action on its intellectuals produces a more historically rooted and more critical knowledge
of the world, and where the intellectuals' action on the people results in
the raising and widening of the cultural level of the people. Such a movement describes a process of innovation and modification that can be pic-
tured as a system of never-ending and open-ended concentric circles,
where each ring of the circle delineates a stage or level of consciousness,
such that each outer ring represents a higher and broader sphere of consciousness. The outer rings, as they represent a higher stage of culture and
knowledge, encompass the inner rings. Consequently, the overcoming and
the transcendence of the inner spheres do not imply their total destruction and complete annihilation; rather, what is overcome is preserved and
retained as a more profound and critical sense of the past, and of the consciousness of the past. The interaction between the people and their intellectuals cannot be schematic and mechanical, nor can such a relation be
superimposed upon the people: it must be organic and dialectical—in the
sense that the movement from one sphere to a higher one is seen and experienced by the popular masses as an unfolding and a flowering from
within the body of the people. The movement is a result of the growth of a
knowledge and a consciousness that are present *hic et nunc* within the
people; the process is an elaboration and an individuation in practice and

34   in history of what is already recognized and germinating *in nuce* within the life activity and praxis of the people.[73]

The democratic philosopher is an organic intellectual because he is, precisely, an "organ" of the people that is in intimate and practical contact with the people. Any break in such a relation will lead to the "crystallization" of culture that Gramsci analyzes with regard to the traditional type of intellectual represented by Croce. The movement from the inner to the outer rings, in an ever-expanding series of circles, is an open-ended process that demands innovation and the critical transformation of social reality. The task of the democratic philosopher is to "determine and to organize a moral and intellectual reform, that is, to relate and adjust culture to practice." On the other hand, those intellectuals that have created an ossified and crystallized culture, such as the traditional intellectuals of the ruling groups, perform a conservative and legitimating function that covers the power structure of society.[74] Thus we have the necessary elements for the formulation: transformation of reality presupposes moral and intellectual reform, which presupposes the development of hegemony, which in turn presupposes the emergence of the democratic philosopher, which embodies the relation organic intellectual/popular masses. In effect, the democratic philosopher is "a historian who interprets the past," and "a political actor [*politico*] who acts within the present."[75] The development of a hegemonic conception of the world is the transformation of reality, which translates into the moral and intellectual reform of the existing society, so that we have *riforma* = *storia in atto* + *filosofia in atto* = the philosophy of praxis. The philosophy of praxis is *riforma in atto*, the critical transformation of social reality and social *facta* (which process, of course, is itself a social *factum*) through the active and dynamic interaction between teacher and student, between the culture of intellectuals and popular culture, where teacher/student, culture/people, together form a conscious and determinate political subject, and where this subject is a hegemonic force because it is "una filosofia che è anche una politica e una politica che è anche una filosofia" ("a philosophy that is also politics, and a politics that is also philosophy").[76]

Chapter 3

Renaissance and Reformation

It is sometimes suggested that the Gramscian notion of intellectual and moral reform is one taken from the work of Renan.[1] However, whatever its immediate antecedents, there is no question that Gramsci makes a historical and political parallel between the *riforma* that the philosophy of praxis is to undertake, and the Lutheran and Protestant Reformation of the sixteenth and early seventeenth centuries.[2] The intellectual and moral renovation that was initiated by the Reformation is critical to Gramsci because it described a type of movement that attempted to bridge the gulf between the church hierarchy and the faithful in a way that embodied a practical and thoroughgoing critique of the Roman church. Such a movement was interpreted by Gramsci as the ideological and sociopolitical renovation that led to the transformation of the medieval and aristocratic conception of the world.[3] The Reformation destroyed the unity of the medieval world by attacking the "universality" of the Roman interpretation of religion on the one hand, and, on the other hand, by discovering and harnessing the political and social forces whose eventual awakening and mobilization transformed the sociopolitical structure of Europe.

The critique of the Roman church, and the demand for its reform, became equivalent to the transformation of the *modi di pensare* ("ways of thinking"), which, once having become *operanti* ("operative" or "active"), involved the radical reinterpretation of the past and the radical restructuring of the present. In their critique of the present (Roman and papal) interpretation of Christianity, Luther and Calvin presented a conception of the faith as the rediscovery and restoration of the truths and values of the original

35

36 founders. The interpretation of the texts, and the critique of the commonly accepted tradition, together meant the appropriation of the past, the re-creation of the past, a task necessary to carry forward the critical transformation of the present by creating a new religious and cultural vision. In turn, this vision is enunciated and taught by the religious reformers in terms of a past that has been "retranslated" in light of the new vision, such that a new past and a new vision are now contrasted and opposed to the *traditio* that supports and represents the power of the established church. The debates and controversies that revolved around the nature of the sacraments, the relative value and weight to be assigned to "faith" and to "good works," were in essence struggles over the definition or redefinition of the nature of the term "church." To accomplish such a redefinition required the transformation of the tradition and past of the Roman church into the tradition and past of a corrupt and self-serving hierarchy whose teachings and practices deviated from those of the original founders, Jesus Christ and Saint Paul. The hierarchy represented a past and a present antithetical and irremediably opposed to the truly Christian notion of the community of the saved—the people as the community of the faithful. Luther and Calvin created a new vision of what this community meant and what it represented, and they opposed it to the power structure and practice of the Roman church, a critique embodied in the radical attack on the validity of the sacraments, and hence on the sacred and sacramental character of the priestly caste.[4]

The attack on tradition, and the recapturing of the past in terms of the retranslation—both literally and exegetically—of the sacred texts, also revealed the church as the negation of the Christian mission. Such an undertaking stressed the gulf that separated the culture of the priests from that of the people in order to eliminate and replace it with the new conception that saw the unity and community of the congregation of the faithful. The new conception saw the relation between reformer and people as one of reciprocity and mutuality: the people as a congregation and as a community assume the educative and pedagogical—that is, hegemonic—activity of the new type of "priest," which, in turn, assumed the real possibility of a people that would "adhere," and actively consent, to the new teaching. The retranslation and redefinition of Christianity brought into relief the role and nature of the people as a community of the faithful during the process of reformation and renovation. In theological and religious terms, the salvation of the soul—which is the meaning, purpose, and end of Christianity—is no longer seen as dependent upon the intervention and mediation of the priestly caste and of the sacraments it administers. The purpose of the ecclesiastical organization, separate and distinct from the ordinary lay Christians, was to provide, by means of the sacraments it controlled, the necessary intercession through which the individual soul would attain spiritual "grace" and ultimately salvation.[5] The reform, however, by eliminating the sacred character of the priest, and by stressing the notion of salvation through faith, established a new relation between the church and the faithful that redefined the meaning and practice of the Christian church. The church as an organization of power, whose mediation between God and the community ensured grace and salvation, was abolished and destroyed. The agent of salvation now became the individual believer united with fellow believers. This agent was therefore the community of the faithful organized into a congregation that expressed within itself the dyad minister/congregant.

The new role that the people assumed in the Christian soteriological enterprise is concretely and culturally exemplified by the Lutheran and Calvinist translations of the sacred texts. These new translations are indicative of the transformation of the Christian world from one political and sociocultural system into another. The translations involved the movement from a language that was the exclusive possession of the ruling castes into one that was the natural vernacular of the people. There is a very definite and "organic" relation between types of language and the Gramscian notion of hegemony. The development of a new hegemonic conception of the world simultaneously requires the development of a language different from the prevailing one.[6] Moral and intellectual reform implies the use of a new and different language in order to express and proliferate the new *modi di pensare* and the new *modi di operare*. The new version of the sacred texts was both a presupposition and a result of the new conception of the world that the *riforma* was undertaking. The vernacular was thus at one and the same time a critical instrument in the undermining of the established conception, and a necessary means by which the new conception would become "life" and assume a central place in the practice and experience of the people.[7]

The vernacular does not simply make the texts more accessible and more understandable to the community; more important, it is intrinsic to the very notion of the community as the carrier and repository of the faith. As such the vernacular symbolizes and embodies the people qua community, for it assumes and captures a past and a tradition different from those of the ruling groups—a tradition embedded in the very syntax and struc-

38 ture of the language spoken by the lower classes. The struggle over the sacred texts, therefore, involved more than a simple scholastic and theological controversy regarding the nature of the scriptures that had occupied the medieval and traditional culture. The texts were a focal point that concentrated in themselves a many-layered conflict, where each layer implied and reinforced the other. The opposition between the Latin of the priestly castes and of the ruling elites, and the vernacular tongues of the majority of the "faithful," finds its parallel in the antithesis between the alliance of aristocratic, princely, and ecclesiastical groups and the lower classes—an antithesis that is further reproduced by the contradictions between the conception of the world entertained by the dominant groups and that held by the subordinate groups. Therefore the translation of the Bible into the various vernaculars does not possess solely a religious significance; it also represents a political, social, and cultural transformation of the existing social and historical reality.[8]

Gramsci's discussion of the nature and role of language is instructive. "Language means also culture and philosophy. . . . we may say that every being who can speak has his own personal language, that is to say, his own way of thinking and feeling."[9] The conflicts over the sacred texts are thus struggles concerning different ways of thinking and experiencing the world. Since language expresses the thought structure and value structure of a social group, the conflict over language is the "cultural struggle to transform the popular 'mentality' and to disseminate philosophical innovations"—innovations that are themselves seen by Gramsci as conceptions of the world.[10] The cultural struggle is determined by the interaction between the "popular mentality" and the innovating philosophy: the language of the people assumes a new character and becomes enriched as the new conception of the world is diffused and expanded throughout the lower classes. Moral and intellectual reform, in effect, assumes the reform and appropriation of a language capable of expressing the new conception of the world, a language able to embody and transmit the new philosophy. The transformation of social reality demands the elaboration of a language that is capable of becoming hegemonic and leading such that it becomes the national-popular language of the overall society.

Since "every language contains elements of a conception of the world or of a given culture," "it is possible to judge the greater or lesser complexity of one's conception of the world from one's particular language. Whoever speaks only a dialect . . . necessarily partakes in an intuition of the world that is more or less restricted and provincial."[11] Latin as a universal language was the possession of a medieval and cosmopolitan "culture of a small intellectual aristocracy"[12] that produced and expressed the wide disparity between the *modo di pensare e di sentire* ("way of thinking and feeling") of the ruling groups and that of the lower classes. What Luther and the Reformation accomplished was the formation of a hegemonic and universal conception of the world that was itself expressed in the language of the people, where the "form" of the language and the "content" of the new way of thinking and acting informed each other within a unified totality that challenged and eventually supplanted the traditional conception of the world. The challenge to the universality of Latin and to the cosmopolitanism of the Roman church and the medieval intellectuals resulted in the creation of a political and social movement that led to the formation of the modern European system of nation-states.[13]

For Gramsci the Reformation is the "classical model" that underlies his notion of moral and intellectual reform because it signaled a radical rupture from the traditional ways of thinking about and experiencing the world. Gramsci saw the transformation of the existing world, and the emergence of an innovating philosophy, as the result of a process grounded on the interaction between the new type of thinker (such as Luther and Calvin) and the community of the faithful. What is significant is that Gramsci introduces his concept of the democratic philosopher in the section that deals with the relation between language and "common sense." Here he discusses the democratic philosopher as the popular educator, and the people as the critical and educative matrix that forms and elaborates the new type of philosopher.[14] Gramsci, of course, does not intend to say that Luther and Calvin are "democratic" or "philosophers" in any modern sense of the term: what he wants to do is to discover and establish parallels between past conceptions of the world that have become *politica* and thus "reality"—that is, that have carried forward a social and cultural transformation of the world—and the philosophy of praxis whose present tasks make it similar to the movement that contributed to the birth of the modern world. In the same way that the Reformation engendered a broad national-popular movement resulting from the innovating and mass-mobilizing activities of the new religious teachers, so too the philosophy of praxis is to initiate a moral and intellectual reform of modern bourgeois society by means of the dialectical and active relation between the popular masses and the democratic philosopher. The motive force that will propel this enterprise is the dialectical unity formed by the democratic philosopher and the people, which embodies itself in a national-popular move-

40 ment that will galvanize and mobilize the masses into a hegemonic force directed toward the reform and renovation of Italian society and culture.

The concept of moral and intellectual reform put forth by Gramsci finds its parallel in passages from Croce's work on the history of the baroque age in Italy. In his *Prison Notebooks*, Gramsci refers to the Crocean interpretation of the Renaissance and the Reformation and attempts to retranslate it in terms of the problems and needs of the philosophy of praxis.[15] Croce sets up a distinction between the Renaissance and the Reformation that exemplifies the basic structure of Crocean idealist philosophy: the opposition between thought and action, and between thought and politics. In his *Storia dell'età barocca in Italia*, Croce writes:

> The Renaissance had remained an aristocratic movement that occurred within certain elite circles; and in Italy, which was the mother and germinator of this movement, it did not move outside the courtly circles, it did not penetrate down into the people, and did not become custom and "prejudice," that is, collective conviction |collettiva persuasione| and faith. On the other hand, the Reformation was able in fact to effect a popular penetration but paid for it through the delay and interruption of its intrinsic further development,

an interruption that impeded the maturation of its "vital germ."[16] The Renaissance was the product of the cultural and intellectual activity of a narrow, aristocratic, and "courtly" stratum far removed from the life of the majority of the people, a movement of rebirth and renewal separated from the "common sense" and "faith" of the people. The Reformation, however, was able to establish itself among the people, and become part of the life of the masses. The Renaissance retained its cultural and intellectual integrity precisely because it was a movement that acted within the *alta cultura* of the princely and aristocratic courts; whereas the very success of the Reformation in the penetration and transformation of the life of the people inhibited and stunted its intellectual and cultural development, and thus "corrupted" its inherent intellectual potential. The Crocean refrain that thought as such ought not to come into contact with the "custom" and "faith" of the people is evident, and becomes the main standard of the interpretation of the Reformation. Thus Croce on Luther:

> And Luther, just as the humanists, deprecates sadness and celebrates happiness, condemns idleness and demands labor; but, on the other hand, he is diffident and hostile against literature and scholarship so that Erasmus was able to assert: *ubicumque regnat lutheranismus, ibi litterarum est interitus*; and certainly, if not solely and simply due to the original aversion of its founder,

German Protestantism for a few centuries was nearly sterile in scholarship, in criticism, and in philosophy.[17]

The contrast is between the Renaissance (the expression of a sophisticated cultural and intellectual movement) and the Reformation (a popular renovation of religion and morality). The sterility of the Reformation is the result of the popular and mass "penetration" of the reformer-founder and his followers. On the one hand, there is the scholarship, critical thinking, and philosophy generated by the *alta cultura* of the Renaissance; on the other, there is the custom, prejudice, faith, and *collettiva persuasione* that exist within the masses.

Gramsci is critically alive to these distinctions posited by Croce, and he attempts to assimilate them in order to employ them for his own political purposes and integrate them into his own political and theoretical project. What is immediately striking is the theoretical continuity and similarity these statements have with the critique that Croce offered on Gramsci almost half a century later. Luther and the Reformation represent the death and sterility of philosophy, in the same way that Marx and the workers' movement marked the decline and corruption of philosophy. Luther and Marx attempted to penetrate into the people, a project that to Croce can only result in the decay and vulgarization of thought and culture. Gramsci accepts the distinction between the Renaissance and the Reformation, but in the process he redefines the relationship between the two, and with this redefinition presents not only a critique of the Crocean view of the Reformation and all similarly popular movements, but also outlines his own interpretation, which points toward the integration of these Crocean opposites.

If Luther and the Reformation represent the interruption of the progress of spirit and philosophy, and if Marx and the socialist movement similarly represent the "corrupt philosophy" that penetrated to the people after the 1840s, then, it is relevant to ask, What is it that Croce and his philosophy represent? If Erasmus could say that Lutheranism signaled the death of learning and culture, then are not Croce and his school repeating the same statement, but directed against a more radical movement that bases itself upon the life and experience of the people? All of which is to say that Croce sees the political and popular element as the main problem and the basic characteristic of both movements—thus: *ubicumque regnat populus, ibi litterarum est interitus*. If Luther, therefore, is equivalent to Marx, then Croce must be equivalent to Erasmus, and "Croce's po-

42   sition is that of the man of the Renaissance against the Protestant Reformation."[18] Gramsci points out, however, that "from the primitive intellectual coarseness of the man of the Reformation there nevertheless gushed forth classical German philosophy and the vast cultural movement from which the modern world was born."[19] The philosophy of praxis embodies within it a historical process whose contours are similar to those of the Reformation: both are founded upon the principle of the people as an aware and responsible actor. Gramsci còmpares the philosophy of praxis to the liberalism of Croce, a theoretical and political position that reproduces the narrowness and the limited particularity of the Renaissance into a small stratum of intellectuals. In addition, such a position has demonstrated its political and moral-intellectual weakness in its confrontation and eventual capitulation to the forces of Roman Catholicism, and later to the acquiescence in the advent of fascism.[20] Croce, in a manner similar to that of the humanists of the Renaissance, cannot establish any relation with the people and with politics. Croce's Erasmian position makes it impossible for his liberal philosophy to become the "faith" of the people and an educative and moral force in the life of the people. While Luther and the Reformation effected the generation, by means of its national and popular character, of a group of intellectuals linked to the people and to the community, what Croce and the liberals accomplished is the re-creation of a cosmopolitan intellectual analogous to that of the Middle Ages. In this sense, Croce is the typical Italian intellectual, one without any connection to the national and popular bases of his society, a cosmopolitan who in the premodern world would enter the service of the international church, and who in modern times remains aloof in his self-described intellectual and cultural superiority. Culturally and politically, Gramsci compares the Crocean type of intellectual to the intellectual-cleric of the medieval and "universal" church so that the former becomes the modern and secular equivalent of the latter.[21]

It is in this sense—in the nature of intellectuals and in the nature of philosophy and culture as they interact with society and politics—that Gramsci interprets Italian history and politics. The history of Italy is characterized by the failure and inability to generate and develop a specifically "popular" and "national" group of intellectuals. From the cosmopolitanism of the ancient Roman empire, to the "catholicism" of the medieval church, to the secular humanism of the Renaissance, and finally to the European liberalism of Croce and his school, Italian intellectuals have gravitated between the two poles of provincialism and parochialism on the one hand,

and internationalism and cosmopolitanism on the other. Both, it should be understood, are a function of the social, cultural, and political fragmentation that determined the major part of Italian history. Both the fragmentation and the special nature of the intellectuals that is its reflection and product can be traced to the absence of the national-popular element, to an aversion to, and fear of, the people.[22]

The mutually exclusive distinctions—Renaissance/Reformation and Erasmus/Luther—that are employed by Croce to criticize the mass and socialist movements of the modern world are appropriated by Gramsci in order to uncover and criticize the political and social role of intellectuals in modern bourgeois Italy. What results from the appropriation of these opposite forces is the Gramscian polarity between the "cosmopolitan intellectual" and the "national-popular intellectual." The first is the equivalent of the traditional intellectual discussed earlier, the second of the organic intellectual or democratic philosopher: I say equivalent, but it should be noted that these terms, which describe types of intellectual, are aspects or moments that in their historical and concrete reality define the particular type.[23]

The distinction described by Renaissance/Reformation is the dyad through which Gramsci sees the movement of Italian history, especially the development of those European states that managed to create a national, popular basis for their culture and politics. In its Italian context, the thought and culture of the Renaissance remained within the ambit of a narrow and closed circle, a situation that reproduced itself in nineteenth-and twentieth-century Italian society: in both historical periods the thought and activity of the intellectuals failed to develop into the *collettiva persuasione* and into the "common sense" of the people. Thus Gramsci gives a new meaning to the original Crocean polarities, and assigns a new cultural and political value to each pole of the dyad. What in Croce represents the pinnacle of cultural and intellectual life in the Renaissance is transformed in Gramsci into the product and result of the disintegration and degeneration of Italian life and politics.[24] What is regarded in Croce as the flowering of literary and aesthetic sensibility is translated in Gramsci into the stagnation and death of Italian politics, into the subjection of the Italian cities to the external power of Spain and France, and into the reaction of the Counter-Reformation.[25] As Gramsci puts it:

> While the progressive movement in Italy after 1000 was closely linked to the Communes, it was precisely in Italy that such a movement petered out—and

44   that the Communes degenerated was due precisely to humanism and to the Renaissance. Whereas, in the rest of Europe, the general movement culminated in the emergence and rise of the national states, which was followed by the world expansion of Spain, France, England, and Portugal. In Italy, rather than having a national state as achieved by these countries, there existed the Papacy organized into an absolute state—a process begun under Alexander VI—an organization that destroyed the rest of Italy.[26]

In addition, the northern Italian city-states—from which emerged the secularism and humanism of the Renaissance—could not jettison and free themselves from the cosmopolitan and medieval conceptions of the world expressed in the imperialism of the pope and the cleric, and in the thought and culture of the humanist thinkers such as Guicciardini and Leonardo.[27] The humanism of the Renaissance could not develop into a popular movement because the conception of the world it expressed could not transcend the artificiality of the *alta cultura/cultura popolare* distinction.

The Crocean equation of Lutheranism and Marxism (where both lead to a corrupted and sterile culture) is redirected against Croce and against his interpretation of the Renaissance and the Reformation. Such an interpretation leads Croce into a contradiction from which he cannot escape. For if the philosophy of praxis is the corrupt philosophy that issues from a social and democratic mass movement, and if, similarly, the Lutheran and Protestant Reformations resulted in the vulgarization of culture and philosophy, then it must be asked, What process, and under whose auspices, described the transition from a medieval to a modern sociocultural and sociopolitical reality? If the Reformation unleashed social and political forces that led to the profound transformation of the world and of humanity's interpretation of that world, then to equate the Reformation with the socialist and proletarian movement would be to assign to the latter a similar, and parallel, transformative character. The "anti-intellectual" and "anticultural" elements of the Reformation as a sociopolitical movement blind Croce to the discovery and identification of the liberating and transforming seeds nascent within it. Without the popular movement of the Reformation, the process that culminated in the destruction of the feudal social order and of the feudal conception of the world could not have occurred; nor could such a process have prepared the ground for the birth of classical German philosophy and the Enlightenment. In effect, in political and historical terms, the liberal-bourgeois and idealist philosophy whose autonomy is so necessary to Croce is the product of a historical and sociopolitical process that issued from the very Reformation whose thought and culture Croce describes as sterile and vulgar. On the other hand, it is the culture and humanism of the Renaissance that are revealed to be sterile since their thought did not transcend its narrow sociopolitical base, nor did it transform its culture into a national-popular movement. Thus Gramsci writes: "That a mass of men be led to think coherently and in a unitary manner an existing reality |*il reale presente*| is a 'philosophical' fact much more important and 'original' than the discovery by a philosophical 'genius' of a new truth that remains the property |*patrimonio*| of small groups of intellectuals."[28]

In the same way that the cultural achievements of the Renaissance remained the "property" of a small circle of clerics and courtly humanists, so too in modern Italian history the culture and thought of the liberals and their allies are the exclusive possessions of the educated and leading groups. The philosophy of praxis is that conception of the world that will lead the masses to the formulation of a coherent and rational view of *il reale presente*; and the unity of this conception with the masses is embodied in a modern version of the Reformation, which, by means of the new democratic philosopher that is created by this unity, will generate that "vast" movement necessary to the overcoming of the existing social reality.

Such a reform represents the negation of all Italian history up to the present, a history defined by the Erasmus/Croce relation: the people, mobilized and organized into a national-popular movement, are not present in Italian history, and this absence is explained by the cosmopolitan, traditional nature of Italian intellectuals and Italian culture. Rome, the Empire, the medieval church, the Renaissance, the Papacy as an absolute monarchy, the twilight and decline of Italy and its subjection to external powers, the Counter-Reformation, the French Revolution and Napoleon, the Risorgimento, *trasformismo*, liberalism and nationalism, the philosophy and figure of Croce: the major and significant elements that characterize these successive stages of Italian history are given by what failed to occur, rather than by what did occur—the absence of the national-popular, the absence of the democratic philosopher, the absence of a *riforma*. The emergence of Europe into the modern age began with the transformation of the feudal, cosmopolitan intellectuals into the national-popular, organic intellectuals who disseminated among the people a new conception of the world, which together formed the basis for a territorial and centralized state that developed eventually into the modern bourgeois nation-state. This process presupposed and necessitated the emergence of a new type of intellectual

46   who would "lead masses of men" to a coherent, integrated conception of existing reality in order to change and transcend it.

If, however, Italian history and politics are the characteristic products of Croce's prototypical *distacco* between culture and people, and if they are described by the absence of a moral and intellectual reform such as that initiated by the Lutheran and Protestant Reformations, Gramsci nevertheless locates and identifies, within the very Renaissance that he has just interpreted as representing the degeneration and corruption of Italian politics and culture, an intellectual figure and a politico-theoretical project that encapsulate embryonically the potentiality inherent within the Renaissance, a potentiality that achieved its historical and political realization not in Italy, but outside of it. This figure theorized and elaborated a conception of the world that attained a ruling and hegemonic supremacy not within its country of origin but rather in those very countries that underwent the sociocultural and sociopolitical changes sparked by the Protestant Reformation. Such a figure is Machiavelli, and his project was to identify and institute "new modes and orders" in order to overcome and transform *il reale presente*.

Gramsci's critique of the Crocean liberal philosophy and of its underlying dyads—Renaissance/Reformation, Erasmus/Luther, philosophy/politics, theory/practice—is resumed and summarized under his interpretation of Machiavelli and of his political thought. It is through Machiavelli that Gramsci carries forward the negation of the Crocean position and formulates what he calls an "anti-Croce."[29] This "anti-Croce" is not a simple or mechanical opposition of Croce's philosophy to the philosophy of praxis. Gramsci attempts to generate a critique of Croce that originates within the internal structure of Crocean liberalism, an "anti-Croce" that unfolds from within Croce's own historical and philosophical formulations. To do this means to locate within Italian history and culture a figure whose thought and project point to the overcoming of Croce. This transcendence, in turn, presupposes a figure whose work actively negates the fundamental antithesis of Italian history, which, we have seen, is represented and embodied by Croce: the divorce between the people and the philosopher-intellectual, and between the people and culture.

In addition, to show that Croce is the modern equivalent of Erasmus, and that the philosophy of praxis is the contemporary parallel to the Protestant Reformation, Gramsci must present an alternative figure, and an alternative philosophy, derived not from sources external to the Italian experience, but rather that issue from the cultural, intellectual, and political dynamics of Italian history. It is not enough to equate the philosophy of praxis with the Reformation, and Marx with Luther (as indeed Croce does from his liberal bourgeois perspective).[30] The refutation of Croce, and thereby the refutation of Italian idealist thought, necessitates a specifically Italian figure to mediate the Erasmus/Luther, Croce/Marx, and Renaissance/Reformation antinomies. In the Crocean interpretation, the first term represents culture or philosophy, the second term politics or practice. Thus, if the distinction is posited between "true" philosophy and a sterile or corrupt philosophy, then Gramsci must find a common term that will connect these dyads in a way that will describe the historical and ideological parallels between Croce's position and his interpretation of Italian politics and history.

To Gramsci, the figure of Machiavelli represents the negation of Croce's thought, as well as the negation of Italian political practice. Machiavelli is the anti-Croce in the precise sense that Gramsci looks at the Machiavellian enterprise as a project that attempts to initiate a moral and intellectual reformation in order to transform Italian society and politics. What is central to Gramsci is that the *rinnovazione* that defined Machiavelli's project is not seen as an abstract and narrowly "cultural" renovation, as a scholastic or literary exercise of the intellectual circles of the period. On the contrary, this Machiavelli proposes to accomplish what to Croce, and to Erasmus, would mean the death of culture and learning—namely, to lead a "mass of men" to understand *il presente reale* and thereby transcend it.[31]

To the cosmopolitan and traditional intellectual epitomized by Croce, Gramsci opposes the national-popular and organic intellectual epitomized by the figure of Machiavelli. In Gramsci, the democratic philosopher that failed to emerge as a collective, social force within the actual history and politics of Italy is theorized and prefigured in the thought of Machiavelli. Machiavelli thus emerges as the democratic philosopher who engages in an educational relationship with the people, who educates the people and is in turn educated by them. He represents that element within the Renaissance and humanist tradition—especially that arising from the communal experience and practice of Florence—that recognizes and theorizes the need to transform the traditional categories of thought and the customary ways of acting into a new vision of society and politics, a vision that will transcend the stale, sterile culture that remained anchored within the traditional boundaries of Empire and church.

To Gramsci, Machiavelli is the representative of a specific humanism that was "politico-ethical, and not artistic," a humanism that inquired into

48   the underlying "bases of an 'Italian State,' which should have been born simultaneously and parallel with the states of France, Spain, and England. In this sense Machiavelli is the most expressive and representative exponent of Humanism and the Renaissance. |Such a humanism| was 'Ciceronian' . . . that is, it found its particular bases within the period |of Roman history| that preceded the Empire, the imperial *cosmopolis*."[32] Here we have the contrast between the national-popular—Cicero, who comes from the people, the *homo novus* who wants to preserve the "people's affair" (the *res publica*) from the military despots who want to destroy it—and the cosmopolitan, the intellectual who derives existence and thought from the imperial structure of power in opposition to the people. Gramsci continues: "Machiavelli is the representative in Italy of the knowledge that the Renaissance cannot be such—a 'rebirth'—without the founding of a national State. But as a man, he is a theorist of what occurs outside Italy, and not a theorist of Italian events."[33] The "founding of a national State" is contrasted with the cosmopolitan and international nature of medieval culture and politics as represented by the Holy Roman Empire and by the Catholic Church.[34] In this sense, the Renaissance is a progressive movement to the extent that it destroyed the bases for the traditional society and the traditional worldview, and to the extent that it provided within Europe the elements necessary for the establishment of a new system of power and a new vision of the world. As a European phenomenon, therefore, Gramsci sees the Renaissance as a necessary and innovating movement that contributed to the formation of a new Europe comprised of national, bourgeois states. This new Europe was envisioned by Machiavelli's project to initiate a *rinnovazione*: he attempted to inquire into the political elements necessary for the reconstruction of a popular state, of a state that would be "Italian" and Ciceronian in character. This new political order would be neither "universal" in the feudal and Catholic sense, nor cosmopolitan in the imperial Roman sense.

The distinction that Gramsci makes between Cicero and Caesar—one that is made by de Sanctis in his discussion of Machiavellian thought[35]—is indicative of his understanding of the Machiavellian project. Cicero represents the national-popular elements of Roman-Italian society who are opposed to the autocracy of Caesar, whose power base rests on the cosmopolitan and non-Italian groups that reside in the provinces of the Empire. Whether or not such an interpretation of the class and power struggles that preceded the fall of the Roman republic and the rise of imperial rule is historically accurate is not the issue.[36] The fact that Gramsci sees the rise

of Caesar and the fall of the aristocratic republic in terms of the rise of a
new cosmopolitan caste of bureaucratic intellectuals that ruled the Empire, and the corresponding decline of a group of republican intellectuals
that was rooted within the Italian peninsular society, becomes especially
significant when this interpretation is related to Machiavelli's praise of the
innovator who founds a *vivere politico* and to his condemnation of those who,
like Caesar, destroyed this form of political life.[37] To Gramsci, Machiavelli
represents the potential in Italian history to develop a group of organic intellectuals or democratic philosophers who, by mobilizing the people and
by translating their knowledge into the "life and sense" of the masses, can
generate a moral and intellectual reform of the existing social reality and
achieve a superior conception of the world that will replace the established one. This is the nature of the "Ciceronian" aspect of Machiavelli's
enterprise: it refers not to the moralistic and aristocratic pretenses put
forth by the defenders (one of whom was Cicero himself) of the *optimates*
against the *populares*, but rather to the sociopolitical and sociocultural links
to the Italian municipalities. As such, the cosmopolitan/national-popular
distinction that operates throughout Gramsci's works[38] is what should be
taken as the defining characteristic of Machiavelli's Cicero.[39] Machiavelli's
romanitas and *humanitas*, therefore, are political and ethical aspects of a dynamic activist conception of the world that envisions man as the "sensu-
ous" and conscious creator of his own world; they are not in any way related
to artistic and literary sensibilities, which are only passive, uncritical reflections of a scholastic and courtly humanism whose notion of *imitatio* merely
reproduces the cosmopolitan, antipopular culture of the Empire and the
church. The Machiavellian type of humanism recognizes the hegemonic
and leading—that is, popular and educative—character of the Roman ruling groups as they expanded the Roman republic throughout the Italian
peninsula.

    Machiavelli is the product of a lengthy republican tradition character-
ized by bitter and intense communal struggles that pitted various social
and political forces against each other: the *ottimati* against the *popolo minuto*,
republicans against the *medici*, the rising communal bourgeoisie against the
gentiluomini and the landed feudal lords, the partisans of papal Rome
against the ultramontanists, and those who desired moral, political, and
religious reform against those who supported the established order.[40] In
each instance, Gramsci recognizes within these sociopolitical antagonisms
the problematic defined by the traditional intellectual/democratic philosopher dyad: the sociopolitical struggles of the competing social forces are

50 at one and the same time moral and intellectual struggles between opposing conceptions of the world that seek to establish or to preserve a particular kind of political and ideological supremacy. Machiavelli's thought and work are the representative expressions of this antagonistic historical process. Machiavelli formulates from these struggles a new synthesis—a new conception of the world—that attempts to go beyond and to overcome the accumulated baggage of the past. Thus this Machiavellian synthesis is, in Gramsci's words, "the knowledge that the Renaissance cannot be such . . . without the founding of a national State." What this means is that the cultural, intellectual, moral, and social movement that is collectively known as the Renaissance cannot achieve the impetus and direction of a concrete political reformation unless it becomes translated into a conception of the world that encompasses the life and activity of the people.[41] If the Renaissance is to be a force capable of transforming social reality, then it must address the problem of the founding of a state that embodies the new conception of the world put forth by the new ideas of the Renaissance. But the founding of a national state is at the same time a "philosophical event"[42] —that is, the creation of a new social and political order implies the generation and proliferation of a new conception of the world throughout the popular masses, or simply, hegemony.

It is in this sense that Machiavelli "as a man" is a theorist of "what happens outside Italy": the Renaissance did not culminate in Italy in the creation of a national state. Because it remained the possession of a narrow circle of cosmopolitan intellectuals allied to the various princely courts, communal *signorie*, and to the universalist papacy, Machiavelli's new vision of the world took root and was historically realized in Northern and Western Europe rather than in his native *"provincia."* In Italy the new knowledge remained just that: a knowledge without political, social, and practical consequences. The divorce between Renaissance thought and culture, on the one hand, and the life and beliefs of the masses, on the other, meant that the democratic philosopher necessary to the organization of culture and to the mobilization of the masses could not emerge. The Italian masses, therefore, did not yet exist as a people, as a collective subject. Yet the knowledge that Machiavelli intended to introduce was a knowledge that could not be understood unless the popular masses—*"l'universale"*— are taken as the central and nodal loci within which that knowledge is anchored, and from which it acquires purpose and direction. The *rinnovazione* that was the intention of Machiavelli, and the moral and intellectual reform that is basic to Gramsci's notion of hegemony, together presuppose the people as the necessary force in the founding of a state or of a new social order. The penetration to the masses of a new knowledge constitutes the development of a hegemonic conception of the world, which is the proliferation of moral and intellectual reform, which is, finally, the constitution of an Italian state.[43]

Machiavelli, therefore, is the democratic philosopher who embodies in his thought and in his practical activity the fulfillment of the ideas of the Renaissance; at the same time, such a fulfillment is also the negation of Renaissance humanism. Machiavelli is its fulfillment because his work represents the consciousness that the new vision of man and the world advanced by Renaissance culture cannot develop further, cannot progress to a higher phase—indeed, it is not able to realize the very values and ends that it has posited for itself—unless there is constituted a national-popular and collective movement directed toward the creation of a centralized and national political entity: a specifically "Italian" state. And Machiavelli is the negation of the Renaissance because this thought and this consciousness were realized outside Italy—and against the trends and forces intrinsic to the process during the period of the Renaissance that led to the decline and fall of the Italian communal republics and principalities. The national-popular movement, and the formation within it of a collective will, achieved sociohistorical reality outside Italy. The teaching of Machiavelli remained an academic knowledge in Italy, whereas it flowered in that very soil where the civilization and the *studia humanitatis* of the Renaissance had not yet taken deep root. Hence the paradox: Machiavelli as the fulfillment of the Renaissance becomes realized in those countries removed geographically and culturally from the centers of the Renaissance and from the "school of Italy" (Florence). Machiavelli, the democratic philosopher of Italian politics and history, as the negation of the Renaissance, represents a political knowledge and a conception of the world that eventually become realized through a moral and religious Reformation whose sociopolitical and sociocultural effects are the secularization and modernization of Europe.

Chapter 4

Power and the State
Croce and Gramsci on the Nature of Machiavelli's Politics

The Gramscian formulation that the work and thought of Machiavelli are equivalent to the work and thought of the Protestant reformers—that the enterprise Machiavelli wanted to introduce into Italy was historically carried out and brought to fruition by the Reformation—sees Machiavelli not so much as the discoverer of an "objective" political "science," but rather as the innovator who attempted to initiate a moral and intellectual reform of the beliefs and thought of his period, and who in turn wanted to create and proliferate a new conception of the world in opposition to the established view. Thus the Crocean position that posits a contradiction between the Renaissance and the Reformation is viewed by Gramsci to be one-sided and superficial. The contradiction resolves itself into a false polarity when the figure and thought of Machiavelli are introduced into it as a mediating middle term.[1]

Now such an interpretation cannot be appreciated unless it is understood that Gramsci's analysis is derived, at least in part, from a reading of the Risorgimento historian Francesco de Sanctis. In his magisterial work on the history of Italian literature, de Sanctis contrasts the spirit and culture of the Middle Ages with the moral and intellectual *rinnovamento* ("renovation") that he believes Machiavelli represents.[2] Such a comparison emphasizes the "disharmony" that prevailed during the period that saw in Italy the end of the feudal order and the emergence of the Renaissance, a comparison that underlined the differences between the decadence and corruption of the ecclesiastical and princely courts, and the way of life and practices of the people, a contradiction expressed often by Machiavelli between "the depravity of the Italian, or rather Latin race, and the moral soundness of the German people."[3] In addition, the contradiction between thought and practice, ideal and reality, is highlighted in the sermons of the Florentine reformer Savonarola and in the critical activity of Luther. De Sanctis notes that "the Gospel always remained an undisputed ideal, although it had no real effect in practical life: thought was no longer word, and the word was no longer action; [thus] there was no harmony in life."[4]

In de Sanctis's view, the Lutheran Reformation could not have been a real possibility in Italy because

> Italy had already passed through a theological period, and now no longer believed in anything except science. It would have necessarily perceived Luther and Calvin as new versions of the medieval scholastics. Thus the Reformation could not have taken root among us, and it remained alien and extraneous to our culture. . . . Already liberated from theology, and embracing in a single sweep all religion and all culture, the Italy that gave birth to Pico and to Pomponazzi, seated on the ruins of the Middle Ages, regarded science, and not theology, as the basis for the new edifice.[5]

It should be evident from this quote that the Crocean distinction between Reformation and Renaissance is anticipated or prefigured in the antagonism that de Sanctis, a nineteenth-century Hegelian liberal, posits between theology and science. The de Sanctian polarity, however, is quite different from that of Croce. The theology/science dyad represents an opposition between two conceptions of the world, two ways of life, two "ways of thinking and acting," such that the *rinnovamento* that de Sanctis attributes to Machiavelli contains within itself the revolutionary notion that human thought and human consciousness are independent of any transcendent, extrahistorical authority, and that this consciousness is the self-knowledge of human beings acting in society and in history.[6]

Thus, to de Sanctis Machiavelli is "the consciousness and the thought of the century, and of the society that looks into itself and that questions itself and [thereby] knows itself." Machiavelli represents "the most profound negation of the Middle Ages,"[7] and his innovative project and the new world that it expresses are together the products of the breakdown of feudal society and feudal thought, products that will eventually develop into the modern conception of the world and into a modern notion of science and philosophy. To de Sanctis, Machiavelli is the Italian Luther: "Lutero fu Niccolò Machiavelli."[8] The Italian Luther constructed an innovating knowledge that formed the basis for a new and modern conception of the world that eventually led to the transformation of European thought

54 and life, while the German Luther initiated a moral and religious Reformation whose transformation of traditional religion and established theology led to the foundation of a modern Europe. In both we have the beginning of a moral and intellectual process that revolutionized the thought and activity of European society: in the first case there is a critique of the "disharmony" between the accepted theoretical and political knowledge and the sociopolitical reality this knowledge attempts to understand, and in the second case there is a similar critique of the contradiction between the "word" of the sacred texts and the "action" of practical life.

Although Gramsci does not accept all of the conclusions that de Sanctis draws from his interpretation of Machiavelli, he nevertheless recognizes in the de Sanctian Machiavelli a crucial element that is central to the formation and elaboration of his notion of the organic and national-popular philosopher.[9] To say that Machiavelli is the Italian Luther is to say that Machiavelli is the figure who theorized the necessity for the generation of a moral and intellectual reform that would penetrate to the people, become the life of the people, and thus assume the character of a popular movement. At the same time, such an interpretation provides a political and ideological critique of Croce and of Italian liberal and bourgeois culture. For to envision Machiavelli as the Italian Luther[10] is to deny the Crocean distinction between *philosophus* and *politicus*, and to argue for the elaboration of a philosophy and culture that through their educative and directing activity have become a hegemonic force.

Gramsci accepts as a general principle the de Sanctian formulation that Machiavelli represents the consciousness and self-knowledge of the age. But he historicizes and concretizes it by placing Machiavelli within the political and class context of Florentine history: the new world and the new consciousness discovered and expressed by Machiavelli failed to become the "*costume*" of Italian society, because this new knowledge of ruling did not become the knowledge of Italian social forces—especially of the ruling groups—did not become the hegemonic conception of the communal bourgeoisie, and thus did not become a state, "*il reale presente.*"[11] On the contrary, it is the religious and moral reformers—the Protestant Machiavellians—who are the true historical and political inheritors of the new knowledge. The equation, Luther = Machiavelli, undermines and uproots the liberal bourgeois position that establishes the independence of philosophy from politics, knowledge from action, and the intellectuals from social and economic forces. Gramsci opposes the de Sanctian interpretation of Machiavelli as the Italian Luther to the Crocean distinction between Luther and Erasmus. What such an opposition does is insert within the latter antithesis a middle term—the figure of Machiavelli—such that a synthesis is achieved whereby the thought and philosophy represented by Erasmus (*alta cultura*) and the popular character and beliefs of Luther (*cultura popolare*) resolve themselves into a new and unified totality. It is in the figure of Machiavelli that the opposition is transcended. Such a synthesis may now be expressed by the formulation: Machiavelli = Erasmus + Luther.

But such a transcendence, of course, is regarded by Croce as an impossible self-contradiction, and would be anathema to his philosophical and political position. To posit a unity between Luther and Erasmus would mean the disintegration and collapse of culture and philosophy, and the concurrent elevation of politics and ideology to a level where the latter would become the standards and determiners of what Croce conceives as "Truth" and "Spirit." The elevation of ideology into philosophy, or "error" and "faith" into "truth" and "knowledge," means in fact the initiation of that process that began with the revolutions of the late eighteenth and early nineteenth centuries, and that saw the emergence and spread of the "corrupt philosophy" (Marxian philosophy). Therefore, in order to maintain his position toward politics and the role of the masses, Croce is compelled to offer an interpretation of Machiavelli that denies the popular and democratic character of the Machiavellian enterprise—that is, Croce must deny those elements within the thought and work of Machiavelli that pose the problem concerning the formation of a people and the formation of a way of life that forms and embodies a people. The opposition between Erasmus and Luther, and between the Renaissance and the Reformation, must be maintained, and each term of the relation must be posited as separate and distinct, if the Crocean position is to retain its political and philosophical integrity.

Croce begins by repeating the de Sanctian notion that Machiavelli is a great revolutionary and initiator in the field of historical and political thought. He is the discoverer of a new political knowledge that established the independence and autonomy of his science from all theological, ethical, and philosophical systems.[12] To assert the autonomy of philosophy and culture, Croce must simultaneously assert the autonomy of politics, and he sees in Machiavelli the thinker who theorized and developed this autonomy of the political. Machiavellian thought is a science of politics that transcends any specific historical period and any particular sociopolitical class or group. Thus Croce:

56   Machiavelli discovers the necessity and the autonomy of politics, of a politics
that is beyond, or rather this side of, a moral good and evil, that possesses
its own laws against which it is useless to rebel, a politics that holy water
cannot exorcize and expel from this world. Such a concept permeates his
entire work ... a profoundly philosophical concept that represents the true
and actual foundation of a political philosophy.[13]

The laws and categories of this new political philosophy are eternally and
universally valid, as immutable and unrelenting as the physical laws of nature. They are consequently autonomous and independent from any other
categories or concepts external to themselves, and from any concrete and
historical subject who knows them and knows how to employ them.

The Machiavellian "new modes and orders" constitute a system of
thought radically different from the antecedent philosophy of feudalism
that subordinated politics to ethics, and ethics to theology. Machiavelli is
the discoverer not simply of political thought—for, after all, political thinking has had a long and durable tradition in European history—but rather
of the notion that such thought is a product of categories and concepts pe-
culiar to itself, and does not issue from ethical, religious, theological, and
philosophical systems of which it is a mere constituent. Machiavelli signals
the breakup of the unity of the Middle Ages, and he embodies the consciousness that this rupture requires a new way of thinking about power
and politics. The de Sanctian notion that the Renaissance means the general awakening of the human spirit, the coming to self-consciousness of social man, is interpreted by Croce in terms of the progress of the Spirit in
history.[14] Croce echoes the de Sanctian observation about the role of Machiavelli:

Niccolò Machiavelli is considered the pure expression of the Italian
Renaissance; but at the same time he should be related in some way to the
Reformation, to that general necessity that emerged during his age, both in
and outside Italy, to know man and to inquire into the problem of the soul.[15]

This need for human beings to acquire knowledge of themselves is similar
to the de Sanctian "*nosce te ipsum*," but while Croce links it to the problem
of the soul and of thought, de Sanctis understands self-knowledge not as a
problem exclusively spiritual or philosophical, but rather as one intimately
related to the concrete world, where self-knowledge presupposes "the
knowledge of the world in its reality."[16] In Croce, to the extent that the age
recognized "that general need" for self-knowledge, Machiavelli may "in
some way" be compared to the Reformation—but in what way? In the de

Sanctian interpretation of the Italian Luther who initiates not just an intellectual, but also an ethical and moral reformation, as one who attempted to construct a new conception of the world in order to change the real world? The operative term here is Croce's *"anima"* (soul): both the Reformation and Machiavelli posed the problem of consciousness and self-knowledge in terms of *"anima"*—that is, in terms of pure thought. Thus the autonomy of politics, and the autonomy of political thought, express the general need for self-knowledge, and are located within the *"problema dell-'anima."* Machiavelli and the Reformation do not negate the moral and religious problems of their time, they each in their individual ways free them from their subordination to traditional authority and established theology.

Following his conception of the "dialectic of distincts," Croce sees Machiavelli as the thinker who individuates and develops that moment or aspect of the universal Spirit that embodies and takes the form of political thought.[17] The distinction between philosophy and politics, and between culture and politics, is preserved because the revolution that Machiavelli initiates in politics, and the reform that the Reformation represents, occur not within the real world of social forces struggling against each other, but in the realm of the spirit and of the *"anima."* The Machiavellian enterprise is seen purely in terms of the problems of political philosophy and political science; that is, the subject of this knowledge is located within the moment of thought and culture. Thus the autonomy of politics is the autonomy of a political knowledge from the other moments of Spirit, an autonomy achieved by the individuation and differentiation of this knowledge within philosophy and culture.

Croce writes that "the art and the science of politics—of pure politics—which were developed and brought to maturity by Italians, had become an object of great pride to them, so that to Cardinal Rohan's statement that the Italians did not know anything about war, |Machiavelli| replied that 'the French did not understand the nature of the State |and of politics|.' "[18] But what is the substance of this *pura politica*, what form does it take, and what role does it play? Croce presents an entirely abstract and ahistorical discussion of the nature of politics: *politica* is an activity and an art whose particular sphere is the manipulation and control of the appetitive and economic interests of self-regarding individuals. These interests make it necessary to direct them into orderly, integrative channels that will preserve the overall stability of society. Without the integrating activity of politics the egoistic nature of man will lead to the destruction and dissolution of societal order, where society will degenerate into a Hobbesian

58 *bellum omnium contra omnes.* It is the political art that provides the mechanism and the means through which the struggles among the various groups and individuals within society will be circumscribed within the established forms and institutions.[19]

Political knowledge, therefore, is reduced to a technique and a means, which, by its very nature, does not contain within itself any ends or purposes: as instrument and technique it is ethically and morally neutral. Politics is a cold, purely scientific, logical activity detached from the passions, needs, and interests of conflicting and antagonistic people. The man of politics—*il politico*—is an actor without passion and without emotion. As the practitioner of the political art he is pure calculation, so that he embodies in his action this "pure politics," in the same way that he reflects in the calculating nature of his thought the limpid and stark objectivity of his science. *Pura politica* has no interests and no values except those necessary to its self-constitution and self-preservation as politics and as science. It defines itself and looks to itself: it is an instrumentality whose nature is given by its technique and by its "amorality."[20] "Detachment," "science," and "technique" are the operative terms that constitute the Crocean notion of "pure politics," elements that underlie the liberal and bourgeois— and, as Gramsci points out, fundamentally Giolittian—nature of Croce's politics.[21]

Croce attempts to redeem such a notion from its Hobbesian and individualistic atomism through the appropriation of the Hegelian term "ethical" and transforming it into the "ethico-political." The ethico-political means that the "State" is neither pure force nor pure consent, but is rather an active and dynamic relation between the two, such that it becomes a synthesis of "power" and "morality." The actual state is this synthesis between the two moments of force and ethics—thus the state is ethico-political.[22] The state is a unity of these two moments: it is "pure |*mera*| politics, pure force or power or utility, and amoral; and it is morality and ethical value."[23] The first Croce equates to the Machiavellian moment of *pura politica*, where Machiavelli is said to deny any ethical or moral character to the state, such that the state is pure power, and as such is autonomous from the "rules of Christian piety."[24] This is the "eternal truth" enunciated by Machiavelli, who opposed a "*verità politica*" to the "*verità cristiana*," a truth that was reclaimed and appropriated by Hegel and Marx when they attacked the moral and democratic character of the state as mere illusion and hypocrisy, and who together "reasserted the nature of the State and of politics in terms of authority and a struggle for power (the power of nations or the power of classes, as the case may be)."[25] Thus to Croce there is a common strand that links Machiavelli to Hegel and to Marx; this strand is the conception of the state in terms of pure power, and the consequent interpretation of politics as pure technique and as a struggle for power.

When, therefore, Croce addresses Marx as the Machiavelli of the proletariat, he is saying that the Marxian theory of proletarian revolution is the concrete historical form of that *pura politica* that was originally discovered by Machiavelli.[26] Gramsci only partially accepts such a formulation.[27] For the Crocean equation Marx = Machiavelli implies that Marxism possesses no moral and intellectual content, that it reduces itself to mere political technique, and thus cannot represent the thought and consciousness of a new historical subject whose activity will usher in a new sociopolitical and sociocultural order. We shall see below why the Crocean form of this equation is radically unacceptable to Gramsci. Nevertheless, Gramsci appropriates it and redefines it in terms of moral and intellectual reform, so that Machiavelli = Marx = the democratic philosopher. Gramsci, like Croce and others, opposes the *virtù politica* of Machiavelli to the *virtù morale* of medieval and Christian philosophy.[28] But the meaning and content given to these terms are understood differently in Gramsci and in Croce. For the latter, the nature of political *virtù* is constituted by "prudence," "cunning," and "shrewdness" ("*prudenza*" and "*avvedutezza*")[29]—in other words, those very skills necessary to appetitive man. Such a notion of *virtù* reduces itself to the technique that defines for Croce the nature of the political. Gramsci, however, points out that mere technique does not exhaust the full meaning of political *virtù*: the Machiavellian *virtù* does not simply address the instrumental questions given by the metaphor of the lion and the fox; it does that, but it is also a concept of action that presupposes a moral and ethical posture toward the world. The *virtù* that Machiavelli opposes to the established conception of ethics and morality contains within itself a view of life and a vision of the future such that the opposition is not between power and morality, but rather between two radically opposed conceptions of morality and ways of life.[30] Croce is not able to understand a moral and spiritual dimension unless it is posed in Christian terms; thus the Machiavellian attack on Christian and medieval notions of the ethical life is taken as a critique of morality and ethics in general.

It is indicative of Croce's interpretation of Machiavelli that the opposition between the power state and the ethical state is seen as an antagonism between two different spheres of action whose resolution can only be

60 achieved in thought. The opposing terms must be made "*pensabile*"—"thinkable"—by means of what he calls a "dialectical movement," where the "parallel and juxtaposed duality" is resolved through a spiritual process in such a way that the "State poses itself in a first moment as pure power and utility, and thence it ascends to morality, but at the same time it does not repudiate its former character, but rather negates it—that is, it preserves it by transcending it."[31] This, of course, is a restatement in Hegelian language of the liberal distinction between state and society that has become the prevailing duality in political thought since the advent of modern, bourgeois society. The Hegelian language is simply a superficial device that obscures the undialectical character of the analysis. It is significant that the dyads power/morality, force/consent are not seen by Croce in terms of a dialectical mutual penetration and reciprocity, but are rather posited within entirely separate realms, such that one "ascends" to the level of the other. Such a positing simply reproduces the traditional antithesis between state and church, Reformation and Counter-Reformation, the earthly city and the city of God (these opposing concepts permeate the whole body of Croce's *Etica e politica*).[32]

In effect, the Crocean notion of *pura politica* reclaims, and translates into a modern liberal discourse, the Christian and Augustinian distinction between the state, conceived as the result and remedy of the earthly *bellum omnium*, and the spiritual-ethical realm, seen as the sphere where "true" justice reigns. The Augustinian state is pure force, utility, and coercion. It issues from the sinful and irremediably unregenerate nature of humankind—a conception not very distant from the Crocean antipathy toward the popular masses. The Augustinian Christian kernel within the liberal Crocean notion of the political emerges quite clearly from the following statement: "political men, powerless to change rapidly the nature |*lo stato d'animo*| of the common people |*volgo*|, are led to accept and to approve of them in their words and speech, and to deny them in their actions."[33] The political can be nothing other than the technical method of the lion and the fox (force and fraud) employed to control and repress the nature of the people. Political human beings are powerless to transcend the necessary laws of sociopolitical reality. In a very profound sense politics is as amoral, and a question of technique, to Croce and to the liberal bourgeois philosophers as it is in Augustine and in Christian thought generally.[34] The moral and ethical nature of the state, in Croce as in Augustine, is a function of a spiritual and philosophical realm—of a level of being—external to what they consider to be properly political.

The Augustinian problematic appears in Crocean liberal thought under the guise of a secular and historical elaboration of philosophy and ethics. The state of grace—the *civitas dei*—in Augustine is transformed in Croce into the sphere of philosophy and culture; similarly, the earthly city—the *civitas terrena*—of the former is secularized by the latter into "*lo stato d'animo del volgo*"; in both cases, human and political activity cannot change the nature of reality, and the two realms must remain forever antagonistic and alien to each other. Thus the Crocean state: power, which is necessary to restrain and coerce the appetites and passions of the "*volgo*"; and ethics, a sphere of action to which the philosophers, but not the people, can aspire to attain. In Augustine and in Christian theology and philosophy as a whole, the political activity of human beings can have no transformative character, nor can it generate an educational and moral process by which "virtue" (in the classical and Aristotelian sense) may be attained. The political arises as a consequence of the fall and the unalterable nature of humankind, a nature that is corrupt and "morally" imperfect. What is crucial here is that Augustine posits the general and fundamental question regarding the nature of activity and practice: the action of human beings in this world is inherently and unchangeably value-less; by means of their own will and their own *virtus*, human beings cannot rise to a higher and more meaningful level of existence. The undeserved and free grace of God becomes necessary to reform and to save the "*anima*" of humankind: there is a radical and profound gulf between humans in the state of grace and humans in the *civitas terrena*. The two realms are forever separate and distinct. Thus Christians in the state of grace are *peregrinatores* and strangers to this earthly life: they are *in* the world, but not *for* the world; they live and move in this life, but their ends and final destination are given by an entity external to the world. To be for this world—to entertain ends defined by the earthly city—is precisely to participate in the "corruption" and "amorality" that permeates the very character of human action. The political, which belongs properly within this earthly city, is thus a mere device for the attainment of "earthly peace" (or order and stability)—that is, the channeling and ordering of human passions and interests through the institution of the state. The Augustinian dualism between the two kinds of *civitates* is transformed into the secular and Kantian dualism to which Croce subscribes: the noumenal world of ethics and morality is alien to, and "beyond," the phenomenal world of practical action.[35] To the extent that the Crocean state is ethical, it is not for the world, though it is very much in it. This is how we should understand the statement quoted earlier that

62   "power is preserved and transcended." And the political—"pure power"—
must be preserved in order to coerce and contain the nature of the common people. The "transcendence" into the ethical, therefore, means that
the state creates an order, and a necessary integration, by means of which
the spiritual activity of philosophy and culture may be conducted and constantly renewed and transcended. To Croce, the philosopher and the intellectual are the "elect," the pilgrims who are in this world but not for it.

Notwithstanding Croce's attempt to attain a synthesis between the
state as force and the state as morality, and transcend the duality into the
state as ethico-political, the moments of the duality remain parallel and
juxtaposed to each other, and the two polarities remain locked within their
separate spheres of being. As Gramsci points out, if a transcendence and
synthesis are indeed achieved, then they occur solely within the realm of
thought, within the abstract activity of the Spirit as it moves from one level
to the other.[36] Croce himself notes that the transcendence is realized by
means of a "spiritual process" that makes the synthesis "dialectically
thinkable"—which is to say that the synthesis takes place within the
sphere of philosophy and culture, a sphere, we should remember, that is
distinct from that of politics and the "*volgo.*"[37] But if the resolution occurs
within the moment of thought and philosophy, then the concept of the
state as an ethico-political entity, when inserted into the historical and sociopolitical reality, is a rationalization and legitimation of this reality, for it
endows the state with a value and a purpose that are alien to it. The state
as *etica* is totally divorced from the state as *potenza*, so that the former veils
and mystifies the character of the latter. Such a "synthesis" leads to a notion of the ethico-political that is basically conservative and restorative, a
notion that is historically and socially specific to the late nineteenth and
early twentieth centuries (that is, the concept of the ethico-political justifies the power structure that emerged in Italy after its unification).[38]

It should be noted that the thinkers who Croce believes assert the
view that the "State recognizes no other law than the law of power or
force"[39] are precisely those who attempted to inquire into the conditions
necessary for the transformation of existing reality: Machiavelli, Hegel, and
Marx. On the other hand, he identifies the doctrine of the state as morality
with those thinkers who emerged in periods of history where restoration,
preservation, and conservation had become the paramount questions of
the day.[40] The Crocean relation between the political and the ethical, and
the attempt to arrive at a synthesis, are closely related to Croce's interpretation of the political and historical problems that confronted Italian and

European history: the Counter-Reformation, Italy in the age of the baroque, the failure of the 1799 Neapolitan Revolution, the history of Italy and Europe during the late and early nineteenth century are Crocean subjects of study that emphasize the moment of restoration and preservation as opposed to the moment of innovation and transformation.[41] The age of the baroque, as well as post-1870 Europe, are seen as decisive periods where, in the former, Italian political science reached its "maturity," and where, in the latter, the formation of the Italian liberal state is viewed as a stage in the continual progress and individuation in history of liberty. The concept of history as the story of liberty becomes linked to the concept of the state by means of the ethico-political: in both instances the moment of force and the moment of transformation are "transcended" into the moment of the ethical and the moment of philosophy.[42] In practical and political terms this means that history, and the state that to Croce is the subject of this history, are denuded of their social and economic content; they are "tamed" and reduced to a history wherein struggle and conflict are absent, and to a state whose structure and role are idealized into a mere moment of thought. What Croce achieves is not a synthesis, but its opposite. He intends to relate the moment of the universal to that of the particular by means of the ethico-political viewed as the resolution of the duality of the state;[43] what he in fact achieves is the construction of an ideology that justifies the particular. The particular is not transcended into the universal; rather the universal, since it exists purely in thought and in philosophy, is particularized the instant it comes into contact with historical and political reality. Consequently, the moment of the ethical cannot transform and negate the moment of power as long as the former remains an abstract universal. The ethical does not act to transcend the moment of force, but acts as an ideological "political formula,"[44] through which the force and power of the state are veiled and made acceptable to subordinate and dominated groups.

Such a state, envisioned as the "unity of political life and ethical life," and as the embodiment of an "ethical and moral consciousness" joined with an "economic and political consciousness"—where the former represents the universal, and the latter the particular, moments—is the product of a liberal, bourgeois conception of the world whose concrete, historical incarnation is the Italian state of the late nineteenth and early twentieth centuries.[45] The origins of this state may be traced to the cosmopolitan and nonnational character of Italian culture and intellectuals, so that its claim to universality, and to express the "life of the nation," is an illusion

64 that obscures and covers up the narrow and particular character of its social bases. The Crocean unity between political life and ethical life is not a unity in the Hegelian and Marxian sense of a dialectical synthesis, but is rather an artifical, mechanical juxtaposition between the particular seen as the political moment and the universal viewed as the moral and ethical moment. The two moments are crystallized within their respective polarities and values. In addition, they remain separated and unrelated to each other because the ethical is posited as a sphere superior to the political, so that the latter is reduced to an instrument and means of the former. The dyad *politica/etica* resolves itself into pure *etica* since to Croce *politica* acquires meaning and content through its subordination to the former category.[46]

This notion of the ethical parallels the conception of philosophy and the philosopher; to Croce, they embody the march of history in space and time. We should remember that philosophy represents the sole activity in history that is creative and innovating. Philosophy, culture, and ethics represent in history the universal consciousness; the political is a one-sided moment that needs to be fulfilled by the totality of the former—it is an aspect of a particular consciousness that results in what Croce calls mere "passion."[47] The particular and "unilateral nature" of political action, when directed by the ethical consciousness, is transformed into the universality of the "total" state: "With this elevation of pure politics into ethics, even the word 'State' acquires a new meaning: it is no longer a simple utilitarian relation, a synthesis of force and consent, and of authority and liberty, but rather it becomes the incarnation of the human ethos and is thus the ethical State or a cultural State."[48] In effect, politics is not a self-sufficient moment of action: it is realized through ethics and culture such that it is raised to the level of philosophy and thought. But although it is so raised, the nature of politics remains an alien form within this level, for it still retains its particular character. Thus there emerges a paradox whereby the political is autonomous and distinct from the ethical precisely because the former's meaning and end are given by the latter. The instrumental and technical nature of politics presupposes a political knowledge whose methods and procedures are quite different and independent from those of ethics and philosophy. But since this knowledge is utilitarian, one relating to means rather than ends, it is a knowledge whose purpose and significance are determined by values located outside itself.[49]

Since the essence of the political—of *pura politica*—is reduced to an instrumentality, and since, consequently, it is morally and ethically neutral, the essence of political knowledge is also reduced to a technical knowledge that describes the methods by which a ruler or a "prince" attains or maintains power. The science of politics is the knowledge of the manipulation and deception of the "volgo"—for the attainment of ends posited by those who possess such a knowledge. The philosopher, however (or the logos of which he is the incarnation), does not descend immediately and directly to the world of practice and of the "volgo"; philosophy must ever remain distinct from politics. It is the political actor—"il politico" ("politician") or "l'uomo di Stato" ("statesman")—who puts into practice the political knowledge given by the notion of pure politics. The activity of the politico becomes purposive and is redeemed through the activity of philosophy and culture. The politico translates the methods and rules of political knowledge into action and practice: it is he who "soils" his hands within the world of struggle and conflict.

The political actor is the agent who possesses the arcana imperii—the political knowledge that describes the modes of action and the instrumenta regni proper to his sphere of activity. It is significant that the function and role of the political actor is not to svelare (uncover) the arcana imperii in order to "make political action transparent and conscious"; rather it is "to keep the arcana imperii secret and mysterious."[50] Thus the defining characteristic of the political actor is to make certain that this political knowledge remains in the hands of "those who know" (chi sa). For it is not possible to open this knowledge—to make it transparent—to the popular masses. Such an unveiling would lead to the unraveling and undermining of the sociocultural and sociopolitical structure of power embodied in the "State." Any attempt to reveal the arcana imperii and teach the people such knowledge—any attempt to transform "those who do not know" (chi non sa) into "those who know"—is self-contradictory and would be rendered useless, for it would assume a level of culture and of intellectual-moral awareness that the volgo will always lack. In other words, the alta cultura that defines the life of those who possess philosophy and knowledge is to remain "superior" to the cultura popolare of the common people. The political, and the knowledge appropriate to it, are to maintain in practice this distinction between philosophy and culture on the one hand, and politics and the volgo on the other.[51]

The nature of the common people is such that any revelation of political knowledge would result not only in the annihilation of the uomini di politica, but also would lead to the destruction of that sociocultural space necessary to philosophy and to thought. The consciousness of the masses cannot attain the level necessary to understand and accept (both morally

66 and intellectually) the stark reality of political action. The consciousness of the people is a form of error, which always exists at the level of "passion" and sentiment. And to teach political knowledge to them would be to destroy the very basis of such knowledge. Indeed, if the knowledge of the *politico* is to fulfill its directive and ruling function, the consciousness of the *volgo* must remain ignorant of the methods and techniques employed to shape and manipulate it. In effect, in the same manner that politics is the subordinate instrument of ethics and philosophy, and the *politico* is the instrument of the "great thinker," so too the masses are the raw material and the instrument of the political actor (a formulation that reproduces the platonic relation between the philosopher and the people).[52] Thus political knowledge is a method by which the contradictions between the ruler and the ruled, philosophy and practice, the "word" and the action, are covered and rendered opaque.

In a review of Burnham's *Machiavellians*, half a century after he first formulated his position on Machiavelli and the nature of politics, Croce registers his full agreement with Burnham's call for a "realistic political theory": "this pure political theory, discovered once and for all by Machiavelli, is to be found repeated by many who, consciously or not, have recently followed his tradition." This tradition teaches that history and experience "prove" that democracy is impossible; and since "we have no reason to suppose that the tendencies and conditions which have prevented the realization of democracy in all periods of human history will disappear in the future, we must, as scientific thinkers, expect that future to have as little democracy as the past." The "hard doctrine" of the Machiavellian tradition has proved to be the "only scientific theory of politics; in the political world it is the truth." This truth which is taught by Machiavelli "is opposed to the masses, who can never be induced to think scientifically and critically, to see realistically or to argue logically at the sacrifice of passion sometimes fickle and sometimes obstinate, but always violent."[53]

The popular masses represent and embody "feeling" (*sentire*) and passion. As in Plato, so too in Croce the people can never "think" and deliberate, and therefore can never acquire an autonomous and self-determining will—the *volgo* in itself can never create a world that is "for itself" and that is the embodiment of its life and its values. But if this is the case, then this would imply that to the extent that the people cannot think and determine for themselves the form and shape of their social existence, then to that extent the people will never attain the realm of the ethical and the moral. The slave in Aristotle is a being whose nature lacks the faculty of reason and moral deliberation, which only the master—the autonomous citizen—can provide him; the people in Croce are an entity than can acquire moral and ethical purpose only through the leadership of "those who know."[54] What this means is that within the social totality described by the ethico-political "State," the ethical moment is realized through the intellectual and cultural activity of those who possess knowledge and know how to rule, while the political moment (technique, force, power) delineates the realm wherein the *volgo* exists as a subordinate entity, whose life and consciousness are determined by the moral and intellectual elite. Autonomy and freedom presuppose moral and intellectual knowledge, and since the masses can never aspire to such a cultural and ethical consciousness, they will remain immersed within the "realm of necessity," where mere nature—passion, feeling, and violence—reigns. On the other hand, "those who know," who possess a superior consciousness, are able to develop a moral and autonomous will through which is established the "realm of freedom" where nature and violence are transcended. Although Croce is fond of using the Hegelian terminology of "dialectics" and "transcendence," he most tellingly fails to understand the basic Hegelian proposition that the freedom of a given subject presupposes at the same time the freedom of the Other; whereas Croce constructs a dialectic that posits the freedom of the subject as dependent upon, and requiring, the domination of others and their subordination to necessity and nature.[55]

The metaphysical and theoretical duality (which is quite Kantian and anti-Hegelian) between thought and action, between *pensare* and *sentire*, is socially and politically reproduced by this "pure" political doctrine that posits an essential divorce between the "scientific" and educated elite (the "aristocracy of the intellect"), and the *volgo*, which "does not seek the truth" and thus cannot rule itself.[56] The metaphysical polarity thinking/feeling established by philosophy parallels the cultural dyad philosopher/the "simple" (*i semplici*), which translates into the social antithesis intellectual/common people, which, finally, corresponds to the political dyad ruling/being ruled.[57] These polarities must at all costs be maintained, for there cannot be "liberty without necessity."[58] Any attempt to overcome the antitheses would result not in the annihilation of necessity and the universalization of liberty, but in the destruction of the realm of freedom and the return to nature; that is, the people as a political force signals the destruction of culture and ethical life, and the intrusion into society of nature and violence.

68   It is the political, the pure political theory discovered by Machiavelli, that acts as the vehicle through which these distinctions are maintained and constantly reproduced. Given the nature of the masses—for whom even the efforts of popular, public education to raise their level have proved futile, and who will ever remain ignorant of philosophical and political knowledge—"the only course . . . is to put our trust in that part of the ruling elite that is scientifically educated. . . . We must trust the class called the 'intellectuals,' as Hegel acknowledged by calling them the 'universal class,' or the 'unclassed' [*classe non classe*]."[59] This universal class, ever open to receiving new members rising from below, will renew and rejuvenate itself constantly (this is not dissimilar to Mosca's "circulation of elites").[60] In the Crocean vision of "democracy" (which in American political thought translates into pluralism and the theory of groups and organizations), the intellectuals, as the universal class, will establish an "aristo-democracy" that will produce the sociocultural and sociopolitical conditions necessary for further historical development.[61] Such development depends upon the continued subordination of the *volgo* to the intellectuals, and upon the continual reproduction of the moral and intellectual distance that the Crocean liberal "State" guarantees between *cultura popolare* and *alta cultura*—that is, between "feeling" and "thinking."

The masses as a sociopolitical force will act to undermine the intellectuals as the universal class. In the same way that philosophy, when directly linked to politics, is corrupted and transformed into ideology and error, the intellectuals will lose their autonomy as a sociopolitical group and become the appendages and satellites of the particularistic interests of societal groups and classes: they will lose their universality and descend to the particularity of the class conflicts and power struggles of society. But what is an outcome to Croce is to Marx and Gramsci the general, existing condition of philosophy and thought in a society where the contradiction between the moral-ethical freedom of the few is made possible, and grounded in, the brute necessity of the many.

To Croce, the very nature of philosophers and intellectuals—the antithesis of the nature of the common people—determines their social status as the universal class. They are the social and cultural expression of thought and "truth," the subjects whose activity is to think and to deliberate, such that "*il pensiero pensa*." To establish a popular, mass base for philosophy and for the intellectuals, to demand that philosophers not only go to the people but issue from the life of the people, would mean that "thought does not think"—it would mean the transformation of "thinking" into "feeling," and "feeling" into "thinking."[62] The function of the political is to establish the conditions under which "thought thinks." The political is to order and manipulate the passions and emotions of the people, to dominate and control the people; but it cannot seek to discover the conditions existing within the social reality that would transform the *volgo* into an active agent of history.

The movement from thinking to feeling, and from feeling to thinking, is a mutual, reciprocal relation that parallels the relation established between the educator and the student. It is a movement whose theoretical and critical elaboration—not to mention its social and practical realization—presupposes a concept of the political that does not limit itself to mere power and utility, but rather understands political activity as hegemonic activity, as moral and intellectual reform. The latter does not posit a static, mechanical distinction between ethics and politics, thought and action; it understands feeling, thinking, seeing, and acting as mutually related and mutually dependent aspects of a totality that is constantly becoming. The Crocean "dialectic," as it proclaims the autonomy of "pure politics," at the same time reduces it to the status of a technical instrument dependent upon ends posited by ethics and philosophy. The political is ossified into an abstract "science" that teaches a body of knowledge conceived as immutable and universal "truth"—a truth that, given its "scientific" character, is socially and ideologically neutral. In such a notion, the truth taught by Machiavelli is not dependent upon the political subject that knows it and seeks to use it; it is there, ready to be used by the tyrant or the democrat, the bourgeois or the proletarian.[63]

Gramsci criticizes the "Machiavellianism" posited by Croce as being ahistorical and "bookish."[64] He believes that the knowledge Machiavelli intended to teach, and the political project he intended to introduce, are intimately related, so that the "science" of politics cannot be understood unless it is inserted "within its concrete context (as well as within its logical formulation) and seen as an organism in the process of becoming."[65] Gramsci translates the Crocean "pure politics," and its autonomy of political science, into what he calls an "active politics" (*politica attiva*), and thus into the autonomy of political action—where action is now precisely the concretization of the reciprocal movement between *pensare* and *sentire*, philosophy and practice.[66] "Politics is an autonomous activity," which, though it certainly follows rational methods proper to itself, at the same time "innovates the conception of morality and religion—that is, it innovates the entire conception of the world."[67] To Gramsci it is the political that gives

70 meaning and purpose to the world, and that establishes the conditions and goals through which the social and historical transformation of reality is attained. Such a conception is diametrically opposed to the Crocean "pure politics," which lacks any transformative or educative character. More important, the very fact that Machiavelli's politics is interpreted as "science" and as pure theory (from which have issued over the centuries long and vacuous debates regarding politics and morality, Machiavellianism and anti-Machiavellianism) is an indication that the notion of politics as a transforming, creative activity advanced by Machiavelli has not "succeeded in becoming the 'common sense' of the modern world."[68]

What this means is that Machiavelli's thought has been appropriated throughout the course of Italian history precisely by those elements and groups that have been the strongest and most consistent opponents of the Machiavellian political project. The Crocean school of Machiavelli interpretation—students such as Russo and Chabod[69]—represents a political and philosophical orientation whose emergence could not have been possible without the absence in Italian politics of a popular, mass base. The fact that Machiavelli's thought has remained the possession of Croce and other "high intellectuals," that it has not penetrated to the *volgo* and become the "common sense" of the people, "means that the moral and intellectual revolution whose elements are contained *in nuce* in Machiavelli's thought is not yet actualized. It has not become a public and manifest form of national culture."[70] Thus the very existence of a traditional intellectual, who interprets Machiavelli in terms of a pure science of politics, is a reflection of the social and political contradiction within an Italian society divided between the two cultures of "those who know" and "those who do not know," between the culture of the rulers and that of the ruled. The Crocean interpretation of Machiavelli is the political expression of the liberal, bourgeois antipathy toward the workers and peasants. But it is precisely the people, the transformation of a mass into a people, that is the central Machiavellian and Gramscian problem. Machiavelli and the enterprise he wanted to initiate encompass the revolutionary problematic that seeks the real, concrete conditions for the creation of what Gramsci calls the "national-popular collective will."[71]

To the question whether it is possible to "escape from this contradiction between word and action"—a question posed by de Sanctis in his analysis of the relation between Luther and Machiavelli[72]—Croce answers that the solution may only be addressed at the theoretical level, but that at the practical level there is no possible resolution or synthesis. Harmony between speech and deed would require that "political men should also philosophize, and that the popular masses no longer be the masses" ("far sì che gli uomini politici filosofino anche, e che il volgo cessi di esser volgo").[73] Here Croce identifies the crux of the matter. It is here too that we find the central pivot on which revolves the radical difference in the Gramscian and Crocean interpretation of Machiavelli and of his politics. This statement summarizes the Gramscian political project and its radical critique of Crocean thought, and of Italian culture and politics that such thought expresses.

To state that the political actor should philosophize is to state that politics is not simply pure power or pure utility, but is also the generation of hegemony and reform; it is to state that the political actor is a democratic philosopher (*politicus* + *philosophus*). The democratic philosopher is the politician-intellectual that addresses the Crocean requirement that political beings should also know philosophy (a requirement, of course, first enunciated by Plato). But to ask that politics become philosophy is also to ask that philosophy become politics; it implies that philosophy realizes itself in the world. And the realization of philosophy in practice, within social reality, assumes the concrete existence of a political subject that embodies such a philosophy; by acting in the world, its development and self-becoming as a subject are simultaneously the development and self-realization of philosophy.

In effect, to ask that politics become philosophy is to ask that the "volgo cessi di esser volgo"—it is to ask that the masses transform themselves into a coherent and determinate people possessed of a purpose and will. This people as a political force embodies the activity and thought of its life, such that it is the agent and subject of history, which, through its praxis, determines itself and defines itself both in thought and in practice. It is, indeed, the political-educational—and thus hegemonic—relation between the democratic philosopher and the people (a relation that describes the moral and intellectual reform whose model in the Lutheran Reformation Gramsci attempts to translate into contemporary Italian culture and politics) that makes such a process possible. But what to Gramsci signals the realization of philosophy and the proliferation of a new conception of the world that has become the life and custom of the age, is to Croce the transmogrification of philosophy into popular prejudice and error. "Che il volgo cessi di esser volgo" requires the moral and intellectual reform that the philosophy of praxis is meant to initiate, a political and cultural process that will uncover existing reality in order to transform it—a process

72 that moves toward overcoming and annihilating the sociopractical conditions wherein the contradiction between *"il detto"* (the word) and *"il fatto"* (the deed) is embedded. The Crocean conception of the political as "pure politics" is both product and presupposition of such a contradiction. In opposition to this notion, Gramsci attempts to formulate a notion of the political that is both the product and the carrier of a transformative and innovating praxis.[74] Gramsci takes Machiavellian political thought as the representative thought in Italy of such a conception of politics. Machiavellian thought is the negation of Crocean liberal thought, and Machiavelli is the anti-Croce that exposes and uncovers the antipopular, antidemocratic roots of Italian politics, history, and culture.[75]

The democratic philosopher does not express a simple contradiction of the traditional cosmopolitan intellectual, but is the overcoming and transcendence of the historical, cultural weight that the traditional intellectual represents. The very generation of the democratic philosopher presupposes the political and practical overcoming of the traditional, established way of life and "common sense" through the proliferation of a new conception of the world. But this very formation of a new conception of the world is itself the product and motive force of the moral and intellectual reform sparked by the democratic philosopher/popular masses dyad—an active and reciprocal relation that in its totality and in its reciprocal movement constitutes the national-popular and collective will. The organic and dynamic relation described by such a movement between the educator and the student creates the practical and social bases for that very requirement Croce believes impossible to achieve—the transformation of the *volgo* from a passive, nonconscious entity into a coherent force whose knowledge and activity within the preexisting reality represent the concrete and practical potential for further transformative development inherent within this very reality.[76]

"Che il volgo cessi di esser volgo" is a Crocean formulation intended to show the impossibility of this transformation. Gramsci translates this formulation into the language of the philosophy of praxis and into the language of Machiavellian political theory, such that the Crocean formulation is transformed into the Gramscian and Machiavellian imperative: the formation of a political and revolutionary class in Gramsci, and the formation of "the revolutionary class of the time, the 'people' and the Italian 'nation,' the citizen democracy" in Machiavelli.[77] The "citizen democracy" is diametrically opposed to, and represents the overcoming of, the *volgo* in the same way that a revolutionary class constituted as a political and conscious subject is the negation and transcendence of an indeterminate class de- fined as a mere economic category that unconsciously reflects the prevailing knowledge of the ruling class. The transformation of the Crocean *volgo* into the Machiavellian *democrazia cittadina* is the coming-to-be of the popular masses as a political and hegemonic force. The contrast between the two entities corresponds to the opposition between the Crocean notion of politics as pure technique and the Gramscian notion (which he attributes to Machiavelli) of the political as praxis, as conscious activity.[78] The Crocean *politico* is an actor whose "technical" activity presupposes the people as ignorant and as the "simple"; the Gramscian and Machiavellian *politico* embodies and concretizes a politics whose sphere of action is the transformation of the *volgo* and the coming-to-be of a people as a determinate and collective entity.

In effect, the interpretation of Machiavellian thought is central—and pregnant with political and historical consequences—to both Croce and Gramsci: Machiavelli the discoverer of "pure politics," a scientist and thinker isolated from the masses, one who lives and thinks within the self-enclosed circle of his thought and science; or Machiavelli the man of action, who creates an "active and operating politics" (*politica attiva e operante*), whose knowledge is the embodiment of the people—not of a people envisioned as a static, passive "mass," but of a people that is a constantly becoming subject, a hegemonic force that initiates and carries forward a moral and intellectual reform that lays the basis for the *democrazia cittadina*.[79]

Chapter 5

Hegemony and Virtù
Moral and Intellectual Reform in Gramsci and Machiavelli

The antithesis established between the Crocean Machiavelli and the Gramscian Machiavelli underlines the fundamental opposition between the liberal conception of the world, which takes itself to be the "last word" and end of European thought, and a "neo-humanist" conception of the world, which sees itself as emerging from within the very contradictions that the former conception has posited as the immutable products of knowledge and science.[1] The debate over the nature of Machiavelli as a theorist, and the controversy over the nature and significance of his political knowledge, are the focal points around which revolves the struggle between the two antagonistic conceptions. The political and historical ramifications are evident: the liberal Croce sees in the Italian social and political structure that emerged after the Risorgimento a firm ground for the progress of liberty; the Marxist Gramsci sees in the very same power structure the negation of liberty and the oppression of the popular masses. One sees the Italian state as already constituted and the basis for the further development of Italian society; the other sees a nonstate and a nonsociety because the *volgo* as a people does not yet exist.

In both Croce and Gramsci these political and ideological differences are embodied in the figure of Machiavelli. What is the nature of his political knowledge, and in what way does it differ from that of his predecessors and contemporaries? What is the nature of the Machiavellian political project, and how is this project related to the knowledge that he intends to impart? Indeed, what is Machiavelli's intention—is it to establish the rules and methods of an "objective" political science, or is it to introduce within existing reality a new political and social order? Is there a necessary relation

74

between the new political knowledge and the new political order, or can one accept the validity of one without being logically compelled to accept that of the other—that is to say, is the new political knowledge such that its emergence and existence presuppose a new order of things, and is the latter a reality whose coming-to-be is a real potentiality whose necessity is given by this new political knowledge? Is the new knowledge independent of Machiavelli's intention?[2] Does the intention affect the status of this new knowledge? If Machiavelli's thought is an autonomous political science, does the nature of the subject who knows and acts upon this thought influence the character of the knowledge? In other words, who—or what—is the object of Machiavelli's thought? Is it the internal categories and concepts that make up this knowledge? Is he attempting to discover the rules and methods of a "pure politics," such that the object of his thought is the science of politics? Or, on the other hand, is the object of Machiavelli's "new modes and orders" a particular and concrete subject whose existence is discovered by his political thought?

These questions (which summarize the discussion in chapter 4 regarding the nature of politics and its relation to ethics and philosophy) presuppose a knowledge of the problematic attendant upon this relation, and at the same time they concretize the problematic by inserting it within a specific topos: what is it that Machiavelli knows, to whom is it addressed, and how are these two questions related to Machiavelli's theoretical and political project? But all this is simply to elaborate on the central question: what is the evidence in the Machiavellian text that enables Gramsci to challenge the liberal and Crocean interpretation? Is there a textual—as well as theoretical—foundation to the interpretation that sees Machiavelli as the democratic philosopher, and that sees his thought as the knowledge that seeks to generate a national-popular collective will socially and politically constituted into the "citizen democracy"? What are the elements in the Machiavellian text that enable Gramsci to envision him as the "anti-Croce" that explodes the contradictions of contemporary liberal and bourgeois politics? What are the elements that describe the democratic philosopher and the citizen democracy in opposition to the traditional intellectual and the "aristo-democracy"? If the citizen democracy is the object of Machiavelli's project, then what are the political and rational elements that constitute it? And, finally, if the national-popular and collective will is what describes the democratic and popular character of Machiavellian thought, then it becomes necessary to identify such a will as an entity that emerges from within the structure of the Machiavellian enter-

76 prise, and the new knowledge must be able to identify and elaborate the process by which the collective will is generated and formed.

It is legitimate to ask what is "new" about this knowledge, what sets it apart from past knowledge and from that of Machiavelli's contemporaries. In what sense can we say—or indeed can Machiavelli say—that the teaching of this knowledge is different from that of medieval thought or the thought of the Renaissance humanists? Machiavelli clearly sets out his "intention" in *The Prince* (chapter 15): he wants to base his new knowledge on the *"verità effettuale delle cose"* ("the effective truth of things") rather than on an "imagined truth" (*"cose imaginate"*). He intends to uncover the "operative reality" in order to "see what ought to be the rules and methods for a prince." He is aware that "many have written of this," and he fears he might appear "presumptuous" since his argument will depart greatly from the opinions of others.[3] But since, in constructing and developing his argument, he intends to use neither authority nor force, we know that he will not follow the traditional scholastic methods, whose arguments depend upon authority and tradition.[4] And if the argument is not based on authority and on the methods of those who have come before him, then he must present a method that is opposed to the prevailing methods of "disputation." Those who have come before are the "many" that have "imagined republics and principalities never seen or known to exist in reality." He wants to leave the latter aside and consider the *verità effettuale*, where a distinction is immediately established between "what is done" and "what ought to be done." To leave the former for the latter is to invite ruin and destruction. For a prince to maintain himself, he must discard notions of what an imaginary prince ought to do and address himself to the existing reality (*"cose vere"*).

Thus we have an opposition between "what is" (*essere*) and "what ought to be" (*dover essere*): one looks toward a realistic interpretation of the world, and the other provides a moral or ethical interpretation.[5] Students of Machiavelli (such as Croce, Chabod, and Russo) have seized upon this distinction and turned it into the organizing theme of the Machiavellian project. Others, such as Strauss and his school—who in Italy and Europe have gone under the name of "anti-Machiavellianism" and are closely associated (in Italy, but not in France and Protestant Europe) with the Counter-Reformation and the baroque age[6]—see the *essere/dover essere* dyad as the dividing line between "modern" and "premodern" political thought (where the latter is seen, at least by the Croceans and the Straussians, as encompassing both classical and medieval thought).[7] To Strauss, Machiavelli is the "teacher of evil" who represents a radical departure from the philosophical, moral, and political ideas of Christian theology and classical thought (an interpretation not far from Croce's, except that the latter attempts to maintain a "detached" and morally "neutral" stance toward the new teaching).[8]

All of these interpreters view the "imagined" (*cose imaginate*) and the "real" (*cose vere*) as a mutually exclusive and irreconcilable antinomy, so that when Machiavelli attacks the former they understand him to criticize the thematic concern of classical thought with the "good life" on the one hand, and with the traditional concern of medieval philosophy with theology and spiritual life on the other. In both cases Machiavelli is seen to focus his attention on "life" and "preservation." *Cose vere* and *cose imaginate* respectively parallel the "what is done" and the "what ought to be done": the second set of terms of the antithesis describes the traditional and established views of the "many," and the first set of terms refers to the new knowledge of Machiavelli. This knowledge does not concern itself with the moral and ethical problems of the world: it exists within boundaries defined by the "effective truth," and the world of the ethical is a world this knowledge cannot reach ("*non aggiunge*") and does not want to understand (*The Prince*, chapter 11).

Whether one hails Machiavelli as the discoverer of political science and political technique (Croce) or attacks him as the revolutionary prophet of an "evil" message (Strauss); whether one sees in him the embodiment of reason (Russo) and self-consciousness (de Sanctis) opposed to medieval mysticism and scholasticism, or discerns in him a calculating yet passionate spirit given to a utopianism that alternates with pessimism (Guicciardini, Chabod, Sasso), the opposition between the *essere* and *dover essere*, and between the "true nature of things" and their "imagined" nature, is understood by most students to be the major point of departure in Machiavelli.[9]

But such a way of posing the issue begs the question and misinterprets the distinction that Machiavelli is making. The very distinction between the "is" and the "ought" presupposes the existence of a particular kind of knowledge whose methods will enable one to see and to posit the antinomy. The issue is not between a medieval form of knowledge that looks to the *dover essere* and a Machiavellian form that acknowledges only the *essere*. The question is what kind of knowledge will enable one to see a distinction between the two ways of looking at the world. In order to posit this distinction one must have a knowledge of both the *essere* and the *dover*

78 *essere*, a knowledge that is able to pose not just the problem of "reality" but also the problem of the genesis of this reality. What, indeed, is the *essere*? How is it constituted? How did it originate? Is the "effective truth" an entity that exists as a brute fact, a reality that is independent of human beings? Is the "true nature of things" a reality given by a particular form of knowledge without which it could not be recognized? If this reality is independent of human beings, what is the process by which they come to know it—and if they do come to know it, what effect would it have on them, since it exists independently of their knowledge of it? If the new knowledge poses the problem of the *essere* regarding the internal dynamics of this reality, then it must also pose the problem of the *dover essere*—that is, the problem of the development of a given structure of reality and its transformation into another configuration.

Gramsci, of course, refuses to take Machiavelli's new knowledge as the precursor of a "positive" science in the modern sense, a science whose methods and categories are "value-neutral" and "nonnormative." Such a science tries to maintain a certain distance from its object of inquiry in order not to taint with emotion, passion, or engagement the "objectivity" to which it aspires. De Sanctis compares Machiavelli's new political knowledge to Galileo's "new science," and says that the former originated what the latter brought to further development. To de Sanctis, "prose begins with Machiavelli"; that is, the world begins to awaken and understand itself, after the long poetic night of the feudal period.[10] Such a comparison is correct, if it is understood that the "prose" first discovered by Machiavelli in the political world, and later deepened by Galileo in the study of nature, represents a revolutionary rupture and a radical discontinuity with the medieval methods of investigating the *essere*. But to take this "prose," as Croce does, and transform it into an autonomous science that dispassionately seeks to understand reality is to distort the basic Hegelian sense of the de Sanctian statement. As Gramsci puts it:

> Machiavelli is not a mere scientist; he is partisan, a man of powerful passions, a committed political actor engaged in the world |*politico in atto*|, who wants to create new relations of force and thus cannot but address the question of the "*dover essere*," but certainly not one understood in any moralistic sense. ... Political man is a creator ... but he does not create out of nothing. He acts within an effective reality |*realtà effettuale*|, but what is this effective reality? Is it something static and immobile, or rather isn't it a relation of forces in continual movement where the balance of forces is constantly changing?[11]

Thus to Gramsci the *dover essere* is the engagement of the will within the *essere* in order to create a new equilibrium and a new relation of forces. It is the "concretization" of the will—what Machiavelli calls *ordinata virtù*—within the existing reality in order to "dominate and overcome it." The "what ought to be," therefore, is a product of a realistic and historical interpretation of the "what is": it is "history in action and philosophy in action [*storia in atto e filosofia in atto*], and thus it is politics."[12]

There is no question that an inquiry into the *verità delle cose* was an important component of Machiavelli's knowledge. The point, however, is that to discover the nature of this reality, to uncover the nature of the *essere*, cannot but be a revolutionary act, for such a task would require the formulation of methods that could simultaneously encompass the "is" and the "ought" within the reality that is to be uncovered. Galileo and Machiavelli represent not simply the methods and reason of a new science that proclaimed its independence from tradition and established authority. This very demand for autonomy from the prevailing philosophical and value systems is in itself an affirmation of an opposing conception of the world. Science as an autonomous mode of activity presupposes a sociocultural and political environment markedly different from the Thomistic and feudal understanding of reality. To argue, therefore, for the autonomy of science is at the same time to argue for a specific sociocultural and sociopolitical conception of the world.[13] The new knowledge cannot be separated from, nor understood, apart from the new order that is to be seen as both the product and the foundation of this knowledge. Thus the new knowledge is both the creator and the creature of the new order. It is simultaneously a means by which the new conception of the world is translated into an existing sociopolitical reality, and an end product of the new worldview. The intimate connection between science and worldview is revealed by the fate suffered in Italy by Galileo's new science, especially when this fate is contrasted to the experience and history of the new science in those countries that underwent the kind of moral and political resurgence that Machiavelli had wanted for Italy.[14] The fate of both Galileo and Machiavelli suggests that the notion of the autonomy of science is a concept historically and socially rooted, dependent upon the character of the established worldview and the prevailing sociopolitical structure.

The political knowledge that Machiavelli intends to teach is a product of both "*continua lezione*" (continual study, that is, theoretical activity) and "*lunga pratica*" (long experience or practice, that is, social and political activity).[15] Machiavelli's knowledge is not a passive, merely reflecting product

80   of reality that simply registers events, nor is it an empty receptacle filled by the action upon it of an external reality. This reality and the new knowledge presuppose each other, such that one acts reciprocally on the other. The reality and the knowledge taken together constitute a relation that sees the world both as it is and as it will be—that is, both actually and potentially. Machiavelli understands experience and "empirical reality" not as an objective "fact" that imposes itself on human beings and their knowledge, but rather as being mediated by the new knowledge, such that both *lunga pratica* and *continua lezione* form the totality of the new knowledge, which is able to act as a guide to action and as a springboard from which the existing reality may be transformed. What are described by Galileo as the secondary or nonessential characteristics of reality are to Machiavelli the primary material around which reality is organized and ordered: emotion, passion, thought, beliefs, prejudices—the entire complex of sociocultural structures without which reality cannot exist or be understood. Machiavelli attempts to construct a knowledge of reality that recognizes within this reality the potential for overcoming what is given by present and past experience. The categories of this knowledge do not simply reproduce the reality given by experience. The knowledge is informed by an active and critical orientation, and the analysis of the *verità effettuale delle cose* looks toward those elements of the given situation that are dynamically poised to generate a new *verità*.

Thus Machiavelli's project is to change the reality, not merely to reflect it or to "study" it. His type of knowledge cannot be understood if it is separated from his "intention"—"quello che io intenderò."[16] Both the purpose of the project and the knowledge contain each other. The *Discourses* outlines a particular interpretation of the past and the present that is simultaneously a product of "continual study" and "long research." But it is also a product of the intention of the subject who is doing the theorizing and the acting. Knowledge of "primary objects"—reality stripped of the human factor—is not possible to Machiavelli. What this means is that the new knowledge is a product of the relation between human intention—ends, goals, values—and the "effective truth of things," such that knowledge is always a human knowledge, a product of conscious human activity.[17] Such a posture toward knowledge and reality pervades the totality of Machiavelli's writings: sociopolitical reality cannot be considered in the abstract, but is rather an ever-changing structure that issues from action. Action, in turn, results from the knowledge of the proper relation between what is and what ought to be. Thus the relation between the *essere* and the *dover essere* is described by Machiavelli's intention. The *essere* is given by the analysis of the past and the present, and the *dover essere* is given by the intention of Machiavelli, which looks toward a future that he believes is present within the *essere*. Such an intention is itself an aspect of the analysis. In the same way, the analysis develops as it does, and perceives the reality as it does, because it is an aspect of the intention.

As Machiavelli states:

> I shall boldly and openly say |*sarò animoso in dire manifestamente*| what I think of the former times and of the present, so as to excite in the minds of the young men who may read my writings the desire to avoid the evils of the latter, and to prepare themselves to imitate the virtues of the former, whenever fortune presents them the occasion.[18]

What Machiavelli intends is to establish a form of knowledge that contains within itself the conditions for action, conditions whose unfolding depends not simply on "occasion" but also on the proliferation of such knowledge within the life and "spirit" of the young. Machiavelli's writings are therefore not a simple "scientific" and "analytical" treatise on the rules and laws of political activity: they are that, and more; they are a social and political teaching that intends to inform its readers of the possibility—and the necessity—for a radical, new stance toward the "effective truth." The analysis is a necessary preamble to the "preparation" and the "imitation."

"To read my writings" and "to prepare and to imitate" the *virtù* of the ancient Romans are two moments that together constitute the knowledge that Machiavelli desires to introduce. The teaching of this knowledge is itself a moment in the movement toward the introduction of "new orders and systems."[19] The preparation and imitation are closely linked to "the desire to avoid the evils of the present"—that is, the possibility of changing the present emerges from the knowledge and understanding of the past. Machiavelli is offering a reading—or, rather, a rereading—of the past (classical times) as a means of presenting and developing his new knowledge. And a reading of this knowledge, which he makes clear is a synthesis of the present and the past, is intended as an education, as a moral and intellectual "discipline" that will change the nature and character of those who submit to it. But to submit to it is to accept the intellectual argument and to subscribe to the value judgment of Machiavelli's intention—the present is decadent and corrupt and must therefore be transformed.

What Machiavelli intends to say, and what he wants to be read, are not a scholarly disquisition delivered *sine ira et studio*, a calm and dispassionate

82 presentation of an abstract argument. He is *"animoso in dire"* what he intends to argue and analyze; his presentation must be animated and "spirited" because his teaching is not simply a "pure science," as Croce would have it, but also passion and will, a dynamic knowledge that produces engagement and commitment—what he calls *"azione feroce e gagliarda"* (fierce and vigorous action).[20] It is significant that in the introduction to Book 2 of the *Discourses* Machiavelli brings up the possibility of error in the formulation of his teaching: the possibility exists, but he dismisses it because "the thing" is "so evident" (*così manifesta*): "the *virtù* of ancient times, and the vice of the present age" are "clearer" to him "than the sun." This clarity is not a simple product that issues from an analytical inquiry; it is an aspect of Machiavelli's intention to prepare those who will follow in his footsteps. The intention and the reasoned argument are simultaneous moments of Machiavellian knowledge. Machiavelli is addressing those who—like the young—are willing to envision a different and radical conception of what constitutes value and *virtù*: it is the difference in conception that enables Machiavelli to contrast the vice and degradation of the present with the virtue and greatness of the past.

Yet what is clear to Machiavelli is not so clear to contemporaries such as Guicciardini. And if the latter is taken as the representative of the younger generation, then Machiavelli's intention to transform the present is unique and anamolous for his times. As both Gramsci and Croce recognize, Guicciardini and Machiavelli are thinkers who express differing and opposing conceptions of the world. The *virtù animosa* of Machiavelli provides a sharp contrast to the "pessimism" and "skepticism" of Guicciardini.[21] The fact that events proved Machiavelli wrong, and that the future development of Renaissance Italy "empirically" justified the Guicciardinian orientation toward resignation and a way of life absorbed with the "virtues" of *il particulare* (private life) does not negate the Machiavellian project to overcome the values and thought of the present—indeed, it reinforces the Gramscian argument that Machiavelli is the thinker of events that occurred and were to occur outside Italy.[22] On the other hand, the conception of the world epitomized by Guicciardini—a retreat into the private sphere of self-interest, and a way of life devoted to the abstract analysis and contemplation of external events—is precisely that orientation whose prevalence throughout Renaissance Italy contributed to the fall of the Italian city-states and to the victory of the Counter-Reformation.

What is clear to Machiavelli is the opposite of what is clear to Guicciardini: both orientations are rooted within the same reality. Machiavelli interprets Roman history and politics in order to discover within the present "relations of force" the seeds for the transformation of reality. His interpretation of the past is an aspect of his intention to transform the present, an intention that is, in turn, intimately related to a conception of *virtù* and action opposed to the Christian and medieval notions of virtue and conduct.[23] The aristocratic skepticism of Guicciardini describes a conception of the world and an orientation toward the established sociopolitical structure that posit the "effective reality" and the "effective truth" as givens that cannot be transcended through human action and *virtù*. To Guicciardini, reality and history are not a product of human action—rather it is human beings who are the creatures and "playthings" of this reality, such that their activity and knowledge become a reflection and mirror of a reality fundamentally external and always opposed to humanity. Thus any attempt to transform this reality is not simply utopian, but will merely lead to a reproduction of the preexisting form of reality. Such an orientation is what enabled Guicciardini to produce works on history and politics that historiographically and "scientifically" are more reliable and more "faithful" to the historical events than those of Machiavelli.[24]

Guicciardini observes human activity dispassionately and analytically because his knowledge always remains within the value structure and the thought structure given by the existing reality. This objective detachment, however, leads to an acceptance of reality that is as "partisan" as the Machiavellian engagement to negate and overcome it. If a true science of politics was indeed discovered by Italians, as Croce claims, it is Guicciardini, and not Machiavelli, who should be hailed as its founder and expert practitioner. Guicciardini's political knowledge is of a type that seeks to discover the rules and methods necessary to a political activity that accepts the sociopolitical structure as immutable. It describes a political technique whereby the actor will be able to maneuver and pursue interests within the accepted reality. Guicciardininian political knowledge is a product of the sociopolitical and moral exhaustion of Renaissance civilization in Italy, an exhaustion that led to the decline of the Italian "international" state system, whose final and irrevocable disintegration was heralded by the sack of Rome in 1527 (the year of Machiavelli's death).[25]

But to overcome the established system is to overcome the accumulated weight of the past;[26] it is a project that requires a total immersion within the very consciousness that reflects this reality. In order to overcome it one must subordinate it and redefine it—that is, assimilate it and make it one's own. Both Machiavelli and Guicciardini initiate a historical inquiry

84   into the past and a political analysis of the "relations of force" that obtain in the present. The "facts" and the "events" in themselves are not in question; yet what is as clear as day to Machiavelli is pure illusion to Guicciardini. When the latter, in his critique of Machiavelli's *Discourses*, asserts that Machiavelli is too enamored of the Romans, he does not dispute the greatness of Rome and the *virtus* by means of which the Romans established a "durable" sociopolitical order.[27] Both Machiavelli and Guicciardini reflected the long humanist tradition that looked to the classical age for the "renovation" and rebirth of culture and literature.[28] To Guicciardini, the Machiavellian attempt to recover the Roman values of republican *virtù*, and to introduce political and military institutions based on Roman models, is an impossibility. The fascination with Rome has led Machiavelli to misinterpret the past, and to mistake contemporary political reality for an idealized, imaginary reconstruction of it. To attempt to introduce the ancient "orders" within contemporary history results in bad history and an incorrect analysis of the present world.

Such a criticism—whatever the empirical and "objective" grounds for its validity—fundamentally misunderstands the nature and intent of the Machiavellian project.[29] Machiavelli's passionate interest in the moral, cultural, and political institutions of the Romans was inspired by neither scholastic nor literary concerns comparable to those of the Renaissance humanists. Nor, for that matter, was the interest founded upon a simple belief in the reproduction within contemporary Italy of Roman values and practices. What Machiavelli attempts is to recapture the past, not to reproduce it. To recapture the past, in Gramsci's words, is to "operate in the present" in order to transform the present.[30] Such an attempt is a process that involves the selection and filtering of "objective" facts and events: the past becomes for Machiavelli an aspect of the present. But the present is a reality that is in constant movement, a product of social and political struggles for power, in the same way that the Roman "effective reality" or "truth" was constituted by power and political struggles. Thus to recapture the past is to assimilate it, to transform it in terms of the social and political imperatives of the contemporary struggles within the existing society. The question therefore becomes: for whom, for what actor or group existing within the "present reality," is Machiavelli attempting to recapture the past in order to transform the present?[31]

It is at this point that Machiavelli's attempt to reinterpret Livy and Roman history acquires political and theoretical significance. The question that Machiavelli addresses—whether the greatness of the Romans was a product of *fortuna* or of Roman *virtus*—is central to his overall project, for on **85** its answer depended the kind of present and future Italy would have. If glory and greatness in the past were attained by means of one's own activity, then such a condition may be recaptured—certainly not reproduced—by an inquiry into the factors that had made it originally possible. On the other hand, if *fortuna* is the mistress of human events, if the glory of the Romans was the product of the favors of *fortuna*, then the need to transform the present is a futile self-deception (which is precisely the accusation Guicciardini leveled against Machiavelli).

The discussion of *fortuna* in *The Prince* is related to the discussion of Roman *virtù* in the *Discourses*. Machiavelli criticizes in the former work the "many" who

> have been and are of the opinion that worldly events are so governed by fortune and by God, that men cannot by their prudence change them, and that on the contrary there is no remedy whatever, and for this they may judge it to be useless to toil much about them, but let things be ruled by chance. This opinion has been held more in our day.[32]

The critique is echoed in the *Discourses*, where Machiavelli argues against the very same "many" (both modern and ancient) who

> have held the opinion that the people of Rome were more indebted in the acquisition of their empire to the favors of Fortune than to their own merits |*virtù*|. . . . It was the valor of her armies that achieved those conquests, but it was the wisdom of her conduct and the nature of her institutions, as established by her first legislator, that enabled her to preserve these acquisitions. . . . And those people who will observe the same mode of proceeding will find that they have less need of fortune than those who do not.[33]

With these two quotes we can see that the "mode of proceeding" of the Romans—their *virtù*—is a means by which Machiavelli criticizes and refutes the established opinion of his time. The tribulations and degradation that Italy is undergoing are not the result of the inscrutable will of God or the caprices of *fortuna*, but are rather the outcome of a reality created by the actions of human beings who do not possess *virtù* and who lack the knowledge of the "mode of proceeding." To establish *virtù* as the important factor for the greatness of Rome is to establish both the cause and the remedy for the ravaged state of contemporary Italy, and, at the same time, to deny to the "many" the intellectual and moral grounds for a theory that

86 justifies passivity and inaction. In these two passages is revealed the dual nature of the Machiavellian enterprise: to recapture the past in order to remake the present, and to engage the accepted opinion and established conception of the world in order to capture the past and seize it as one's own.

Machiavelli's belief that human "freedom |is| not entirely extinguished" is opposed to the accepted opinion that human beings in this world "have no remedy whatever." But the contrast between the two underlines Machiavelli's point that action seems futile precisely because human beings "let things be ruled by chance." That this opinion is the prevailing conception of the time is both cause and effect of the social and political troubles that afflict Italy. It is the cause because it has rendered Italy a prey to forces—both internal and external—that could have been resisted had it not been for the "vices" and "indolence" that such an attitude fostered; and it is an effect because the belief faithfully reflects the actual state of corruption and disunity expressed by the moral, political, and cultural life of the Italian states.

In *The Prince* Machiavelli compares *fortuna* to a raging river overflowing its banks, and *virtù* to the planning and building of dykes and dams that will channel the flood and render it both harmless and useful. Machiavelli says that *fortuna* shows her power where "no measures have been taken |*non è ordinata virtù*| to resist her"; and in the next sentence he connects this to contemporary Italian events:

> And if you regard Italy, which has been the seat of these changes, and who has given the impulse to them, you will see her to be a country without dykes or banks of any kind. If she had been protected by proper measures, like Germany, Spain, and France, this inundation would not have caused the great changes that it has, or would not have happened at all.[34]

The remedy—dykes and banks—presupposes an *ordinata virtù*; but this in turn presupposes a form of activity that is structured and directed toward an end posited by human beings. *Ordinata virtù* is structured action; it is social action directed by a purposive, conscious will. The construction of banks and dykes requires a knowledge that will enable one to anticipate the future flooding of the river—which assumes a knowledge of the past and present course of the river. But more important, the intention and the project to erect these dykes demand not simply the technical and scientific knowledge necessary to the project, but also the moral and political

knowledge that will enable one to *ordinare* and organize an activity that is   **87**
inherently social and political.

It is this *ordinata virtù*—the defining and essential characteristic of political and social action—that will redeem *"questa provincia"* (Italy) from the
external and alien forces of *fortuna*. But such an orientation toward
action—a consciousness of one's relation to the objectivity of the world,
and a purposive will that "subjectifies" this objectivity and transforms it
into a humanized and social reality—assumes the introduction and proliferation of a particular form of knowledge that understands the necesssary
relation between *virtù* and *fortuna*. It is this relation that describes one of
the most recurring terms within the writings of Machiavelli—*necessità*—a
term that adumbrates the relation between the consciousness of the objectivity of the world, and the *virtù* or purposive will that humanizes it.[35] To
humanize the alien and objective forces of *fortuna* is precisely to intervene
actively and dynamically within the *essere*. It is, in Gramsci's terms, to "operate within the present" in order to reorder it and recreate it.[36]

The problem with the Guicciardinian conception of the relation between *virtù* and *fortuna* is that the opposition between the two is posited as
an absolute antithesis, such that the two poles of the dyad, frozen into an
unchanging and eternal antinomy, lose the tension necessary for the transformation of the relation. As a consequence, Guicciardini's concept of *virtù*
envisions it as a reactive and merely prudential quality. Since historical
and political events assume an objectivity and a force external to human
beings, since these forces are not a product of human *virtù*, then the latter
can only function within the limits and structure imposed by *fortuna*. *Virtù*
will never overcome the existing reality. It can only seek to adapt and ac-
commodate itself within a reality that is not, and can never be, the conscious product of human action. Therefore, such a reality will always remain
alien to human beings. Such a conception of *fortuna*—as an alien and external power—bears a close resemblance to the medieval Christian view,
where it either becomes a power subordinated to providence or to God, or
is simply translated into the will of God.[37]

On the other hand, the Machiavellian relation between *virtù* and *fortuna* establishes a reciprocal and dynamic interaction in which *fortuna* no
longer appears as an external power, but rather as an aspect of *virtù*. *Fortuna*
appears as the existing objectivity of the *essere*, an objectivity that results
from the action of human beings in the world. *Virtù* is the conscious and
purposive will that recognizes itself in this objectivity, because the latter is
the product of this will. *Fortuna* appears as an alien force only when, and

88 because, *virtù* has disintegrated and degenerated. But it should be noted that even with this disintegration *fortuna*, while acquiring a power over human activity, nevertheless still remains an aspect of *virtù*: in this case the former now appears as the objective force of events over which human beings believe they have no control. Thus the subordination of human beings to *fortuna* is a function of *virtù* itself: to the extent that *virtù* is active and operative, to the extent that it is embodied in the concrete activity of human beings in the world, then to that extent the objective forces of *fortuna* are overcome and directed toward human ends. As Gramsci puts it,

> According to Russo, for Machiavelli *fortuna* possesses a double meaning, both objective and subjective. *Fortuna* is the natural force of reality |*delle cose*| (that is, the causal relation), the propitious concurrence of events, what to Vico will become Providence, or that transcendent power mythologized by the old medieval doctrine of God. |But| for Machiavelli this is simply the very same *virtù* of the individual, and its power springs from the very same will of man.[38]

These differing conceptions of the relation between *virtù* and *fortuna* establish, in Gramsci's view, the basic opposition between Machiavelli and Guicciardini. The former is a *politico* who acts upon the existing reality in order to transcend it and establish a new structure; the latter is a *diplomatico*, who "can only move within |the existing structure| of effective reality, because his specific activity is not directed toward the creation of new structures |*equilibri*|, but rather toward the preservation within certain juridical boundaries of the existing structure of power."[39] Guicciardini's attitude toward Machiavelli anticipates Croce's attitude toward the philosophy of praxis, in the same way that Croce's interpretation of the relation between political action and thought is a modern version of Guicciardini's: both Croce and Guicciardini look at politics as a technique useful for maneuvering within the given reality, but one that is always subject to the laws that govern this reality (Croce), or to the external power of *fortuna* (Guicciardini). Both regard any attempt to transform this reality as not only impossible, but also dangerous, for any such action will destabilize the existing structure and unleash the unpredictable and violent forces of *fortuna*.

It is not an accident that to both Guicciardini and Croce such violence and unpredictability are products of the active intervention of the people into the sociopolitical reality.[40] Since the nature of the existing reality is immutable, and since the nature of the *volgo* is always opposed to thought (Croce) and to "wisdom" (Guicciardini), the emergence of the masses will disintegrate the existing structure of power, which to them depends for its stability and durability on the permanent divorce of the "wise" rulers from the ignorant people. From this perspective, the Guicciardinian and Crocean critique, issuing from a basically conservative and "restorative" interpretation of history and politics, represents an element of the contemporary reality against which Machiavelli and Gramsci are struggling. The latter's attempt to recapture the past in order to change the present is at the same time an attempt to deny the very same past to those who, like Guicciardini and Croce, would employ it to justify the prevailing conception of the world and to maintain the established system or "equilibrium" of forces. A Guicciardini who supports the rule of the *ottimati* and argues for the establishment in Florence of a *governo stretto* envisions a Roman past and its relation to the Italian present quite differently from a Machiavelli who supports the *popolo minuto* and argues for the formation of a *governo largo*.[41] The former understands historical and political change as the result of the uncontrollable forces unleashed by *fortuna*, whereas the latter sees such change as the product of an interaction between *virtù* and *fortuna*, such that sociopolitical reality is open to the transformative efforts of political action. The *ottimati*, being more cultured and possessed of more *virtù* (that is, more disciplined and "prudent") than the common people, will be able to create a stable and more durable state that will be able to lessen the deleterious effects of *fortuna*. To expand the base of the *governo*, to subject the state to the popular participation of the people, would be to destabilize the foundations of the state (which can only rest on the "wisdom" and prudential knowledge of the *ottimati*), and thus to destroy the narrow space necessary for the aristocracy to pursue its cultural and social endeavors.[42] If human beings are subject to the action of *fortuna*, then the expansion of political participation through the introduction of the *populo minuto* into the government will mean the expansion and intensification of the forces of *fortuna*. The *governo stretto* of Guicciardini translates into the "aristo-democracy" of Croce: both are seen as necessary to the establishment and preservation of a realm of culture and thought.

In both cases, the nature of the people is as unchangeable as the nature of the "aristocracy of the intellect." The underlying assumption that supports both perspectives is a belief that posits a profound gulf between knowledge and action, a position that posits a superior value to thought and contemplation precisely because thought is seen as an activity isolated from sociopolitical action. To both Croce and Guicciardini, not only is the "word" always antithetical to the "deed," but the deed itself can never

90 redeem the brute necessity of worldly events, so that salvation is possible only through the word, and by retreating into the private world. Thus Gramsci asserts that there is in Croce

> the will not "to commit oneself" at all, which is the mode of looking to one's own *particulare*, a modern Guicciardinism peculiar to many intellectuals for whom the "word" is quite sufficient: "*Dixi, et salvavi animam meam.*" But the soul will not be saved merely through the word. Works are needed.[43]

The parallel between the Machiavellian attack on the "many" who believe human actions cannot remedy the nature of things and the Gramscian critique of Croce is noteworthy. The former assert that "there is no remedy whatever, and for this they may judge it useless to toil much about them,"[44] and Croce's separation of philosophy from practice reduces itself to the will not to engage the world. The will not to commit oneself in Croce's case, and the will to retreat into the private realm of the *particulare* in Guicciardini's, are translated, within the political and social context of struggle and competition, into the will to support a concrete social group and a concrete structure of power. In the first case, the liberal philosophy that posits the political as technique and as "pure" science envisions a divorce between the rulers and the ruled, the intellectuals and the *volgo*—a divorce necessary to attain and maintain a "liberty" founded on the "aristo-democracy." In the second case, Guicciardini's historical and political thought similarly posits a distinction between "those who know" (the oligarchic families of Florence) and "those who do not know" (the *populo minuto*), which must be preserved if stability and liberty are to be achieved. Crocean thought posits the existing Italian state and the existing social relations of power as the culmination of the nineteenth-century liberal movement; Guicciardini posits the *governo stretto* of the great Florentine houses as the only possible means of avoiding the violence of the people and the tyranny of the despot. It is significant that both Croce and Guicciardini, within their respective time periods, felt it necessary to support, or at least acquiesce to, the reaction of the fascists and the despotism of the Medici (restored to power by papal and foreign armies).[45]

The Machiavellian conception of the *virtù/fortuna* dyad presupposes an active will engaged in the world, a will that sees the world as its own creation. Consequently, the relation between the *essere* and the *dover essere* establishes a conception of politics in which the latter is seen as emerging from the former, in which the realization of the latter necessitates sociopolitical engagement within the former. In Machiavelli the *dover essere* is not a realm whose meaning and purpose are actualized within the private realm, and the *essere* is a world in which the iron laws of events are impermeable and intractable to the value-creating activity of human *virtù*. In Machiavelli there can be no retreat to the realm of the private: all value and all creative activity emerge from within the realm of the public; that is, the political is the activity by which the *dover essere* that is latent within the *essere* is transformed into a new *verità delle cose*. The Machiavellian political knowledge, therefore, must of necessity be a "public" knowledge that both teaches the "new principles and orders" and attempts, by means of this teaching, to "animate" the will and *virtù* of human beings.

Thus Machiavelli asserts in the *Discourses* that "sarò animoso in dire manifestamente"—he will speak out openly and passionately and reveal the fruits of *lunga pratica* and *continua lezione*, that is, the new political knowledge that encompasses both history and politics.[46] And in *The Prince* he also makes it clear that the "modes and orders" that previously were covertly taught by the Centaur he now intends to teach openly.[47] The political as technique is not what is new to Machiavelli's knowledge; what is new is that now he is openly teaching it. But this *manifestamente* is crucial to the entire body of Machiavelli's project: the new knowledge must be an open and public knowledge because it teaches a dynamic and active *virtù* inserted within the very structure of social reality, a *virtù* that transforms the *essere* into the *dover essere*. It must be open and public because such knowledge cannot be developed within the Guicciardinian *particulare*, but rather must be addressed to an audience that the new knowledge recognizes has the potential to realize itself within the *essere* and within the "effective reality." The *manifestamente* of Machiavelli's knowledge is a necessary moment of the movement from the Guicciardinian *particulare* to the political world conceived as activity that creates new values. Similarly, the *animoso* is a necessary posture for the creation of a *virtù* directed toward the transformation of the established system.

The opposition between the retreat into the sphere of the private and the active intervention into the "effective reality," the antithesis between the Machiavellian *virtù/fortuna* dyad and the Guicciardinian one, are no more sharply contrasted than in those sections of Machiavelli's works where he discusses the various types of religion and their relation to action and to politics. In the *Discourses*, where he analyzes the role of liberty in making the Roman people great, Machiavelli says that

in ancient times the people were more devoted to liberty than in the present ... |because| men were stronger in those days, which is attributable to the difference of education, founded upon the difference of their religion and ours. For, as our religion teaches us the truth and the true way of life, it causes us to attach less value to the honors and possessions of this world; whilst the Pagans, esteeming those things as the highest good, were more energetic and ferocious in their actions ... our religion glorifies more the humble and the contemplative men than the men of action |who are more valued by the Romans|. Our religion ... places the supreme happiness in humility, lowliness, and a contempt for worldly objects, whilst the ... |Roman| places the supreme good in grandeur of soul, strength of body ... and if our religion claims of us fortitude of soul, it is more to enable us to suffer than to achieve great deeds. Such a way of life has made men feeble, and made them an easy prey to evil-minded men, who can control them more securely, seeing that the great body of men, for the sake of gaining Paradise, are more disposed to endure injuries than to avenge them.[48]

I have quoted Machiavelli at length because within this chapter of the *Discourses* emerges the fundamental conception of the world that Machiavelli's knowledge teaches and intends to introduce. In addition, the chapter posits an antinomy between the conception of the world entertained by the pagans—the religion of the Romans—and the conception of the world advanced by the Christian religion. It is noteworthy that in this discussion of religion Machiavelli relates a belief system and a "way of life" to what he calls education. It is through education that the way of life and the conception of the world are concretized and reproduced within society. Education implies a knowledge that is to be taught, and a practice that expresses and animates the new knowledge—a totality that presupposes an "end" and a "good" that are generated by the new moral and intellectual system. What Machiavelli finds unacceptable in Christian thought and practice is the negation of the world and the negation of action in the world. "Il *sommo bene*" (the supreme good) is located outside the world of human events. The Christian good is the standard by which the world and political action are interpreted, such that the "world has been weakened and made effeminate, and Heaven is disarmed."[49] The condition of the world "*nel temporale*," and the particular type of moral and intellectual education, are closely connected. "Our religion" (Christianity) does not simply posit an irreconcilable duality between the world of thought and the world of experience, but the thought itself requires for its continued existence a form of education that maintains the duality while at the same time negating the Christian good in the world of experience and political action.

The continued existence of the Christian way of life, therefore, is based on the "disharmony" between the word and the deed (to use de Sanctis's term).[50]

The cutting edge of the critique is the opposition between active and passive, pride and humility, action and contemplation, *virtù* and *ozio*, the world existing *nel temporale* and a reality given by "the truth and the true way." The attack is all-encompassing, since the critique of "our religion" is basically a critique of a conception of the world that posits the "disharmony" between thought and action, and that elevates the former to a moral and ethical realm superior to that of the latter. This is evident when Machiavelli attacks those "who have interpreted our religion according to the promptings of indolence rather those of *virtù*. For if we were to reflect that our religion permits us to exalt and defend our country, we should see that according to it we ought also to love and honor our country, and prepare ourselves so as to be capable of defending it."[51] There are traces in this passage that anticipate the national, antipapal, and anti-Empire elements that were later harnessed by the Lutheran Reformation. It recognizes the possibility that the Christian religion may be reinterpreted away from, and against, the feudal and medieval conception of the world so that it may be wedded to the interests and needs of the emerging rulers of the various territorial states, and opposed to the interests of the supranational church and Empire.[52] Whereas in the past the Christian fathers and doctors reinterpreted the classical notions of *virtus* and *aretè* and transformed them into Christian concepts of value, Machiavelli intends to reverse the process: he reinterprets the Christian religion in order to assimilate it into his concept of *virtù* and his notion of politics.[53] In any case, the point is unambiguous: a particular interpretation of Christianity, according to which heaven is "disarmed" (that is, the end or good is located outside the realm of historical and political action), has rendered the present world weak and subject to the forces of *fortuna*. Thus, a different interpretation of Christianity, based on a new conception of *virtù*, will rearm heaven, locate the supreme good within the *essere*, and consequently remake the world through the actualization of the *dover essere* ("*il sommo bene*").

It should be noted that the Christian good—the salvation of the soul—is a religious and theological version of the *particulare* toward which action is directed by the Guicciardinian concept of *virtù*. Guicciardini, of course, entertains a secular and humanist notion of *virtù*. But since this *virtù* is a reactive capacity subject to the overwhelming forces of *fortuna*, its pessimistic and skeptical attitude toward action resembles the Christian and

94 Augustinian belief that willing and acting cannot change the nature and structure of worldly events. Thus, in one we have the retreat into the religious *particulare* of faith and the salvation of the individual soul, and in the other we have the retreat into the secular *particulare* of individual and economic self-interest; in both, the *bene* is individual, particular, and narrow—a consequence of the basic futility of human action to redress the disharmony between word and deed (a futility based in the first on the consequences of the Fall, and in the second on the primacy of *fortuna* over *virtù*, which makes it impossible to relate in any meaningful way *pratica* to *lezione*). Thus the Machiavellian critique encompasses the past and the present: it attacks the *caritas* of a Saint Francis of Assisi as well as the secular humanism of the Renaissance papal and princely courts; it rejects the *vita contemplativa* of classical and medieval philosophy as well as the merely (or solely) literary erudition of the Renaissance humanists; and it negates the retreat into Christian self-interest (the salvation of the soul) as well as the retreat into the Guicciardinian *particulare*.[54]

But the critique of the Christian conception of the world, and the critique of the humanist concern with the narrow and particular interests, are at the same time accompanied by the formulation of a new conception of the world that contains within it an opposing vision of the good. It is the "common good rather than the particular good that makes cities great. And certainly the common good is recognized nowhere but in republics."[55] The common good—the underlying, thematic question that is addressed by the *Discourses*—is presented as the antithesis of the particular good. The former makes a *vivere civile* and a *vivere politico* ("civil and political life") possible, while the latter is a good that belongs within the realm of the private. Thus the inculcation of a given conception of *virtù* is a necessary condition for what Machiavelli calls the *vivere libero* and the *vivere comune*—a life based on liberty and on common action. A "way of life"—"*modo del vivere*"—cannot be separated from the social and political education that presupposes it. In Machiavelli such an education refers to the moral, intellectual, and cultural structure that is actively and experientially embedded within a specific way of life. The emphasis on this type of education is found throughout Machiavelli's works, which make numerous references to "religion," "good education," and "good laws," which make for "good arms," which in turn lead to "good laws" and "good education."[56]

The prevailing conception of the world, whether expressed by the feudal interpretation of Christianity or by the Renaissance humanist preoccupation with the *particulare*, posits a way of life antithetical to the general and common good necessary for a *vivere politico*. Thus Machiavelli: "It is this education, then, and this false interpretation of our religion, that is the cause of there not being so many republics nowadays as there were anciently; and that there is no longer the same love of liberty amongst the people now as there was then."[57] An education and a religion that teach a *sommo bene* within the world, that celebrate and inculcate human action and practice, and that place a moral and political value on the "civil" and "political" way of life, assume a moral and intellectual perspective whose necessity is given by the new political knowledge that Machiavelli intends to introduce. On the other hand, the existing state of affairs presupposes a sociopolitical and sociocultural conception of the world that is antithetical to the Machiavellian form of knowledge, a perspective whose frame of reference and terms of discourse describe and "fix" a field of vision wherein the very notions of *vivere politico* and *vivere civile* lose their meaning and intelligibility.

What this means is that to pose the question of the *bene comune* as a way of life that embodies the *vivere politico* is to negate the prevailing conception of the world. The introduction of "new modes and orders" presupposes a conception whose terms of discourse are radically different from those of the existing reality, a mode of discourse that establishes a new way of seeing the world and a new way of acting in the world. Machiavelli's new perspective is given by the end, and this end is at the same time the object in sight, because it is produced and elaborated by the new conception. A *vivere politico* is not conceivable without a new way of seeing and acting; and this new way of interpreting the world cannot become a way of life without the introduction of the new political order. Machiavelli presents two kinds of *sommo bene*, antagonistic and mutually exclusive, each a product and an expression of a specific conception of the world—one embodying the prevailing structure of reality (the *essere*) supported by the weight and authority of the past in all its social, moral, educational, and cultural encrustations, the other embodying an embryonic seed and an end (the *dover essere*). This second kind of *sommo bene*, which is both potentiality and necessity, is embedded within the reality, and yet in its unfolding constitutes the negation of this reality.

The common strand that links these terms together is the notion of education as a moral and intellectual discipline, without which sociocultural and sociopolitical life is impossible. The point is what type of education will embody in practice a conception of the world that looks to a way of life based on the *vivere civile* and the *vivere politico*. Since such a conception

96 of the world envisions a notion of *virtù* opposed to the established notion, the problem the *Discourses* poses is the organization of *virtù* within a people, which is an aspect of the organization of education. But this is another way of asking who is to be the subject of this education, what entity possesses the necessary capacity to become *virtuoso*. Is there an entity within the *essere* that, by means of this education and this *virtù*, will create a civil and political life based on the common rather than the particular good? Or, to put it another way, what is the process by which one is able to move from the particular good located within the Guicciardinian (humanist) and Christian (feudal) realms of the private to the common and universal good located within the public and open realm of the political?

The critique of the established conception of the world, and the attack on what is assumed as a given—whether it is the skepticism of Guicciardinian political knowledge or the feudal and scholastic type of Christianity—are translated by Machiavelli into a political and military critique of the Renaissance ruling class, which he holds responsible for the weakened and enslaved condition of Italy. In comparing the ancient "orders" to those of the present, Machiavelli is calling for the formation of a new type of political actor that will embody the new political knowledge put forth in the *Discourses*. Italy is a *provincia*, he says in *The Prince*, "without a head, without order, beaten, despoiled, lacerated, and overrun," yet he believes that "there is not lacking scope |*materia*| in Italy for the introduction of every kind of new organisation |*ogni formi*|. Here there is great virtue in the members, if it were not wanting in the heads."[58] It should be noted that *virtù* is not lacking in Italy when directed to particular and individualistic ends. The problem is to translate this form of *virtù*, which exists within the particular and private sphere, into a political and public *virtù*, into an "ordered *virtù*" consciously directed toward the common good. But "no one has arisen who knew how to discover new |orders (*ordini*)|."[59] Machiavelli intends to discover a subject or entity that is able to introduce the new orders given by his new knowledge.

The Machiavellian project to create a new political and historical subject emerges when we juxtapose the statement just cited from *The Prince* to the intention stated in the dedication to the *Discourses*:

> I . . . do not address myself to such as are princes, but to those who by their infinite good qualities are worthy to be such . . . |and| to those who would know how to govern states, rather than those who have the right to govern, but lack the knowledge.[60]

The new ruler addressed by Machiavelli's knowledge will not be bound by the practice and "opinion" of the present, nor be tied to the preexisting system of power. Machiavelli locates the new political actor outside the established and customarily recognized centers of power. Machiavelli addresses himself to those who, though not princes by the standards and practices of the age, nevertheless have the potential to be princes. The established princes do not deserve to rule because they are rooted within the moral, intellectual, and cultural totality corrupted by vice, "proud indolence," and idleness.[61] The servile condition of Italy reflects the true character of its ruling groups, who would rather study and practice the courtly arts and manners, rather than the arts of war and of ruling.[62]

The distinction between those "who are princes" and those who "are worthy to be such" presupposes a political knowledge that is simultaneously a critique of the present and a prefiguration or anticipation of the future.[63] The former are located within an existing reality (the *essere*), which is defined by a past and present whose values, ideas, beliefs, and practices together constitute the totality against which Machiavelli is reacting; and the latter, as they emerge from within this totality, represent the *dover essere*, which is the result and the negation of the established structure. The critique, although originating within the intellectual, social, and cultural complex of the established totality, transcends this totality and attempts to formulate novel moral and intellectual criteria that define the nature of ruling and the nature of the subject that rules. In effect, the new knowledge reformulates and redefines the concept of ruling and the nature of power. The established princes are not worthy of rule, not because they lack the knowledge of political technique—the *arcana imperii*—but because they lack Machiavelli's new knowledge. The latter attempts to overcome the traditional and customary terms of discourse within which political technique is inserted. Thus Machiavelli asserts that he has "departed from the ordinary usage |*uscito fuori dell'uso comune*| of writers."[64] This departure signals the independence of the Machiavellian project from the established reality: rooted within the historical present, it looks to undermine and destroy it by locating within it a new subject able to carry forward the introduction of the new modes and orders. In Gramsci's words, Machiavelli recognizes the necessity "to break the unity |of the existing reality| created by the traditional ideology, |for| without such a rupture the new force will not be able to achieve the consciousness of itself as an independent subject |*personalità*|."[65]

98   The burden of the argument presented in the dedication and in the introductions of the *Discourses* is the opposition between those who ought to rule as a consequence of moral and intellectual force (*virtù*), and those who do in fact rule simply because they possess the power, force, and resources of the established system ("*avere il regno*"). The dominant groups in Italy do not possess moral and intellectual authority, for they understand the nature of rule—and of the political—only in terms of the immediate and particular good. Their rule is a consequence of the conception of the world that Machiavelli identifies with "our religion" and with the "opinion of the many." Therefore, the established rulers "do not know" because their values and activity are determined by a worldview that "esteems the private" more than the public, and therefore employs the *arcana imperii* for private ends rather than for public and common ends.[66]

"To go outside common usage" represents a double departure: on the one hand, in opposition to his predecessors and contemporaries,[67] Machiavelli intends to introduce a knowledge that represents the negation of the established forms of thought and practice; and, on the other, this knowledge will address itself not to established rulers and princes, but rather to those that are identified by this very knowledge as "worthy to be rulers." Those who are outside the established practices and beliefs are the "real" rulers and princes, whereas those who are within are merely the "apparent" rulers; that the former ought to rule is given by the new knowledge, and that the latter rule, yet do not know how to rule, is also given by this knowledge. Machiavelli thus establishes a radical opposition between two kinds of knowledge and two kinds of subject. The Machiavellian project demands a new subject—a "new prince"—that expresses in action and in practice the new political knowledge.[68] Since this knowledge opposes the established conception of the world, it requires a new subject that will oppose the established rulers. It is the subject to which the new knowledge is addressed that will carry forward the transformative and innovating project. The knowledge, and the subject it addresses, together constitute the overcoming of the established system and the movement toward the creation of a new reality.

Chapter 6

Machiavelli and the Democratic Philosopher

The Relation between Machiavelli's "New Modes and Orders" and Gramsci's Hegemony

The relation between Machiavelli's thought and the subject to whom it is addressed is fundamental to understanding the Machiavellian enterprise. The new knowledge is not a disembodied thought that exists eternally and universally. It represents a form of consciousness, and a conception of the world, whose meaning and purpose are given by the subject to whom it is addressed, and within whom this knowledge is concretized and put into practice. The knowledge is the consciousness that defines, in Gramsci's words, the *personalità* of the subject, and the subject is the embodiment of this knowledge in the world and in struggle.[1] Thus the problem of *address* is crucial: it presupposes a dialogue between Machiavelli and the subject he is addressing. Such a dialogue, in turn, presupposes an interaction that is necessarily based upon mutual recognition and mutual speech. In effect, to ask the question who or what Machiavelli's knowledge is addressing is to ask what the nature and role of this knowledge is, and how it is related to practice and to action.

We have already noted that Machiavelli goes outside the accepted custom of his predecessors and his contemporaries. He does not address himself to the existing rulers; rather, he specifically dedicates his writings to those who are within the private sphere (*nel privato*), and who, though not rulers, "are worthy to be such."[2] Those who deserve to rule are represented in the *Discourses* by Zanobi Buondelmonte and Cosimo Rucellai, to whom Machiavelli formally dedicates the work. Machiavelli says that although it is customary to dedicate works of this kind to a prince or ruler he will depart from the *uso comune* and address his work to those who do not have power and who live in the private sphere. Buondelmonte and Rucellai are friends of Machiavelli who had urged him to write the *Discourses*. Machiavelli often frequented the Orti Oricellari, where he engaged in conversation and discussion concerning political, historical, and literary subjects; he may have read portions of the *Discourses* to the group assembled in the Gardens.[3]

In the dedication it is made clear that the "gift" Machiavelli offers to his friends is one that springs from "obligations" the writer owes to the reader-friends. At the very beginning, Machiavelli establishes a relation between himself and those he addresses that is based on the mutual obligations friends owe to each other: "take it, then, as one accepts whatever comes from friends." The relation between the subject and Machiavelli the teacher is thus one of equality and reciprocity. Machiavelli signals that he intends to be a teacher of political knowledge utterly different from his predecessors. If we accept Strauss"s interpretation (that Machiavelli writes the *Discourses* in order to transform and retranslate Livy's works to use them in the same way that Christianity retranslated the Hebrew scriptures and the works of the classical world for its own ends), then it must also be added that Machiavelli does not assert a nature radically superior to that of his readers.[4] Machiavelli teaches in the name of no divine or earthly authority; nor does he assert divine election or any special faculty or quality not possessed by others. In contrast to the teaching of Christianity, Machiavelli's teaching is not a "free" gift bestowed on the subject by an act of grace. It is a gift, but one that is "owed" by him to his friends. Indeed, Machiavelli is "forced" to write by the very friends he is addressing: "you have forced me to write what I should never have attempted on my own accord."[5]

In Machiavelli, the subject is not the product of an external "revelation"; on the contrary, the new knowledge is seen by Machiavelli to be closely related to the subject it addresses. And Machiavelli the teacher issues from the very same subject that he intends to teach. This becomes clear when we realize that Machiavelli is forced to write that which is desired by the very same subject he has "chosen" to address. Thus the knowledge that Machiavelli is attempting to formulate openly and boldly is in part a consequence of the subject, in the same way that the subject emerges as a consequence of the knowledge. The "having chosen you" is equivalent to the "you have forced me to write" and to the "you yourselves have desired it" (*Discourses*, dedication). What is desired is what Machiavelli is forced to write, which, once written, identifies as the carrier of the knowledge the very subject that had originally sparked the enterprise. Both recognize each other as necessary aspects of the new knowledge. Thus Machiavelli's choice is a necessary choice, where this necessity is a reciprocal necessity: it issues from the identification of the subject by the new knowledge, and simultaneously from the subject as the agent that forces the formulation of this knowledge and that recognizes it as a knowledge specific to itself.

It is significant that Machiavelli asserts the primacy of reason over authority, tradition, or God in the chapter of the *Discourses* where he discusses the nature of the people ("The people are wiser and more constant than princes").[6] In this chapter Machiavelli defends the people against those writers (both classical and contemporary) who see them as the *vulgus* whose nature leads to the violent destruction of stable rule.[7] Such a defense, he knows, is contrary to the thought of "all writers"; yet he will maintain that reason shows that "the governments of the people are better than those of princes." Machiavelli "thinks, and ever shall think, that it cannot be wrong to defend one's opinion with arguments founded upon reason, without employing force or authority." "To go outside the common usage" is to "reason without employing force or authority." It is precisely such a kind of reason that enables him to see the superiority of a popular government. It is a reason that establishes a knowledge not given by any traditional source, such as revelation, authority (secular or religious), or the absolute Reason posited by Platonism and Stoicism.[8] Machiavelli's knowledge is given by "long experience and continual study": an experience that reflects the practice of contemporary Florentine and Italian sociopolitical struggles, and a study that is the product of a "conversation" between Machiavelli and ancient writers such as Cicero, Livy, Tacitus, and Sallust (a conversation, in other words, between past and present, which is one element that constitutes Machiavelli's knowledge).[9] The terms of the relation—of the conversation—between Machiavelli and his readers imply each other and are essentially interchangeable. Rucellai, Buondelmonte, and Machiavelli together express a common nature and a common purpose.

It is because of this relation that Machiavelli can write: "I feel a satisfaction in this, that, even if I have often erred in the course of this work, I have assuredly made no mistake [*in questa sola so*] in having chosen you above all others to whom to dedicate [*indirizzi*] these discourses."[10] Machiavelli admits of error in the formulation of his analyses, but there is no error in the choice of subject. A knowledge that wants to argue with reason recognizes the possibility of error, and can make no absolute statements regarding the nature of truth and error. But this knowledge recognizes itself

102 and unfolds within a subject that is the carrier of this knowledge. It is the relationship between Machiavelli and the subject—a relationship of friendship and mutual interests—that provides the certainty in the choice of subject. Machiavelli is free from error not because he possesses a knowledge that has discovered "scientifically" the objective and eternal laws of reality, but because this knowledge is a product of the relation between himself and those to whom he is sending it. Machiavelli is certain because the knowledge he is formulating and the choice of whom to impart it are inherent within each other. The certainty arises from the nature of the subject, which is not an alien entity outside the experience and practice of Machiavelli's knowledge. The educator and the educated are products of each other. Machiavelli recognizes himself in the subject, and the subject, as a friend and reader, recognizes itself in Machiavelli. The subject is to take the knowledge in the same way that "one accepts whatever comes from friends, looking rather to the intention of him who gives, than to the thing offered." The intention would be incomprehensible without the mutual recognition and mutual interests that describe the relation.

When Machiavelli writes "*in questa sola so*," this "I know" is a moral and intellectual knowledge that springs from a relation of friendship and equality. What this means is that "I know" becomes possible because it is based upon, and is the product of, "we know." The certainty regarding the subject is necessary because it is this very subject that makes the knowing possible. Thus Machiavelli's knowledge is the product of a moral-intellectual interaction, which is in turn based on a social and political relation. In this sense, Machiavelli's knowledge is fundamentally rooted within the practice and activity of the subject to which it is addressed.

The mutual recognition and interaction are seen in the construction Machiavelli employs to describe the relation between himself and his readers. After referring to his "poor arguments" and "errors," he writes: "This being so, I know not which of us has the greater right to complain—I, that you should have forced me to write what I should never have attempted of my own accord, or you, that I should have written without giving you cause to be satisfied" ("Io a voi, che mi avete forzato a scrivere . . . voi a me, quando, scrivendo"). The "io a voi" ("I to you") and the "voi a me" ("you to me") establish a dynamic interaction between the writer Machiavelli and the reader-subject. It is precisely such a formulation that posits a relation between the knowledge Machiavelli teaches and those who are to be taught, a relation that translates the "I know" into the "we know."

Such a relation finds its parallel in *The Art of War*, where the interaction between the new knowledge and the new subject is symbolized in the literary and stylistic form of a dialogue. This dialogue is a conversation between Fabrizio (an admired soldier-statesman) and a group of "young men" assembled together in the Orti Oricellari.[11] The participants in the dialogue include the same Buondelmonte and Rucellai to whom the *Discourses* are dedicated. The occasion for the dialogue is Rucellai's invitation of Fabrizio to his Gardens, which provide its setting—a secluded setting that stands as a symbol for the private life and private interests against which Fabrizio will argue. Thus in both the *Discourses* and *The Art of War* the conversation and dialogue are initiated by a subject to which, though existing *"nel privato"* (within the private sphere), the knowledge is directed. The theme of the dialogue, of course, is similar to that provided by Machiavelli's "conversation" with the ancient thinkers: "to imitate the ancients in bearing hardships and inconveniences, instead of giving |oneself| up to ease and indolence, in performing such exploits as were done in the sunshine and not in the shade." Such an intention pervades all of Machiavelli's works: knowledge of ancient *virtù* is directed toward open and public ("in the sunshine") action in the present, rather than toward the passive and private ("in the shade") contemplation of history.[12]

The recognition of the necessity to act is immediately linked by Machiavelli to the necessity to present a certain form of knowledge. Rucellai asserts that "you |Fabrizio| have now introduced a subject |voi avete aperto la via a uno ragionamento| which I myself have wished to have discussed, and I therefore implore you to speak freely |sanza rispetto| about the matter, because I, on my part, will just as freely put questions to you |io sanza rispetto vi domanderò|."[13] Rucellai states that Fabrizio has "opened" the discussion, yet it is the former's wish that has brought Fabrizio to introduce the theme of the dialogue. Fabrizio is to speak *"sanza rispetto"*—that is, freely, without regard to established social customs or usages—and Rucellai will in turn ask questions *"sanza rispetto."* The free interaction that will carry forward the *"ragionamento"* (reasoning) is based on the relation between the *"domandare"* (asking or questioning) and the *"parlare"* (speaking). It is through such a relation that one will come to the truth (*"intendere la verità"*). But to speak *"sanza rispetto"* is a method of proceeding that is quite similar to the "difendere alcuna opinione con le ragioni sanza volervi usare o l'autorità o la forza": thus to speak freely is to reason without the use of force or authority. Or, as Fabrizio says, to state "my opinion . . . while speaking with friends" is to engage in reasoned discussion (*"disputare le cose"*). The beginning of Book

104 I in *The Art of War* makes it clear that the conversation and the *ragionamento* can only be conducted within an environment (or social structure) where force and authority (such as established social habits and norms) are excluded. As in the *Discourses*, Fabrizio intends to discuss and to "defend with reason" what he proceeds to teach. Thus the relationship that obtains between Fabrizio and the young interlocutors corresponds to the relation established in the *Discourses* between Machiavelli's new knowledge and the subject to which it is addressed.

It is interesting to note that in both works a parallel correspondence is established between Machiavelli-Fabrizio and the subject to whom they address themselves. The relation between the "io a voi" and the "voi a me" established in the dedication to the *Discourses* is almost exactly reproduced in Book I of *The Art of War*. Fabrizio says to Rucellai: "it will give me great pleasure that you question me. For I will learn through your questions in the same way that you will learn from my replies. Many times a wise questioner will make one consider aspects of a problem—or a new problem entirely—that would never have been recognized had he not been so questioned" ("mi sarà grato mi domandiate; perché io sono per imparare cosí da voi del domandarmi, come voi da me nel rispondervi; perché molte volte uno savio domandatore fa a uno considerare molte cose e conoscerne molte altre, le quali, sanza esserne domandato, non arebbe mai conosciute").[14] The new knowledge that Machiavelli intends to introduce is here established by the relation "io . . . da voi . . . come voi da me" ("I . . . through you . . . as you through me"), a relation that establishes the active dynamism of a knowledge that itself teaches the necessity for action.

This passage is laden with consequences regarding the nature of political knowledge and its relationship to a subject that knows it. In a thinker of the stature and power of Machiavelli it would be a grievous error of interpretation to attribute these parallels between *The Art of War* and the *Discourses* to a simple matter of coincidence—or, which comes to the same thing, to look at them as mere literary and stylistic devices that are repeated because of literary convention and usage.[15] Such an interpretation becomes even more tenuous when we consider the dedication to *The Prince* and relate these parallel dyads to Machiavelli's statement that "it is necessary to be a prince to know thoroughly the nature of the people, and one of the people to know the nature of princes."[16] Machiavelli considers political knowledge to be a product of an active interaction, where the relation between the terms of the dyads is a process through whose unfolding knowledge is developed and constituted.

The parallels, therefore, are significant, and they are so presented to establish a precise point. Fabrizio asserts, as Machiavelli does in the *Discourses*, that error in the presentation of what he knows is quite likely, and that therefore his knowledge is not to be taken as the absolute fount of what is and of what ought to be: "but I shall not pretend to obtrude my opinions upon you as decisive and infallible. When you have heard them, you may judge for yourself" ("il che se sarà vero o no, me ne rapporterò al vostro giudicio").[17] What Fabrizio knows, he himself wants subjected to the criticism and "judgment" of those to whom his knowledge is addressed. The "truth" of his teaching is thus a function of the reason and critical activity of the subject. This knowledge cannot exist outside the relation that gives birth to it. It is not a knowledge constituted by abstract principles whose truth is determined by the degree of their conformity to the "effective reality." When Fabrizio understands the truth of his knowledge to be related to the "judgment" of the subject he is addressing, he is not saying that this truth is a reflection of the empirical and objective conditions of the subject (in this case, the preexisting beliefs, values, and ideas of Rucellai and his friends). There would be no point to the *ragionamento* if Fabrizio were to passively accept the opinions of his friends (as there would be no point were the latter passively to accept Fabrizio's). The "judgment" to which he refers does not merely reside in Rucellai and his friends; rather, it is a product of the relation between those who ask and those who reply.

The relationship that Marx established between the educator and the educated—a relation that Gramsci elaborated in his formulation of the concept of hegemony—finds its antecedent in the Machiavellian relationship between knowledge and the subject to which it is addressed. It should be remembered that Gramsci offered a critique of the Crocean philosophy that posited an irreconcilable rupture between politics and philosophy, and between politics and ethics. The Crocean formulation posits a form of knowledge that exists independently of social and political reality, such that this knowledge does not address a subject rooted within the practice of social life, a subject that emerges and acts "*nel temporale*" (as Machiavelli would put it); rather, this knowledge is capable of recognizing only itself, and the subject it addresses is merely the abstract reflection of itself as it contemplates itself. Gramsci attempts to *svelare* (uncover or reveal) the underlying sociopolitical roots of such a philosophy, in the same way that Machiavelli attempts to *svelare* the political and practical implica-

106   tions of a *studia humanitatis* and a Guicciardinian conception of politics that retreats into the hidden shadows of the private realm.[18]

Both Gramsci and Machiavelli attempt to formulate a form of knowledge that will bring out into the open the political and power bases of the Crocean and Guicciardinian conceptions of knowledge. Such a knowledge, therefore, as it uproots the preexisting and accepted conceptions of the world, presupposes simultaneously rooting itself within a historically specific subject, whose very emergence will represent the negation of the established knowledge. If the latter understands itself as the product of thought and contemplation, and since the new knowledge, which attempts to oppose and overcome it, understands itself as the continual product of an active interaction with social reality—then this new knowledge is necessarily compelled to address a subject existing within the social reality. The critical posture of the Gramscian and the Machiavellian notions of knowledge requires that it address itself to a subject whose activity and consciousness are themselves the carriers of this knowledge. And such a critical knowledge must be a public and open discourse—it must be addressed in "the sunshine and not in the shade"—since its generation and development require the concurrent generation and development of a subject that, as the carrier of this public knowledge, embodies a conception of political action directed toward the overthrow of a political and cultural system whose *sommo bene* is located within the "shade" of the private.

The constructions—the "io a voi"/"voi a me" of the *Discourses*, and the "io ... da voi ... come voi da me" of *The Art of War*—establish what to Gramsci is a hegemonic relationship between Machiavelli-Fabrizio and the young men they address. Machiavelli, therefore, is a democratic philosopher or organic intellectual. The relation between the democratic philosopher and the subject is mutual and reciprocal, where the educator and those who are being educated stand in an active and dynamic posture toward each other, such that each educates the other, and each is the source and spring of the other's consciousness and knowledge. As was explained in chapter 3, the democratic philosopher is a type that issues from the practical and life activity of his sociopolitical environment, where the relationship between Machiavelli and the subject is, in Gramsci's words, equivalent to "the relation between teacher and student ... |an| active relation of reciprocal interaction, |so that| every teacher is a student and every student a teacher."[19] But such a relation cannot be limited to a "specifically 'scholastic' " field of activity. The relation between teacher and student is envisioned by Gramsci as the model through which he understands the

entire complex of social and cultural relationships. The relation is general-
ized throughout society, where he sees it as the motive force of change and
transformation. Thus, to assert that an educational relationship is a social
and political relationship is to assert what is at the same time a hegemonic
relationship: "every relationship of 'hegemony' is necessarily an educational relationship."[20]

This hegemonic and educational relation is seen as active and dynamic because each term of the relation continuously transforms the other,
where the activity of the educator "modifies" the reality of which he or she
is a part, which in turn reacts on the educator-philosopher—a process that
constitutes a "continuous self-criticism."[21] It is a process based on the discourse and "conversation" established by Machiavelli in his major works,
where the object is to arrive together at a common interpretation of reality
("disputare le cose . . . parlando con gli amici"), but also where the process
"constrains" both elements of the dyadic relation ("I to you" and "you to
me") to the formulation and defending of one's position through reason
and free speech.[22]

Machiavelli wants to present his knowledge without the use of force
and authority: but such an argumentation presupposes the simultaneous
existence of a sociopolitical reality that will make the giving of reasons
possible and meaningful. To want to argue without force and without authority is to want to establish a sociopolitical structure wherein force and
authority are excluded—it is to want to destroy or to transform the established complex of sociocultural and sociopolitical reality founded upon
the authority of tradition and past usage. As Gramsci asserts,

> one of the most important demands put forth by modern intellectual groups
> in the political field is that of the so-called "freedom of thought and of the
> expression of thought" ("freedom of the press," and "freedom of
> association"), because only where there exists such a *political condition* will the
> educator-student relation realize itself; only then will the new type of
> philosopher, which may be called the "democratic philosopher," realize itself
> "historically" and concretely.[23]

Thus the nature of the knowledge that Machiavelli intends to introduce (as
well as that of Gramsci) presupposes a form of political reality that both
expresses this knowledge and makes it possible as a concrete and historical reality. In Gramsci's words, "the unity of science and life is an active
unity, in which alone freedom of thought will be realized; it is the teacher-
student relation, one between the philosopher and his cultural environ-

108 ment."[24] A hegemonic relation, such as that established between the democratic philosopher and the subject to which he is related (and from which he emerges), demands a political relation whose characteristic elements provide the ground upon which such a type of educational relationship will fluorish.

The Gramscian equation, educational relation = hegemonic relation = political relation, establishes the necessity for the unity of thought and action, where such a necessity means that a specific form of knowledge presupposes a particular kind of social reality, where this reality represents the concretization in action of the knowledge. It is for this reason that the question of whom the knowledge addresses assumes decisive importance; for it is through the addressing of the subject that the knowledge defines itself and unfolds "*nel temporale.*" The type of knowledge, and the type of subject that is addressed and that knows it, are therefore necessarily of a similar and corresponding character. The knowledge that is the product of an educational relation determined by the "io ... da voi ... come voi da me," where the process requires a free and open form of reasoning and argumentation, is equivalent to the subject that is the product of a political and social relation that is also open and public.

In both Gramsci and Machiavelli "*intendere la verità*"[25] (the knowledge of reality) is a process that assumes a social and collective practice: the "truth" emerges as the product of the reciprocity and mutuality given by the interaction between the democratic philosopher and the subject. This truth, and the knowledge that recognizes it, cannot stand above or outside the interaction. The dyad *parlare/domandare* (speaking and questioning), with which Machiavelli begins *The Art of War*, constitutes a process that negates the accepted conception of the world and the existing form of knowledge. It establishes a practice that negates metaphysical and speculative thought circumscribed within the boundaries of its own solipsism.[26] This process and this dyad are themselves a conception of the world that represents the negation of all existing thought and practice. Such a process, according to Gramsci, is similar to the theory of knowledge put forth by the philosophy of praxis, which "historicizes thought because it sees it as a conception of the world diffused throughout society (and such a diffusion would precisely not have been thinkable without rationality or historicity); it is diffused, moreover, in such a manner that the thought becomes an active norm of purposive action |*norma attiva di condotta*|." The relation between the teacher and student describes a form of knowledge that "teaches that reality does not exist on its own, in and for itself, but rather it exists in a historical relationship with the men who modify it."[27]

Gramsci's *realtà* and Machiavelli's *verità* are themselves aspects or moments of the relation between the democratic philosopher and the people, where this relation is given by the discourse and the conversation that take place between the two. Thus Machiavelli's new knowledge expresses both the understanding of the "effective truth" and the necessity to *"imitar"* (imitate) and *"preparare"* (prepare) the new conception of *virtù* in order to move toward a new reality.[28] Rucellai's desire for knowledge—the *"intendere la verità"*—is translated by Fabrizio into the question of practice, and into the problem of introducing into the present the ancient *virtù* of the Romans. To Fabrizio, to know the *verità* is a function of acting within it, such that the knowing and the acting generate the possibility of creating a new order of things.

It is significant that throughout his writings—but especially in the *Discourses, The Art of War,* and *The Prince*—Machiavelli relates the introduction of the new knowledge to the introduction of a new political order. In all three major works his intention is to educate those whom he addresses in order that they may be prepared to "imitate" the ancient orders and *virtù* of the Roman republic.[29] The subject addressed in all three is the same subject, and the relation between this subject and and the political knowledge is an identical relation. The military discipline that is ostensibly the topic of discussion in *The Art of War,* the *principe nuovo* that Machiavelli addresses in *The Prince,* and the republican *virtù* of the Roman people, which Machiavelli deems necessary to the institution of a free political order, represent Machiavelli's attempt to formulate a new conception of the world in opposition to the existing one, and to introduce it *"nel temporale"* by addressing it to a subject that will, through its practical activity, embody it.

Gramsci's *norma attiva di condotta* (active norm of conduct or purposive action)—which is another way of saying that a conception of the world has become hegemonic—is equivalent to the Machiavellian *virtù,* and to the introduction of a new order of things through the activity of a subject whose consciousness and self-definition (Gramsci's *personalità*) are the knowledge that Machiavelli presents. It is through the subject addressed that the knowledge becomes a *disciplina* and an *educazione,* which, in turn, transform it into practice and action. Education and discipline are two notions constantly stressed by Machiavelli (in both the major and the minor writings).[30] The education and the discipline, which represent the realization of the knowledge within historical reality, presuppose the germination

110 and the "diffusion" of a new conception of the world throughout society, where they become a new practice—in Gramsci's words, a new *"operare"*— that will express a new way of life.[31]

In addition, if the educational relation that obtains between the teacher and the student is the prototype that expresses the emergence and development of a subject that can act and transform society, and if this relationship is universalized throughout society, as Gramsci asserts, then the relationship between the leaders and the led, between the intellectuals and the people, is a hegemonic one: it is hegemonic because it represents the diffusion of a conception of the world that posits a particular form of interaction between rulers and ruled, culture and politics. But if the relation is hegemonic, then it must also be political; that is, the operative and defining characteristic that describes the political relation between the rulers and the people is the interactive construction put forward by Machiavelli in the *Discourses* and in *The Art of War*. The political relation is founded upon the relation "io a voi"/"voi a me" that describes the political knowledge of Machiavelli. Thus the new knowledge and the new politics are coterminous; one implies the other. To reason without force and authority, and to arrive at the truth together by the giving of reasons, demand a vision of politics that transcends the existing sociopolitical structure.[32] The "questioning" and the "replying" *sanza rispetto* (freely and openly) can only occur within a sociopolitical topos that is itself founded upon the very same relation. To address a knowledge that demands a radical posture toward the given, where the process of addressing demands a subject that is critical and questioning, is to introduce a political order in which such an activity will become the *norma attiva di condotta*.

The relation "io a voi"/"voi a me" is simultaneously a moral and intellectual, as well as a political and social, relation: the identity of the two relations establishes the subject of the knowledge as an active and conscious agent engaged in the world. To institute a new political order presupposes a subject conscious of the necessity and of the potentiality inherent within the established order. Thus the unity of the new knowledge and of the new political order is incarnated in the new subject, which focuses within itself the new political praxis. This new subject represents the transformation of the established feudal, traditional sociocultural and sociopolitical order into a new political reality founded upon the *"ordinata virtù"* and the new conception of the world.[33] This new reality is what Machiavelli calls the *vivere politico* and the *vivere civile*, where the latter are characterized precisely by the reciprocal interaction established by Machiavelli between the political knowledge and the subject that knows it. Indeed, the *vivere politico* would be incomprehensible if it were not based on such a relation: it is the reciprocal movement from the *voi* that questions to the *io* that replies, a movement that conditions and modifies in turn each element of the relation, that defines the nature and character of the *vivere politico e civile*.

What Gramsci understands in his notion of the democratic philosopher and in his concept of hegemony is anticipated, and finds its theoretical and historical source, in the Machiavellian *vivere*. Political life represents the overcoming of the thought and practice of the feudal past, the creation of a new conception of the world that puts human beings at the center of the world and the world as their conscious creation. The new knowledge and the new subject together express, in Gramsci's words, "an original conception of the world, which could even be called a 'philosophy of praxis' or 'neo-humanism' |"neo-humanism" because, we should remember, Machiavelli's thought opposes that of contemporary humanists as well as that of feudalism and Christianity| since it does not recognize any transcendent or immanent (in the metaphysical sense) elements, but bases itself entirely on the concrete action of man, who, through his recognition of historical necessity, operates on and transforms reality." Such a conception of the world presents a "critique of the present" in order to create a new "permanent consensus"—that is, a new sociopolitical order.[34] Thus Gramsci makes a direct connection between the new Machiavellian knowledge and Marxism; both express a conception of the world that seeks to initiate a moral and intellectual reform of sociopolitical reality. The philosophy of praxis and the new knowledge of Machiavelli attempt to identify a subject that is present in the world, where this subject is the carrier of this knowledge, which is, in turn, the consciousness and the expression of the subject acting in the world.

Gramsci understands the Machiavellian enterprise as the identification and development of a "progressive force in history" that will "break the |existing| unity based on the traditional ideology"—a destruction necessary to the emergence and self-becoming of the "new force."[35] The "critique of the present" that defines the new knowledge is at the same time the coming-to-be of the new subject; and the coming-to-be of the subject is a process delineated by the active interaction between the subject that bears this knowledge and the world of which the knowledge is a critique. The Gramscian philosophy of praxis and the Machiavellian "neo-humanism" (or "absolute laicism") together represent the emergence and the un-

112   folding of a developmental process whose motive force is the hegemonic activity given by the "I to you"/"you to me" relationship.[36] This relation, as it develops through the interactive movement of its elements, constitutes both the new knowledge and the new subject. The two terms of the relation are not static entities; neither are they immutable givens whose nature is fixed a priori and whose movement is determined by a deus ex machina (or by the Crocean *deus absconditus*).[37] The knowledge is the product of a particular posture toward the world; it is the outcome of a being in movement—indeed, this being in movement is itself what constitutes the knowledge, such that the consciousness of the subject is the consciousness of this active and dynamic becoming.[38]

What this means is that the Machiavellian intention and enterprise cannot be carried out and put into practice by Machiavelli himself. According to Gramsci:

> |Machiavelli| interprets the |existing| reality and indicates the possible line of action. The fact that he was a "private person" defines the boundaries |of his practical activity|. . . . Machiavelli never says that he himself can change reality; he intends simply and concretely to show how the historical forces should have acted if they were to have succeeded.[39]

What Machiavelli initiates is the relation between the new knowledge and the new subject: the relation between the educator and the student, transformed into a relation between knowledge and action, initiates the process by which the subject becomes the agent that will lead the "*impresa*" (enterprise) to its "destination"—that is, the process by which the subject will finally and totally realize the new knowledge in the social reality.[40] In the *Discourses* Machiavelli says that he "has chosen to embark on a road" whose final journey will be completed by "another": his teaching is a guide that will point the "way for someone who, with greater *virtù*, and with more reason and better judgment, will be able to satisfy my intention |to introduce new orders and systems|."[41] A similar intention is found in *The Art of War*, where it is stated by Rucellai that Fabrizio "has opened the road" toward a discourse that the latter had desired, a voyage that will be undertaken by those he is addressing. Thus Fabrizio and Machiavelli are the guides who point the way, but they cannot force the project to its final end. The very relation that Machiavelli establishes between himself (as the "democratic philosopher") and the subject of his new knowledge—the "io a voi"/"voi a me" as well as the "io . . . da voi . . . come voi da me"—indicates that the voyage and the "exploration of unknown seas and continents" are a common, collective enterprise, whose eventual outcome depends on the action of the new subject.[42]

The enterprise and the new knowledge are not introduced by Machiavelli and Fabrizio from a position superior and external to the subject; they do not emerge ab initio and full-blown from Machiavelli's head. Machiavelli describes the group around Rucellai as "friends" who all love one another—"*giovani tutti amati*"—and who ardently love the study of ancient Roman *virtù*.[43] The "*studi ardentissimi*" of the young men is directly related to the "sarò animoso in dire manifestamente" of Machiavelli. What Machiavelli is teaching, and the subject the teaching addresses, are not completely given at the beginning of the argument and the conversation. The conversation does not present a knowledge already constituted, a body of knowledge that exists prior to, and outside, the process of addressing its subject. Fabrizio and Machiavelli do not mechanically transfer this knowledge to the young men. The conversation between Machiavelli-Fabrizio and the young men demonstrates that what is being presented is not a closed system of thought established before the conversation is initiated.

It is true that both in *The Prince* and in the *Discourses* it is stated that the question is the introduction of new rules and methods that look toward the "effective truth of things" rather than to those that are imagined. But there is no assertion that posits the eventual destination of the new way being opened. Machiavelli points to the discovery of new seas and continents, but he does not claim that he knows the geographical and topographical contours, let alone the various forms of life to be found there. It is the nature of the new knowledge that the educator cannot posit the end of the "*impresa*." What is posited is the relation that establishes the interaction between the democratic philosopher and the subject, a relation that opens a process of "questioning" followed by the "replying," each alternating with the other—together in their reciprocal action forming a conscious, purposive subject, and a knowledge that expresses, and is expressed by, this subject. Machiavelli does not impart an elaborated, "positive" body of knowledge because his knowledge and his project are in the process of formation and re-formation—in the same manner that the conversation is in the process of becoming as it is carried forward by the questioning and the answering. Fabrizio and Machiavelli are themselves taught through this conversation. What they know at the beginning of the *ragionamento* is transformed, just as what Rucellai and his friends know is transformed, through the unfolding of the process. And the unfolding of the process is, at the same time, the development of the subject addressed by the knowledge of Machiavelli.

Machiavelli, who, as he says in his letters and in the *Discourses*, is condemned by the "malignity of *fortuna*" to live within the private sphere as a "private person," addresses himself and his knowledge to a subject that is also located within the private.[44] The knowledge and the subject will together engender a movement that will lead to the "resurgence" of Roman *virtù*, and to the reordering of the present state of affairs.[45] Such a transformation thus begins within the sphere of the private: the conversation is located within this sphere, where it initiates a movement that will propel the subject into a new level of being, a level defined by the new knowledge itself. To Rucellai's question—"what are these things you would introduce in imitation of the ancients?"—Fabrizio provides an answer that summarizes Machiavelli's enterprise: "to honor and reward *virtù*; not to scorn poverty; to value good order and discipline in their armies; to oblige citizens to love one another, to decline faction, and to prefer the good of the public to any private interest."[46] The knowledge of Machiavelli teaches the subject to value the "public things" over the private, yet both he and those whom he addresses reside "*nel privato*." It teaches the citizens to love one another, yet the project is initiated precisely because the accepted usage of the times is to prefer one's *particulare* to the *bene comune* of the citizens. It asserts the primacy of action directed toward the "*cose publiche*," yet precisely because faction is not "declined" this "public thing" does not exist. The reality of the times—the *essere*—is such that what exists is the private sphere, and what is valued is the interest of narrow factions and particular groups.

The conversation, therefore, must begin within the private sphere. And the subject addressed, and that carries the dialogue forward, can only be a subject whose existence is defined by the narrow boundaries of this private world. In this sense, Machiavelli is similar to Guicciardini: both recognize the necessity of the private; both understand the power and force of particular and private interests.[47] Unlike Guicciardini, however, who remains mired within the irrefutable "objectivity" of the private and the *particulare*, Machiavelli recognizes within this necessity generated by private interests the potential for its movement toward a higher form of social existence. He recognizes within this world of factions and competing self-interests a subject whose unfolding will lead to the establishment of a *vivere politico* and a *vivere civile*—that is, a subject whose activity will realize the knowledge that teaches the supremacy of the public realm over the private, a subject whose active engagement with the world will negate the *bene particulare* and transform it into the *bene comune*.

This negation of the *particulare* located within the private is the negation of the realm of *fortuna*. It should be recalled that *fortuna* represents the subjection and domination of human beings to forces over which they appear to have little control. It is the subjection of human beings to the "iron" objectivity of external events. Thus the realm of *fortuna* may be seen to correspond to the realm of the private: in both, human beings confront the world as isolated individuals, whose power and *virtù* are not adequate to repulse or overcome the violence and unpredictable forces that surround them. To remain, therefore, within the sphere of the private is to remain subject to forces one does not understand, to forces that appear alien to human ends and values. On the other hand, to move from the private into the public is to move from a condition of domination and subordination to a sphere where external events are, and are recognized to be, the product of *virtù*. Such a movement can only occur when a subject is identified within the private realm that possesses the knowledge and the *virtù* that will engender a movement toward the public and the political. This subject must embody a consciousness that sees this movement as the product of its own activity—of a *virtù* generated within itself, such that the movement is nothing other than the self-formation of the subject.

In effect, the transformation of the particular good into the common good, and the establishment of an order where the public sphere prevails over the private, represent the self-transformation of a subject previously defined by the particularistic forces of the private realm into an entity that sees its self-realization within the realm of the public, and whose nature and end are given by the *vivere politico*. The movement from the private to the public, from the particular to the universal, is a movement that can only occur with the simultaneous transformation of the subject from an entity subject to the forces and necessity of private interests into one that posits itself as the autonomous actor whose interests and activity embody the new political order. To address the subject that is located *nel privato* of the existing reality is to initiate a moral and intellectual reform that will redefine the nature of the subject and restructure the social space. The emergence of a subject, whose practice and consciousness represent the forms of discourse and speech developed by the new knowledge, is equivalent to the emergence of a public realm that makes such speech and discourse socially and politically possible. Thus the development of such a subject signals the dissolution of the previously existing private realm and the concomitant expansion of the public realm.

Chapter 7

The Constitution of the People as a Political Force
Hegemony, *Virtù Ordinata*, and the Citizen Democracy

The distinction that Machiavelli establishes between the *vivere privato* (private life) and the *vivere politico* (political life) is one that defines the Machiavellian problematic. This distinction is reproduced in various forms throughout his writings. It is possible, moreover, to formulate a series of opposing dyadic polarities where the first and second term of one polarity correspond to the first and second term of the succeeding polarities. Thus we have:

vivere privato ⟷	*vivere politico*
forze private ⟷	*forze publiche*
particulare ⟷	*bene comune*
cose private ⟷	*cose publiche*
vivere con sètte ⟷	*vivere civile*
tirannide ⟷	*vivere libero*
fortuna ⟷	*ordinata virtù*[1]

These dyads summarize fundamental questions posed by political theory since its emergence in classical antiquity. These questions address the nature of the political in the construction of a "space" within which man can act as a moral, cultural, and intellectual being. Machiavelli's "return" to the classical texts—especially his reading and "conversation" with the Romans—represents a profound awareness that in contemporary Italy such a state no longer exists. Thus his enterprise—the search for a subject that will embody and concretize his political knowledge—represents an attempt to recover the notion of the political as that public "ground" wherein human beings as collective actors engage the world and whose very en-

116

gagement is the self-definition and self-formation of humanity. Such an awareness, however, also represents the recognition that this ground is alien to the practice and thought of both a feudal system of power and the one that prevailed within the Italian city-states in Machiavelli's time.

Machiavelli criticized both the fundamental bases of feudal society and the political and social structures of contemporary Renaissance society.[2] The criterion he employs in launching his attack is the classical notion of the political. To Machiavelli the "political" has been redefined and transmogrified in such a way that what was considered prepolitical or antipolitical by the Greeks and the Romans is brought into the foreground and elevated as the *uso comune* or as the accepted *norma di condotta*.[3] Politics is no longer seen as the activity that looks toward those goals common to all human beings; it no longer represents the attempt to establish a sociopolitical structure within which they compete for glory and mutual recognition, and through which they pursue public, universal goals. On the contrary, in the modern world, Machiavelli asserts, the political and the public have been exploded, and the prevailing forms of activity are those that he regards as properly belonging to the private sphere.[4] To the Greeks and Romans, the latter existed for the sake of the public sphere, whereas in the contemporary world what passes for the public sphere is used as an instrument to attain merely private ends. Thus Machiavelli laments the corruption of Italian rulers and princes, and addresses himself to those who, though located within the private, deserve to rule because they recognize the distinctions that define the opposition between the corruption of contemporary *virtù* (especially within those groups who in fact rule) and the *vivere politico* made possible by Roman *virtù*.[5]

Machiavelli's emphasis on the "return" to the institutions of classical Rome—especially his attempt to introduce into Florence the institutions and tactics of Roman military practice—is fundamentally an attempt to recapture the notion of the political defined by the *bene comune* and by the public space within which such a good could be attained. The conversation with Livy and the Romans, therefore, represents a search for the conditions within the present reality whereby a new form of rule, and a new relation between "ruling and being ruled," could be established. Such a form of rule, presented in opposition to feudal and contemporary Italian forms, is based upon the relation between the democratic philosopher and the people, a relation that is in turn founded upon the reciprocal interaction between the subject who questions and the knowledge that is addressed to the subject.

118   In classical thought, to be political is to be a free actor within the public space known as the "polis"—an association composed of free citizens who are equal in their mutual recognition and in their citizenship.[6] The internal strife and class conflict in Athens recorded by Thucydides, and in Rome by Livy and Tacitus, as well as the political and theoretical debates between Plato and Aristotle, revolve around this central question: what are the criteria for citizenship, and who is eligible for citizenship within this political association? To be excluded from this public association is to be condemned to the private or prepolitical sphere. Thus the political is the public space or topos that delineates the "realm of freedom," whereas the household and the economy describe that private sphere that constitutes the "realm of necessity" (or what is to Machiavelli the domain of *fortuna*).[7] In the politics and thought of the classical age (Greece and Rome), it is the latter that makes possible the former: it is the necessity of the slave that establishes and insures the freedom of the citizen-master. Put another way, the private sphere is subject to the necessary laws of nature, whereas the public space of the Greek polis or the Roman *civitas* enables the citizen-masters to escape this realm of necessity and consequently to act as free subjects within this artificially created political arena. The masters recognize themselves as citizens—the city-state, in fact, is precisely this association of citizens. On the other hand, no such recognition is possible to those relegated to the private sphere—slaves, wage laborers, women, metics, and the like (in fact, to all those who are subject to the necessity of labor in order to exist). Political beings act (and this "act" is pregnant with loaded energy: competing, striving, struggling) within a public topos, which is the polis or the *civitas*, an association of citizens who mutually recognize each other, which constitutes the realm of freedom—all of which rests upon the nonpolitical or prepolitical private sphere, the realm of necessity.

The political thus becomes the space where speech, language, and discourse are located, and outside this space violence and brute necessity predominate. To the Greeks and Romans (at least in theory) the ruling activity within this space is discourse and rhetoric (or oratory), which in turn presuppose an association of free citizens. Where mutual discourse and recognition are not the bases of a relation between two actors, this relation is one of subjection and domination: the master does not engage in a discourse with the slave, for the slave cannot respond in the same language, but can only submit. In this context, tyranny (or, to use terms more faithful to Greek and Roman political usage, *despoteia* and *dominium*) is that condi-

tion where the *civitas*—the political space where discourse is possible—
has been possessed or appropriated by a particular individual, group, or
class to the exclusion of all others. The despot or master narrows the political space simply and only to himself. The relation, therefore, between
the despot and the others cannot be political, because the relation is no
longer based on discourse and persuasion: mutual recognition and discourse no longer exist. In this sense, all forms of despotism and domination are prepolitical or apolitical (indeed, to Aristotle and to Plato they are
antipolitical).[8] The public space—the realm of freedom—has been reduced to the particular activity of the despot or the dominant group, while
the private sphere—the realm of necessity—extends to and encompasses
everyone but the tyrant or the ruling group. In these terms, therefore, despotism and domination represent the use of the public space for private
ends, which means that the realm of the public has been destroyed.

To Machiavelli, the institutions that defined the public space of republican Rome were the Senate, the magistrates, and the people organized into the popular assemblies.[9] The Senate and its magistrates were
the operative political actors within a public arena that was founded upon
the assemblies of the people. Within this space politics represented the
competitive pursuit of power and glory at the service of the *res publica*—the
common or public business. Discourse and speech—oratory, debate, court
and jury duty, elections—were the primary vehicles through which the
struggle for power was conducted. The public space, in other words, was in
the hands of an oligarchy whose members competed against each other for
magistracies, public recognition, and service to the republic (which provided the justification for the ambition).[10]

Under the republic the powers of the magistrates were strictly limited
and delineated. These powers rested upon a fundamental distinction (one
that was also basic to the Greek polis) that was established between those
powers proper to and exercised within the boundaries of the *civitas* (the *imperium domi*) and those proper to and wielded without and beyond these
boundaries (the *imperium militiae*).[11] The *imperium* of the magistrates was limited within the city by the right of appeal and by the tribunicial veto. In
addition, power within the city was further circumscribed by the limitations
imposed by the systemic and institutional competition resulting from the
plurality of offices and from the principle of collegiality. Outside the con-
fines of the city, however, the *imperium* of the magistrate was unlimited, absolute, and without appeal: the power of a general on campaign. Such a
distinction should be related to the earlier discussion of the political as a

120   public space where mutual recognition and discourse take place, and from which force and violence are excluded.[12]

Machiavelli's discussion of the class wars and civil strife that led to the fall of the republic and the introduction of imperial and despotic rule shows that his notion of the *vivere politico* is based upon this very distinction between the speech and discourse that define power within a political space, and the absolute domination that defines the military power of a general. He notes that a "well-governed kingdom never gives absolute power to its prince in anything but the command of its armies, because sudden resolutions are often necessary in this one sphere [that is, a sphere that is outside the political space and thus most subject to the unpredictable forces of *fortuna*], so that there must be a supreme command [*unica podestà*]. In other matters, a prince should do nothing without his council."[13] But the fall of the republic occurred because the power struggle between the plebeians and the patricians led to the destruction of the space that made this distinction possible. The destruction of the republic represented the introduction into a space originally made politically meaningful by speech and discourse of the military and absolute power of the contending generals. As Machiavelli puts it, "Caesar and Pompey, and almost all the Roman generals who lived after the Second Punic War, acquired their reputation as skillful men, not as good citizens. . . . [for they] made war their sole occupation" by recruiting and arming troops loyal to the personal and private interests of the military leaders.[14]

The destruction of the political space of the republic was signaled, according to Machiavelli, by the "disarming of the citizens" by Augustus and Tiberius and the introduction into Rome of a Praetorian Guard that "served not only to guard the emperor's person but to bridle the people."[15] Thus the decline of the republic was marked by a lengthy process characterized by civil wars, which saw the rise of private citizens who controlled and led personal armies of retainers. The emergence of imperial rule represented the constriction of the public and political space, and this space now became the *res privata* of the emperor. What emerges from Machiavelli's analysis of the class conflict and power struggles of ancient Rome is a theoretical and political construction that enables him to identify the defining elements of the *vivere politico* and the *vivere populare*.[16] The political is defined by what it is not: despotism or tyranny reduces all political space to itself, so that the relation between Caesar and the citizens is no longer one of mutual discourse (as it would be if he were an ordinary magistrate) but has now become equivalent to that between the *pater* or *dominus* and his *familia*; that is to say, the public space has been transformed into that of the private, and the *civitas* has become a *dominium*. The space described by the *dominium* is a private space where the absolute power of the master reigns, a space defined precisely by the use of force and violence over the subjects. Tacitus, writing in the late first century A.D. (over a century after the fall of the republic), provides striking support for the foregoing discussion. Contrasting the oratory—that is, public speech and discourse—of imperial times with that of the republic, he remarks that in the latter there was a "more vigorous eloquence" where the magistrates "even against their own wish had to show themselves before the people. It was little good for them to give a brief vote in the senate without supporting their opinion with ability and eloquence. . . . it was thought a disgrace to seem mute and speechless." On the other hand, under imperial rule "the orator gets an inferior and less splendid renown. . . . What need of long speeches in the senate . . . or of endless harangues to the people, when political questions are decided not by an ignorant multitude, but by one man of pre-eminent wisdom?"[17] To be mute and speechless is to be condemned to the private sphere, the realm of brute nature and *fortuna*, to the household where the slave cannot answer back.

Machiavelli's critique of feudal society and his attack on the sociopolitical, cultural, and military institutions of Renaissance Italy are not unrelated to the discussion of the political. The critique of feudal society represents the attempt to destroy a particular form of rule and of power—a form that to Machiavelli is antithetical to the mutual discourse and free speech necessary to his concept of the political. To Machiavelli, feudal relations of power are equivalent to the master-slave relation that existed within the private sphere of the *familia* in ancient Rome. Since these relations exist only within the private realm, and since they establish a system of power that is essentially founded upon the *dominatio* of the *dominus*, it is impossible to establish a public space characterized by the *vivere politico e libero* without the destruction of these private relations of power, which rest upon the personal subordination of the people to the lords.

The relations of subordination/domination (the *dominatio* that exists in the realm of the private) may be seen in that section of the *Discourses* that discusses the necessary structural and systemic bases of republican government, where Machiavelli asserts that it is least difficult to establish a republic "in that city where the masses are not corrupt" and where equality is a universal condition. He adds that "those republics which have preserved their political existence uncorrupted do not permit any of their citizens to be or to live in the manner of gentlemen, but rather maintain amongst them a perfect equality, and are the most decided enemies of the lords and gentlemen that exist in the country." The "*gentiluomini*" (nobility) and the "*signori*" (lords)

> live idly upon the proceeds of their extensive possessions, without devoting themselves to agriculture or to any other useful pursuit to gain a living. Such men are pernicious to any country or republic; but more pernicious even than these are such as have, besides their other possessions, *castles which they command, and subjects who obey them.* . . . no republic has ever been able to exist in those countries |ruled by such a class of men, as in the Romagna, Naples, Tuscany, and the Papal states|; nor have they been able to preserve any regular political existence |*vivere politico*|, for that class of men are everywhere enemies of all civil government |*civiltà*|.[18]

Thus civil and political life is possible only where the *signori di castella* (lords who possess castles) and the *gentiluomini* do not hold power, or where they have been exterminated.

In order to reform those countries where the lords are entrenched and possess a preponderance of power, Machiavelli deems it necessary to establish a strong monarchical form of government, for there the "body of the people is so thoroughly corrupt |*la materia è tanta corrotta*| that the laws are powerless for restraint."[19] The corruption and servility of both lords and people are such that reform and renovation are possible only through the "*mano regia*" (kingly authority) and the "absolute power" of a prince. It is interesting to note—as Gramsci himself points out[20]—that Machiavelli presents a method that was put into practice by the emerging dynastic monarchs outside of Italy (in France, Spain, and Russia): the creation of a new class whose power and position depended upon the favors of the dynast, and the simultaneous destruction of the traditional lords (such as the boyars in Russia), whose power was independent of the central authority. In any case, to Machiavelli the elimination of the independent lords is essential whether one intends to construct a republic or a civil monarchy; the former requires a condition of equality, which is antithetical to the feudal relations of power, and the latter presupposes a centralized structure of rule, which is opposed to the independent centers of power of the landed nobility. In both instances, the elimination of their power is the primary prerequisite, for the lords are the embodiment of that *ozio* (indolence) and vice against which Machiavelli contrasts his conception of *virtù*.[21]

What is especially odious to Machiavelli is the class of lords ensconced in their castles and in control of their territory—that is, the very nature of lordly rule Machiavelli finds antithetical to his conception of ruling.[22] The relation that obtains between the lord and his subjects is not based on equality and mutual recognition. Such a relation, which defines and fixes the positions of the dominant group and the subordinate "*sudditi*" (subjects), is located outside the realm of mutual discourse and open speech; that is, the relation is not political in the classical sense, but is rather private, prepolitical, and therefore despotic and oppressive. Because the relation is based on *dominatio* and therefore outside the political space (as understood by Machiavelli and the ancients) the interaction between the dominant and subordinate groups revolves around only two possible modes of action: mute passivity, or violent and active resistance. But such action is impossible without the prior establishment within the subordinate group of an autonomous structure of speech/discourse that will empower it to answer back and respond to the actions of the oppressor. Indeed, without the structure of discourse violent resistance is quite literally speechless, and therefore politically meaningless. Speech and discourse are therefore the necessary bases that make violence, force, and fraud possible (in the context of revolution and rapid change).

From the perspective of the subaltern group the demand for mutual recognition must be accompanied by force and violence (or the threat of their use) because the dominant group is defined by a sociocultural and political consciousness different from that of the class it rules: the two groups speak a different language and possess quite different discourse structures. Nor would the dominant group recognize the moral and intellectual validity of the demands and problems posed by the subaltern group if the former understand the language of the latter. Since there is no common political space—that is, since the realm of discourse does not exist as a universal reality—the only possible basis of interaction between the two is force and fraud. To put it another way, there is no political structure that permits the Machiavellian form of ruling, which is based on the ability to "reason without the use of authority and force." Indeed, the very nature of the relationship between the lord and his subject is based on the military force of the lords and on the authority of past usages and customs. The lords assert a "natural" and traditional supremacy over those not of the same class, status, or group. Such a relationship, therefore, precludes any form of dialogue or "conversation" between the two groups—a dia-

124   logue that, to Machiavelli, must be based on *"né sangue né autorità"* ("neither blood nor authority") if it is to be mutual and reciprocal.[23]

It is in the context of the foregoing discussion that the Machiavellian attempt to establish a "new prince" and a "civil principality" is to be understood. The new prince embodies the new knowledge of the Machiavellian Centaur—force and consent, organized violence and a structure of discourse, the *dittatura* and *egemonia* of Gramsci—that will establish a new political order superior to that founded upon feudal relations of power.[24] It is significant that Cesare Borgia, whose methods were greatly admired by Machiavelli, and who some interpreters have seen as the model for the new prince, attempted to create a centralized, rational state within the Romagna, a territory which, according to Machiavelli, was under the domination and rule of the *signori di castella*.[25] Force and violence are required to break the private and personal relations of *dominatio* in order to establish a civil principality whose rule is based on the *vivere civile* of the people. This "method of beasts" is necessary because the new political space is not yet in existence. However, once the new space is established, force and violence, given the premises of Machiavelli's notion of the political, must be excluded from the new order. Machiavelli makes this point very clearly when he says that "kingdoms which depend entirely upon the virtue of one man endure but for a brief time. . . . |and thus| the welfare of a republic or kingdom . . . consists in having |a prince| who will give it such laws |that is, a structure where discourse is possible| that it will maintain itself even after his death."[26] Therefore, to establish a structure of rule where the relation between the rulers and the ruled is no longer based on force, "blood," or authority, it is first necessary to employ force and violence against the preexisting power structure. But once the new structure has been established, the *vivere civile* requires that force and *dominatio* be directed outside and beyond the boundaries of the republic or the civil principality.[27]

Rule defined by force and domination represents the negation of the hegemonic and political rule established by Machiavelli in the relation between the subject who questions and the democratic philosopher who answers and replies. Here rule is private and personal rather than public and universal. Such a system possesses no common political space that defines the relations of ruling and being ruled, and the end to which it is addressed is a particular good rather than a common good. To establish a *vivere politico*, the relations of *dominatio* that prevail within the privatized space described by the master-subject relation must be destroyed, such that the domination/subordination structures—which are personal, nonrational, and enveloped within the legitimizing sanctions of tradition and past usage—are exploded and replaced with differing and superior structures. The overcoming of these relations of domination and the introduction of new relations represent the construction of a new conception of the world that posits a new and radical notion of what it means to rule and to be ruled.[28]

To Machiavelli, therefore, feudal relations of power are equivalent to the relations of *dominatio* that the *pater familias* exercises within the private sphere of his household. The relation between the lord and his subject assumes the same form as that established by Aristotle between the master and slave: the former possess a moral and intellectual personality that is denied to the latter.[29] And since the subordinate subject is stripped of any autonomous cultural and ethical identity, the rule of the master and the lord is fundamentally based on force and authority. It is a rule that describes a structure of power that in Gramsci is expressed by the two notions of *dittatura* and *dominio*: pure domination and pure force. Domination is the form of rule necessary to a system where all social relations are privatized, where there exists no *bene comune* that provides the common ground for the development of rule based on speech and discourse. Such rule, in effect, is identified by an ossified and crystallized relation where those in authority speak, and therefore command, yet those over whom authority is exercised can neither respond nor question, and must therefore simply obey.[30]

In the same way that the conversation between the "I to you" and the "you to me" delineates the Machiavellian concept of the political as a discourse founded upon mutual recognition, the relation that Machiavelli discusses between the lord and his subject establishes a paradigmatic model for a form of rule that is prepolitical and antipolitical. Such a model establishes the fundamental distinction between rule as an activity that occurs within a political structure that makes discourse and the *vivere civile* possible, and rule as an activity characterized by the speechless subordination of the slave to the master. This distinction provides the common strand that links Machiavelli's analysis of the relation between the social and political institutions of the ancient Greeks and Romans and his attempt to introduce a new political knowledge that is reflected within the life and activity of a new political subject.

Machiavelli's conversation with the ancients, and his conversation with his contemporaries, together form the "free and open" process of rea-

126 soning through which the subject that is being addressed comes to be formed and to know itself. The interaction between the subject and Machiavelli, which takes place within a space where force and authority are excluded, is founded upon a relation of mutual recognition and equal speech or discourse. This conversation, which is both the cause and the product of mutual recognition and equality, becomes in Machiavelli the critical and distinguishing relation that delineates his conception of the *vivere politico* and the *vivere libero*, in the same way that the relation between the democratic philosopher and the people is the fundamental basis for the Gramscian notion of the political envisioned as a hegemonic (and thus educational) relationship between the rulers and the ruled.[31] In Machiavelli, as in Gramsci, the political relation—the very concept of ruling and being ruled—is founded upon a moral and intellectual system of discourse that presupposes a mutuality and reciprocity between the "student" and the "teacher" such that the two terms of the relation become interchangeable. As the dynamic movement of the interaction represented by the "I ... through you ... as you through me" construction unfolds, the teacher as teacher becomes superfluous, and the student as conscious and autonomous subject emerges. The classical, especially Aristotelian, parallels are obvious,[32] but what is not as obvious is the Machiavellian retranslation of the ancients in order to establish a political order based upon the widest possible foundation—that is, the people.[33]

The political relation in classical thought is envisioned as a relation based on reason and discourse: as Isocrates puts it, *"logos hegemon panton"* ("speech and language are the ruler and guide of all things"), and both Plato and Aristotle elaborate and expand upon this principle.[34] Aristotle, in particular, identifies the *logos* as both the foundation and the product of the political association.[35] But whether the subject that is the carrier of the *logos* is located within an aristocratic elite, as in Plato, or is identified within a political association formed by a demos narrowly defined and extremely restricted in numbers, as in Aristotle, the ancient thinkers never considered the "people" as a universality possessed of the ability to reason "without force or authority." Indeed, the people considered as a universality, and the people envisioned as a subject capable of moral and intellectual autonomy, did not exist in classical times or in the medieval era.[36] The Roman *populus*, though more universal than the Athenian demos, was nevertheless a people subject to the moral and political authority of the Roman aristocracy.[37]

It is Machiavelli, as both Gramsci and Wolin have pointed out, who recognized the *populo* as a significant and revolutionary force that could transform the sociopolitical contours of the existing reality.[38] Such a recognition was made possible by Machiavelli's conversation with the ancients, a conversation influenced and colored by the new political project he intended to introduce. For although the people as a moral and conscious body had been narrowly defined, and although the Roman aristocracy had reduced the people to an undisciplined mob, the very concept of the people as the basis of rule (either in the Roman *comitiae* or in the Athenian *ekklesia*) was nevertheless present in various guises within classical thought and practice. Machiavelli takes the classical *logos* and identifies it as the product of the interaction between the subject and the teacher; but this subject is a revised version of the Roman *populus*, for Machiavelli does not accept Livy's and the generally aristocratic opinion that views the nature of the people as corrupt, ignorant, and impossible to educate.[39]

Machiavelli, both as a man of action and as a theoretician, goes to great lengths to refute the notion of the people as an "emotional," violent, and unpredictable *volgo* and he does not see the people as a fixed, immutable entity, as a *materia* whose nature and form are predetermined by inevitable laws (as Croce and his school would have it).[40] To Machiavelli, the people is not a mere passive *vulgus* defined by its objective and empirical reality; he sees the people as a force that can move from the preexisting reality and create a new reality, a people become the subject of its activity within this reality. This is Machiavelli's intention, and it is the basis for the discourse on Livy: an attempt to recapture, and in the process redefine, the concept of the people and transform it into the subject of his knowledge and the subject of political rule. The Aristotelian notion of ruling and being ruled in turn, which is based on mutual discourse and reciprocity, is taken by Machiavelli and universalized throughout the *moltitudine*, which undergoes a process of becoming through "discipline" and "education" that eventually changes it into a collective force. Machiavelli's admiration for the "religion of the Romans" (in opposition to "our religion"), and his stress on "good education," point to his attempt to introduce into the mass of the people a new conception of the world whose realization depends upon the emergence of the *moltitudine* as a social and political force. Indeed, in the same manner that Gramsci employs Machiavelli to construct an anti-Croce and launch a critique of the liberal-bourgeois antipathy to the popular masses, Machiavelli's conversation with the ancient writers may be seen as an "anti-Livy" employed as a means to reconstitute the mass as a

128 new political actor: the process of civil strife and civil wars that led to the destruction of the *publica libertà* with the fall of the Roman republic and the emergence of despotic rule (in the exact classical sense) under the emperors is simultaneously the process through which the Roman *populus* as an organized people degenerated into an inert mass.

Thus in the *Discourses* Machiavelli takes issue with the opinion of Livy and "other historians" that the people are unstable and unreliable:

> The difference |in the conduct between the princes and the people| is not due to any difference in their nature (for that is the same, and if there be any difference for good, it is on the side of the people); but to the greater or less respect they have for the laws under which they respectively live. ... The excesses of the people are directed against those whom they suspect of interfering with the public good; whilst those of princes are against apprehended interference with their individual interests.[41]

The nature of the people is not inferior to that of princes; indeed, the people, when educated and disciplined, is superior to them, for the former look to the *bene comune*, while the latter look to the *il bene proprio* (the private and particular interest). It should be remembered that it is in this same chapter (Book I, chapter 58) that Machiavelli presents his intention to reason without the use of force and authority, a statement that acquires not just theoretical but also practical-political significance when it is linked to an observation regarding the people: "words suffice to correct |the defects| of the people, whilst those of the prince can only be corrected by violence." A "good man"—that is, an educator, or the Gramscian democratic philosopher—may talk to a "licentious" and "tumultuous" people: the people may be transformed by means of speech and discourse into a disciplined and collective entity. On the other hand, to reform a prince who does not "possess the friendship of the people"—that is, whose rule is based on relations of domination—violence and force are necessary.[42] The phrase "defects of a prince" points to the transformation of a civil principality based on the mutual discourse between prince and people into a despotism founded upon the relation between master and slave, lord and subject.

The reformation of a prince is nothing other than the introduction of a form of rule that is directed toward the *bene comune*, which is the good that defines the character of the people. Thus to reform the established rulers means to establish a new form of rule based on mutual discourse and on speech. Machiavelli makes a specific and direct connection between the *moltitudine sciolta* and the prince who looks to the private and particular interest: in both cases the *vivere politico*, as Machiavelli understands it, is lacking.[43] In the first instance, the masses viewed as an "undisciplined multitude" means that the people as a collective and purposive subject does not exist; the mass is a mere aggregation or collection of individuals who look to their own private or particular interest in opposition to that of others. In the second case, the prince whose rule is defined by the *bene particulare* is not a prince who knows how to rule, for ruling to Machiavelli means the mobilization and organization of a collectivity directed toward a common end. Such a concept of ruling necessarily implies that the transformation of the masses into a collective subject is at the same time the transformation of the ruler into one who functions within a public space defined by the *bene comune*; similarly, the transformation of a ruler into a "new prince" who rules according to the new Machiavellian knowledge is simultaneously the transformation of the *moltitudine sciolta* into a *populo*.

It is significant that the "new principality" outlined in *The Prince* (chapter 9), the republic discussed in the *Discourses*, and the military institutions (the *vita militare*) presented in *The Art of War* each represent to Machiavelli a *vivere politico* and a *vivere civile*. These works address the problem of the movement from the *bene particulare* to the *bene comune*, from the private to the public, from the individual to the universal.[44] In all three, Machiavelli "openly and freely" addresses what is the fundamental and common element that organizes the various arguments and directs them toward his goal: the resurgence of ancient *virtù*. This common element—which is also found in the minor political works—is the nature and role of the masses, or rather, the problem regarding the process whereby the *moltitudine* or the *universale* becomes the *populo*. Whether Machiavelli formally addresses himself to a prince by means of the stylistic device of the "mirror of princes," or addresses the problem of military tactics and valor, or inquires into the elements that generally constitute the nature of politics and of ruling, the underlying theme is that there can be no *vivere politico* without first establishing a structure that looks to the *bene comune*, and there can be no such structure without the emergence and development of the masses into a people that "esteems more the public than the private."[45] As Gramsci points out, there is no contradiction between *The Prince* and the *Discourses*: the former is a "treatise on dictatorship (the moment of authority and of the individual)," and the latter is a work on "hegemony (the moment of the universal and of liberty. . . . although even in *The Prince* there are signs and allusions to the moment of hegemony or of consent juxtaposed to those of

130   authority or of force. . . . thus |there is no| contradiction in principle between principality and republic."[46]

What connects the two is precisely the Machiavellian conception of rule and of the political, which is defined by its relation to the people. In both works there can be no rule in the Machiavellian sense without the emergence of the people as a political and historical subject. In both, the problem regarding the construction of the *vivere politico* is posed in terms of the generation of a subject that is not only conscious of the *bene comune*, but is also politically and militarily organized to realize it in practice. The moment of hegemony is the proliferation and universalization of the interactive and reciprocal relation between Machiavelli the democratic philosopher and the subject that carries the consciousness of the new knowledge that is itself constituted by this relation. The *vivere politico* and the *vivere libero* are given by this relation: they are the end toward which the hegemonic process moves. Thus the *vivere politico* presupposes the educational and hegemonic relation, while the latter can only realize itself through the introduction and construction of the former within the existing reality. The moment of force—or the political, understood in the narrow and Crocean sense of "pure politics" or pure technique—is a contingent moment defined by its instrumental character: if the end is the construction of a *vivere libero* (the moment of the universal), then the moment of force is a technical problem whose solution is contingent upon the relation between the end and the means. The moment of force and of the individual, as Gramsci recognizes, is translated by Machiavelli into the moment of liberty and of the universal through the creation of a people as a "hegemonic force." What this means is that the private and particular interests of the *moltitudine*— which is always acting within the sphere of the private since there is no universalizing principle to make it into a collective subject—must be transcended and transformed, so that the discrete individuals of which the mass is composed acquire an autonomous and moral personality as a subject. But this universalizing principle can be nothing other than the hegemonic relationship established between the subject addressed by Machiavelli "*nel privato*" and the new knowledge that teaches the primacy of the public over the private, and the *bene comune* over the *bene particulare*.

The movement from the private to the public and from the particular interest to the common interest is realized within the moment of hegemony. For it is the hegemonic relationship described by the mutual recognition and the mutual discourse outlined earlier that creates a new form of political action and a new type of subject that together constitute the new sociopolitical reality characterized by the *vivere politico* and the *vivere libero*. The moment of hegemony exists within the circle created and defined by the new political subject. It is within this circle that discourse and speech are possible; and it is outside this circle that the moment of force becomes necessary and meaningful. In other words, violence and force presuppose a condition where the *vivere politico e civile* are not yet the operative and defining principles of political action, a condition where the hegemonic relation is not yet universalized. As such, the moment of force—or the Crocean "pure politics"—is a moment prevalent within that area where action is not based on mutual discourse and equal speech, and where to reason "without the use of force or authority" is not politically and socially possible. The moment of force becomes transformed into the moment of hegemony only within the new political structure, where speech and discourse are possible. Such a transformation occurs when authority and force are no longer subject to the individual and particular interests of the private sphere, but are rather subordinated to the public and political space created by the new subject.

But it is important to realize that the transcendence of the moment of force is equivalent to the transformation of the *moltitudine* into the *populo*, and to the universalization of the new knowledge by the conscious activity of the subject that expresses it. The moment of force loses its individual and particular character when it becomes the instrument of the new subject organized and mobilized into the collective and public force of the people. The point at which the moment of force achieves such a transformation and transvaluation is precisely the point where in Machiavelli the *moltitudine* coalesces into the *populo armato*—that is, the point where force and the conduct of war have become the public and open activity of the people organized into a citizen army.

If, therefore, there is no contradiction between *The Prince* and the *Discourses*—between the moment of force and that of hegemony—it is because the vehicle for the resolution is provided by the mediation of the people envisioned as the collective, armed subject. Thus *The Art of War* provides the link between the first two works. The former, indeed, may be seen as a discourse on the transvaluation of force from an instrument subordinated to the *privato* and to the *bene particulare* into one determined and directed by the *publico* and the *bene comune*. The organization and deployment of force—whether by the "new prince," whose power is based on the collective action of the people, or by the republic, which is the political space coextensive with the *populo*—is viewed by Machiavelli as a problem that re-

132   quires the "resurgence" of the ancient *virtù*, without which the Romans would never have established a stable and successful "armed republic."[47] To Machiavelli, the moment of force is always the moment of organized violence—that is, the deployment and organization of the popular masses. But such an organization presupposes the prior existence of the people as a political force. In turn, the people organized into a political subject implies the creation of a *vivere politico* as the space where discourse and speech without the use of force or authority can take place.

In *The Art of War*, Machiavelli makes it clear that the moment of force—military organization and military tactics—is a means to the erection of a political and civil space, an end that conditions and determines the nature and character of the military art.[48] Without such an end, the military art becomes merely a particular form of action defined by narrow and limited interests. The transformation of the particularity of the military art into an activity that serves the public and common good is the object of the argumentation and the conversation between Fabrizio the general and the young men of the Rucellai Gardens. As Gramsci notes:

> Even in *The Art of War* Machiavelli should be seen as a political actor |*politico*| who must concern himself with military theory and practice. . . . the center of his interest and of his thought is not found in the question of military technique; rather, he considers the latter only to the extent that it is necessary to his political construction.[49]

To Gramsci, as to Machiavelli, it is the construction of a political edifice that defines the nature of the military problem. The problem that Machiavelli poses is the translation of military *virtù* into political *virtù*. To state it somewhat differently, it is to reform a military institution whose activity in the Italy of Machiavelli's day was directed toward the particular interest of the mercenary captains. The military *virtù* of these *"compagnie di ventura"* (mercenary armies) Machiavelli saw as a prime factor contributing to the instability, weakness, and corruption of the Italian states. The existing military arrangements, rather than making the Italians master of their own country, subjected them to the violent power of *fortuna*.[50]

Those interpreters of Machiavelli who engage in pointless debates regarding the "nature" or essential quality of Machiavelli's *virtù*—whether it is an aristocratic and purely military notion, whether its meaning is exhausted by the bellicose nature of man (courage, impetuosity, audacity, force)—fail to consider the movement and direction of the Machiavellian project.[51] Neal Wood, for example, asserts that Machiavelli redefines the concept in such a way that *virtù* becomes "a pattern of behavior distinctively exhibited under what might be described as battlefield conditions."[52] Felix Gilbert, in his classic *Machiavelli and Guicciardini*, understands the Machiavellian critique of the contemporary age as an attempt to establish the importance of "brute power" in politics.[53] In a similar vein, Quentin Skinner argues that *virtù* is redefined in such a way that Machiavelli must in part give "an exceptionally strong emphasis on the military prowess of the prince."[54] In addition, Federico Chabod asserts that the only novelty in *The Prince* is the demand that the prince possess his own militia—a demand that is repeated in both the *Discourses* and *The Art of War*.[55] To Chabod, the Machiavellian political and theoretical project sets up as the sole criterion for the interpretation of history and politics a military principle regarding the organization of the militia.[56] This critique is based on Chabod's discovery of a "profound" contradiction between Machiavelli's call for the reform of the militia and the lack of recognition that such a demand would entail radical changes in the "political and moral system" of contemporary Italy.[57] These students of Machiavelli, in effect, are echoing in different ways the fundamental interpretation of Machiavellian politics originally advanced by Croce: politics as pure force and politics as an instrumentality.

Yet the reduction of the Machiavellian renovation to brute force or to mere military *virtù* is possible only if one overlooks the role of the particular good and the private in Machiavelli's discussion of the theory and practice of war. To Machiavelli the "art" (*l'arte*) of war has a precise meaning: the art of war should be understood in the sense that most Renaissance thinkers understood the particular actions and operations that defined a given craft.[58] Thus the *arte* in *The Art of War* refers to a craft, in the same sense that Machiavelli would refer to a craft when discussing the *arte della lana* (the craft of woolmaking). But the woolmaking craft is more than the skill required to perform the particular activity. The concept of craft also refers to a concrete and historically specific social group: the activity of woolmaking is a social activity embodied in the organization of the guild.[59] Renaissance society, especially in Florence, was organized into various guilds whose struggle and competition for power formed the political experience of most Italian communes. The struggle for power among the various particular interests of the guilds is recounted by Machiavelli in his *Florentine Histories*, where he sees the collapse of republican liberty and the rise of the despotism of the Medici as the results of the inability to tran-

134 scend the narrow and private interests of the guilds in the interests of the common good of the republic.[60]

If, therefore, the art of war is understood in the sense not merely of military skill but also as a social institution, then it will be seen that the reform of the military is not a question of mere technique, and that the *virtù* necessary for such a reform is more than pure "brute power." The *virtù* of the military craft, as that of woolmaking or silkmaking, recognizes the *bene particulare* of its own corporate and social activity. To assert that military *virtù* is the foundation of Machiavelli's new knowledge is to assert that Machiavelli reduces the *vivere politico* and the *vivere civile* to the absolute power (the *"unica podestà"* or the *imperium militiae*) that a general must possess during the conduct of military operations against an enemy. The reduction of the political to an aspect of military *virtù* would mean the transformation of the public space that makes speech and discourse possible into a space where relations of force and *dominatio* prevail. It would make the private and individual good of a particular social group or guild into the universal *bene comune* that defines political life. As Machiavelli says in the *proemio* to The Art *of War*, there is an intimate relation between politics and war, between political institutions and military organization.[61] But precisely because of this intimate relation, it becomes necessary to construct military institutions that will not vitiate the *vivere politico* through which these institutions acquire purpose and meaning.

It should be noted that the demand to "value military discipline" is linked by Fabrizio with the demand to "value more the public than the private," which in turn is linked to the demand that citizens reject factionalism.[62] Thus to reject factionalism—which is to reject the particular good for the common good—is to value the "public things" over the private. The military discipline that should be valued is one conducive to the establishment of the supremacy of the public over the private. Military institutions and the practice of war in Machiavelli are stripped of their private and particular character—which prevailed throughout the feudal era (in the form of armies composed of the private retainers of lords and aristocrats) and throughout the Renaissance (in the form of mercenary troops led by the *condottieri*). To destroy the particular character of the established military system is at the same time to establish a social and political body that expresses and represents the common and universal interests of society. To demand that the military should be subordinated to the political presupposes that the political exists as a structure that can direct the military art to universal ends; that is, in order to subordinate the military to a public good and purpose, the public (both as a value and as sociopolitical order) must also exist. The reform of the military is defined by the attempt to move from the private to the public; in concrete terms, it is to remove the military—both as a practical art and as a social organization—from the realm of the private, and transfer it to the public sphere, so that it comes under the control and direction of the political will of the society:

> War should not be followed as a business by anyone but a prince or governor of a republic; and if he is a wise ruler, he will not allow any of his subjects or citizens to make that his particular profession; indeed, no good man has ever practiced or made war into his private or particular profession.[63]

The social and political history of Florence during the twelfth and thirteenth centuries was characterized by the struggle of the communal bourgeoisie to destroy the power of the landed aristocracy (the "*magnati*"). To the extent that these magnates were eliminated as a force within the city-state, a *res publica*—that is, a public realm that defined the *bene comune*—was brought into being as a tangible reality. Such a transformation, as Machiavelli points out, was accompanied by a concurrent change in the military institutions of the new communal republic.[64] The elimination of the private rule of the landed lords also meant the elimination of the military system that had prevailed under a feudal system of power. Thus the victory of the people in their struggle against the domination of the aristocratic lords meant the subordination of the military organization to the newly established public sphere. The military organization, however, is but the political association of free citizens that establishes itself as the *populo armato*. Machiavelli's *Florentine Histories* describes the process by which the communal republic degenerated into the Medici despotism through the disintegration of the people into factional and civil strife, a process that was simultaneously paralleled in the destruction of the citizen army and the introduction of mercenary troops. The *Histories* echoes and summarizes the political and theoretical arguments Machiavelli presents in his political writings: the struggle for power between the *grandi* and the *populo*, the problem of factions and its relation to the creation or degeneration of the public space, the relation between the *populo armato* and a free political order.[65] Machiavelli addresses these themes by presenting Florentine history as the cumulative corruption of the political *virtù* of the commune; the culmination of this long degeneration is reached during the last decades of the fifteenth century, when Florence as an independent state lost its freedom

136 of movement and became subject, together with the other Renaissance city-states, either to external powers or to the Papacy.[66]

The "ravaged" and "despoiled" state of Italy is not a simple outcome of the lack of military technique and practice. Machiavelli links the military weakness of the Italian states to a conception of the world—and to a notion of *virtù*—that locates the *summum bonum* within the private and the particular. It is not that Italians lack the skill and technique to wage war successfully; it is that war in Italy is a profession undertaken by private individuals in the pursuit of the *bene particulare*.[67] The socioeconomic competition for self-interest that defined the power struggles of the Renaissance city-states is similar to the military and diplomatic competition pursued by the various leaders of the mercenary bands: both take place within an environment where no *bene comune* exists, and where, as a consequence, military action and social struggles merely result in the further reproduction of factionalism and the anarchy of civil war. The existence of private armies, whether in the form of feudal retainers or of *compagnie di ventura*, represents the material embodiment of the forces of *fortuna*: it means the predominance of the private over the public, and therefore signals the destruction of the political space that makes a *vivere civile* possible.

The relation between the new art of war and the new political order is expressed by Machiavelli in those passages where he criticizes the erection of fortresses.[68] Machiavelli compares the methods and practices of "my Romans" (who, as long as they were free |*"mentre che Roma visse libera"*|, never had recourse to fortresses) to those of contemporary times (where reliance on fortresses is the established custom). Fortresses are both useless and dangerous because they embody the divorce between the rulers and the ruled, and this divorce is expressed by the relation of domination between the ruler and the people. As Machiavelli puts it: "whenever either princes or republics are afraid lest their subjects should revolt, it results mainly from the hatred of the subjects on account of the bad treatment experienced from those who govern them; and this comes from either the belief that they can best be controlled by force, or from the lack of sound judgement in governing them." Thus a fortress expresses a form of rule based on force and coercion. But "all the measures of force and violence |employed| to hold a people amount to nothing . . . either you must keep a good army always ready to take the field, as the Romans did; or you must scatter, disorganize, and destroy the people so completely |*dissipi, spenga, disordini e disgiunga*| that they can in no way injure you." It is not fortresses but the "will of men" that is the basis for stable and well-ordered rule:

"non le fortezze, ma la volontà degli uomini mantenevono i principi in stato."[69] This argument is echoed in *The Prince*, where it is asserted that a new prince will always arm his people, but only a prince "who fears his own people more than foreigners ought to build fortresses. ... Therefore the best fortress is to be found in the love of the people, for although you have fortresses they will not save you if you are hated by the people."[70]

These passages establish a direct connection between the *dominatio* of the lord-subject relation, which exists in the sphere of the private, and the privatization of the public that occurred with the breakdown of the Roman republic and the advent of tyrannical rule. Princes and rulers who rely on fortresses, and who hire mercenary troops, are equivalent to the *signori di castella* who wage war through the use of private and personal retainers; both forms of military organization and military conduct presuppose and express a type of rule that is the negation of the political rule Machiavelli's new knowledge teaches. In both instances, the public space of speech and discourse is transformed into the private space where the people are rendered "mute and speechless."

Such a privatization signals the destruction of the people—"scatter, disorganize, and destroy"—as a collectivity and their reduction to a disaggregated mass of individuals subject to the domination of the lord or the tyrant. Fortresses and mercenary armies imply a form of ruling that is dependent on the nonexistence of the people as an organized and collective force. Whether the ruler is a feudal lord, a *condottiere* who has seized power (such as the Sforza in Milan), or an *ottimato* who has acquired power through the manipulation of internal factional strife (such as the Medici in Florence), the necessary preconditions are identical: in each case, the people as subject must be destroyed and transformed into a *"materia tanta corrotta."* It is the nonexistence, or the disintegration, of a people and its transformation into a mere series of isolated (*"disgiunga"*) and competing individuals that is the foundation of a nonpolitical and a prepolitical form of rule. The distinction between the people as a moral and collective body, and the people as an amorphous amalgam particularized and reduced to "sudditi," finds its complementary parallel in the distinction between a military institution founded upon the people as an organized and disciplined entity, and a military system dependent upon the private organization of mercenaries and the erection of fortresses whose very essence is to ensure the domination of the despot or the *condottiere*.

On the other hand, a new prince and the new form of rule he embod-

138   ies establish military institutions—a citizen army—that will both reflect and presuppose this new form of rule. Thus, Machiavelli writes,

> A new prince has never been known to disarm his subjects, on the contrary, when he has found them disarmed he has always armed them, for by arming them these arms become your own, those that you suspected become faithful and those that were faithful remain so, and from being merely subjects become your partisans. . . . |therefore| a new prince in a new principality always has his subjects armed.[71]

This quote acquires full significance when it is related to the passage from the *Discourses* cited earlier: "either you must keep a good army always ready to take the field, as the Romans did; or you must" destroy and scatter the people. Machiavelli establishes an antithesis between a "good army" (which is equivalent to his often-repeated "good arms") and a well-constituted and disciplined people (*"populo ordinato"*).[72] It is an organized people that leads to an effective and loyal military institution, and it is a people constituted as an armed and disciplined army that leads to a well-ordered form of rule. The people armed is the foundation for that political space wherein speech and mutual discourse are the prevailing modes of interaction between the rulers and the ruled. The "new principality" embodies such a relation between the military institutions and the political order, a relation that finds its common denominator in the people as a collective subject and an active political entity: the people is the foundation of the new military institution organized as a mass and popular army, and the people is the foundation of the public space that is defined by the *bene publico e comune*, which is, in turn, the moral and intellectual bond through which a "multitude" becomes a people.[73]

It is precisely the mass and popular nature of the new political form of rule that defines the essential character of the "new principality," a novel political order which establishes—or reestablishes—the activity of ruling and being ruled on a basis similar, but not identical, to the political and social structure of the ancient Roman republic. The transformation of the *"sudditi"* into "partisans"—the call to institute a rule based on the "friendship" and "love" of the people—implies the reformulation and redefinition of the established sociopolitical reality, whose continued existence required the production and reproduction of a moral and intellectual conception of the world that posited the *volgo* or the *universale* as a subordinate and static entity. Indeed, in feudal society—in those countries where the *signori di castella* hold sway—the very notion of the people as a "mass" or as a "bulk" is alien to its sociocultural and moral-intellectual structures: the master-subject relation precludes the emergence of the people considered either as an unruly multitude or as a collective and disciplined body. Thus the Machiavellian call for the establishment of a civil principality represents the recognition that the *populo*, whether as an undifferentiated mass or as an *ordinata materia*, has become a force whose political and practical consequences depend upon the nature and character of the mass. The people understood as an unthinking and uneducable mass—"*disgiunta*" and "*dissipata*"—leads to a conception of the world that assumes the necessary and inevitable relations of domination and subordination that form the core of both despotic and lordly rule. On the other hand, the people, envisioned as an entity whose nature is the product of its own activity in the world—a nature that is thus constantly becoming—leads to a conception of politics that posits itself as the product of the very activity of the people.

Chapter 8

Conclusion
Hegemony and Power

Hegemony is defined by Gramsci as intellectual and moral leadership (*direzione*) whose principal constituting elements are consent and persuasion. A social group or class can be said to assume a hegemonic role to the extent that it articulates and proliferates throughout society cultural and ideological belief systems whose teachings are accepted as universally valid by the general population. Ideology, culture, philosophy, and their "organizers"—the intellectuals—are thus intrinsic to the notion of hegemony. Since, to Gramsci, reality is perceived, and knowledge is acquired, through moral, cultural, and ideological "prisms" or "filters" by means of which society acquires form and meaning, hegemony necessarily implies the creation of a particular structure of knowledge and a particular system of values. The social group or class that is capable of forming its own particular knowledge and value systems, and of transforming them into general and universally applicable conceptions of the world, is the group that exercises intellectual and moral leadership.

The intellectuals, therefore, are the organizers and educators of society. They are the intermediaries through which the dominant class and the subordinate classes are "organically" linked. As "experts in legitimation,"[1] they resolve the contradiction that Gramsci believes to exist between *alta cultura* (the culture of the ruling groups) and *cultura popolare* (the culture of the subaltern masses). By so doing they render the existing power structure acceptable to allied and subordinate groups. Society is a stable, functioning organism precisely because the "organization of culture" elaborated by the intellectuals universalizes the values and ideas of the ruling social group. In other words, the function of intellectuals is not

only to create a particular way of life and a particular conception of the 141
world, but also to translate the interests and values of a specific social
group into general, "common" values and interests.

Hegemony is thus conceived as the vehicle whereby the dominant
social groups establish a system of "permanent consent" that legitimates a
prevailing social order by encompassing a complex network of mutually re-
inforcing and interwoven ideas affirmed and articulated by intellectuals.[2]
Diametrically opposed to rule through intellectual and moral leadership is
rule through *dominio* (pure domination or coercion). Gramsci asserts:

> The supremacy of a social group is manifested in two ways: as "domination"
> and as "intellectual and moral leadership." A social group is dominant over
> those antagonistic groups it wants to "liquidate" or to subdue even with
> armed force, and it is leading with respect to those groups that are
> associated and allied with it.[3]

Thus a sociopolitical order—what Gramsci calls the "integral State"[4]—is
characterized by a hegemonic equilibrium based on a "combination of
force and consent, which are balanced in varying proportions, without force
prevailing too greatly over consent."[5]

It should be noted that Gramsci uses the terms "alliance" and "association" when he refers to a system of reciprocal links and relations
whose common elements are consent and persuasion. Leadership is exercised over allies and associates, that is, precisely over those groups who
consent to be led. In other words, the "alliance" is based on a mutuality of
interests and an affinity of values. This is seen most clearly when Gramsci
writes:

> Among the many meanings ascribed to democracy, the more concrete and
> realistic is the one which may be related to the concept of hegemony. In the
> hegemonic system, there exists democracy between the leading group and
> the groups which are led, to the extent that the development of the
> economy, and thus the legislation which expresses such development, favor
> the molecular passage from the led to the leading group. In the Roman
> Empire, there was an imperial-territorial democracy in the concession of
> citizenship to the conquered peoples, etc. Democracy could not exist under
> feudalism, because of the constitution of the closed groups, etc.[6]

The concession of citizenship, and what Gramsci calls "imperial-territorial
democracy," refer to the Roman practice of transforming those peoples
whom they had conquered or subdued with "armed force" into "allies" and

142   "friends" of the Roman people. A relation of this kind was normally the first step in a process that could lead ultimately to the granting of citizenship rights. Thus, the Roman *imperium* may be viewed as a system of alliances between and among the Roman *populus* and other nations. Indeed, as both Machiavelli and Gramsci (not to mention the Romans themselves) realized, the Roman people itself is the product of an alliance of various groups— most especially that between the patricians and the plebeians. Such an original alliance progressively expanded to include more groups, such that the *imperium* may be seen as a *societas Romana* constituted by *amici* (friends) and *socii* (allies and associates).[7] In effect, the *societas*, understood as an interrelated network of *socii*, is a hegemonic system. And Gramsci's hegemony may be said to have been prefigured in the ancient Roman notion (and practice) of *societas*.[8] Similarly, it may also be understood as a direct parallel to Gramsci's concept of civil society, a sphere or space within which voluntary associations (such as churches, political parties, trade unions, schools, etc.) based on consent and persuasion predominate.

   Such a reading of Gramsci's hegemony finds a textual antecedent in Machiavelli's *Discourses* (Book 2, chapters 3, 4), where he discusses the methods by which ancient Rome expanded and grew to greatness, to which he compares those of the Spartans, Athenians, and Etruscans. According to Machiavelli, there are "three methods of aggrandizement." One, practiced by the Etruscans, the Achaeans, and the Aetolians, is by means of a confederation or a league of several republics. The second, followed by the Romans, is to "make associates of other states," reserving to themselves the rights of sovereignty. And the third, employed by the Athenians and the Spartans, is "to make the conquered peoples immediately subjects, and not associates." Machiavelli continues:

> Of these three methods the latter is perfectly useless, as was proved by
> |Sparta and Athens|, who perished from no other cause than from having
> made conquests they could not maintain. For to undertake the government of
> conquered cities by violence, especially when they have been accustomed to
> the enjoyment of liberty, is a most difficult and troublesome task; and unless
> you are powerfully armed, you will never secure their obedience nor be able
> to govern them. And to be able to be thus powerful it becomes necessary to
> have associates |*compagni*| by whose aid you can increase the population of
> your own city. . . . Rome . . . followed the second plan, and did both things,
> and consequently rose to such exceeding power. . . . Having created for
> herself many associates throughout Italy, she granted to them in many
> respects an almost entire equality |*i quali in di molte cose con equali legge vivevano*

seco|, always, however, reserving to herself the seat of empire and the right of command. (*Discourses*, Book 2, chapter 4)

To "increase the population of your own city" is to "have associates," which, in turn, is to transform the other peoples into friends and allies— and, in some cases, into citizens—of the Roman *civitas*. Here Gramsci's "imperial-territorial democracy" and the "concession of citizenship" are comparable to Machiavelli's notion of "making associates of other states" and granting to them an "almost entire equality"—that is, the constitution of a system of alliances and associations grounded upon a reciprocity of interest.

On the other hand, Machiavelli makes it quite clear that "violence" or simple coercive power is not sufficient to attain and maintain empire. It becomes necessary to develop methods by which one is able to transform one's enemies into allies. Of course, the very capacity to use overwhelming armed force presupposes a system of alliances and associated states whose stability and continuity rest on something more than mere domination.

What is immediately striking in Gramsci's notions of leadership and domination is their almost exact similarity to Machiavelli's famous characterization of the centaur in chapter 18 of *The Prince*:

> You must know, then, that there are two methods of fighting, the one by law,
> the other by force: the first method is that of men, the second of beasts; but
> as the first method is often insufficient, one must have recourse to the
> second. It is therefore necessary for a prince to know well how to use both
> the beast and the man. This was covertly taught to rulers by ancient writers,
> who relate how Achilles and many others of those ancient princes were given
> to Chiron the centaur to be brought up and educated under his discipline.
> The parable of this semi-animal, semi-human teacher is meant to indicate
> that a prince must know how to use both natures, and that the one without
> the other is not durable.[9]

The dual nature of Machiavelli's centaur represents the two aspects or "moments" of politics: force and consent, *dominio* and *direzione*. This double nature of power leads Gramsci to redefine and to broaden the typically Marxist and Leninist theory of the state. He does not envision it as a simple coercive instrument employed by the ruling class to maintain its domination over the proletariat. In Gramsci, the state is conceived as "dictatorship + hegemony," and as "political society + civil society," where the first term represents the element of force and the second that of con-

144 sent.[10] The state is thus something more than domination or coercion. A social group or class whose power is based solely on the coercive apparatus of the state cannot achieve a lasting rule over society. It is only when the social group constructs a sociopolitical order capable of instilling its particular cultural and moral beliefs in the consciousness of the people that it can be assured of a permanent and stable hegemony. The social group must exercise intellectual and moral leadership to impress upon the people a particular moral consciousness, a particular culture, and a particular conception of the world. As a result, the state acquires an ethical content that transforms its repressive, class nature into one perceived as moral and universal. Thus the Gramscian state cannot rest on pure force; violence and coercion must always be mediated by the legitimating moments of consent and persuasion.

Machiavelli himself underlines the importance of consent and morality in his discussion of the religion of the ancient Romans in the *Discourses* (Book I, chapter 11):

> Numa, finding a very savage people, and wishing to reduce them to civil obedience by the arts of peace, had recourse to religion as the most necessary and assured support of any civil society |*civiltà*|; . . . for where religion exists it is easy to introduce armies and discipline, but where there are armies and no religion it is difficult to introduce the latter. . . . for this religion gave rise to good laws, and good laws bring good fortune.

Here Machiavelli contrasts Numa Pompilius, who represents the element of consent, to Romulus, who represents the element of force. Thus the founding of a great state such as Rome, based on firm foundations and sound principles, requires the knowledge of the proper use of force and consent: what is their relation to each other, and what is their proper and necessary proportion? For if it is true that the state has its origins in force and violence, it is equally true that violence qua violence is highly unstable, unpredictable, and costly. The universalization of force and violence into the general principles of the state defeats their original purpose. They must be related to "religion" or consent (Gramsci's ideological and cultural "hegemonic apparatus"), which makes them both meaningful and possible.[11]

On the other hand, Machiavelli places equal emphasis on the necessary exercise of force and violence (*dominio* and *dittatura* are their Gramscian equivalents). He writes in the *Discourses* (Book I, chapter 9):

> I say that many will perhaps consider it an evil example that the founder of a

civil society, as Romulus was, should first have killed his brother, and then consented to the death of Titus Tatius, . . . |but| a wise mind will never censure any one for having employed any extraordinary means for the purpose of establishing a kingdom or constituting a republic.

The point is driven home in *The Prince* (chapter 6):

When they |innovators and founders of states| can depend on their own strength and are able to use force they rarely fail. Thus it comes about that all armed prophets have conquered and unarmed ones failed.

The very term "armed prophets" expresses and summarizes the interwoven and mutually reciprocal—Gramsci would say dialectical—moments of force and consent, *dominio* and *direzione*.

Since Gramsci's dyads—political society and civil society, dictatorship and hegemony, *dominio* and *direzione*, violence and persuasion, force and consent—represent the double nature of power and the state, the articulation and inculcation of culture and ideology are essential for a revolutionary politics and a revolutionary consciousness. In other words, Machiavelli's Centaur is an educator and teacher, and as such represents the overriding importance of developing a class consciousness and a revolutionary ideology opposed to those of the dominant class: to Gramsci, an educational relationship is a political relationship.

In Gramsci, Machiavelli is not seen as a scholar or "scientist" isolated and immersed within the abstract categories of his own thought.[12] He is, rather, the prototype of the Gramscian intellectual, one who is in close and direct relation to the people.[13] Machiavelli is not a compiler of treatises circumscribed by the traditional categories of the Middle Ages and the Renaissance. Nor is his thought simply the possession of an intellectual aristocracy, a monopoly of thinkers working in "Olympian" isolation, but is rather a knowledge issuing from the life and activity of the people—a political knowledge that emerged from the class conflicts and power struggles of the Florentine people.[14] Gramsci interprets Machiavelli as the intellectual whose knowledge presupposes the very subject he attempts to teach. Gramsci sees Machiavelli as the "democratic philosopher"—the very term is laden with cultural, philosophical, and historical layers of meaning that can be traced eventually to Plato and Aristotle (the question of the relation between the statesman and the philosopher in Cicero, the problem of the relation between action and thought in Marx, to take but two examples)[15]—who attempts to teach "those who do not know" ("*chi non*

146 *sa"*)—the people—"the methods and rules" (*The Prince*, chapter 15) by which they could organize a collective will in order to establish a new state.
Gramsci asserts that throughout *The Prince*

> Machiavelli deals with how the Prince should act to lead the people to the founding of a new State ... in his conclusion |the exhortation| Machiavelli himself becomes the people, identifies himself with the people, but not with a people "generically" understood, but with the people Machiavelli has convinced with his preceding arguments, with whom he merges and feels himself to be the conscious expression, and with whom he feels himself united: it seems that all the "logical" work is but the self-reflection of the people, an internal rational discourse, which takes place within the consciousness of the people and concludes with a passionate, direct cry |for action and for *riforma*|.[16]

The "self-reflection of the people" is an "internal rational discourse," which is in turn a process that occurs "within the consciousness of the people." The founding of a new state is an activity that necessitates the coming-to-be of a people as a moral and cultural force, possessed of a consciousness defined by rational discourse. It is precisely the Gramscian concept of the democratic philosopher that describes Machiavelli as the teacher who addresses the people in order to initiate a process of mutual discourse within the consciousness of the masses.

In addition, the democratic philosopher, in order to initiate this process of moral and intellectual reform, must be a person of action—*un politico* as opposed to *un diplomatico*—who uses the style of a political "manifesto" to educate politically "those who do not know"; and that group, which is not yet conscious, is the revolutionary class of his time, the people of a fragmented Italian nation. As Machiavelli makes clear, political knowledge "was covertly taught to rulers by ancient writers"; he, however, writes a work openly addressed to the people and to the prince, for, as he says in the dedication to *The Prince*,

> in the same way that landscape painters station themselves in the valleys in order to draw mountains or high ground, and ascend an eminence in order to get a good view of the plains, so it is necessary to be a prince to know thoroughly the nature of the people, and one of the populace to know the nature of princes.

Thus, it is precisely this reciprocal relation between prince and people that defines the Machiavellian notion of the *principe nuovo*. The new prince embodies a new form of rule whose characteristic signature is the *populo*, without whose support and active consent the Machiavellian prince is transformed into a mere feudal lord. Prince and people presuppose each other, for both emerge from the political knowledge that Machiavelli is "animoso in dire manifestamente," a knowledge that addresses the very subject—the people—that gives such knowledge meaning and that is defined and formed by it. It is the triadic interaction among these three elements that constitutes the radical revolutionary transformation of the existing sociopolitical order and the prevailing balance of power: political knowledge, people, and new prince. Machiavelli's new knowledge is the mediating instrument that connects people and prince, a mediation, indeed, that transforms both prince and people into mirror images of each other, such that each implies and informs the other. What this means is that the new prince cannot come into being without the simultaneous coming into being of a people that carries within it the consciousness embodied by the new political knowledge; and this people—or rather the emergence of the people as a political force, what Wolin calls the "discovery of the mass"[17]—which is the subject of this new knowledge, necessitates the emergence of a new prince, and of a new form of rule, whose basis is precisely the reciprocal and interactive relation between prince and people.

In effect, the people and the collective will that defines the people as a determinate political entity are both the subject and the object of Machiavelli's *principe nuovo*: they are the object because the new prince finds them in a divided and atomistic condition that must be overcome; and they are the subject because, through the educational and hegemonic activity of the prince, they become the conscious agents that forge a new political and historical movement (*rinnovazione* to Machiavelli, and *riforma intellettuale e morale* to Gramsci) whose goal is the transformation of Italian society into a superior sociopolitical and sociocultural order.[18]

The new prince thus emerges as the hegemonic innovator and reformer, closely and inextricably linked with the people, and, together with the people, uses the new political knowledge to engage the *verità effettuale* and by so doing transform reality—"*creare il reale*," as Gramsci puts it.[19] And Machiavelli's civil principality, viewed as an organic relation between prince and people, becomes the new social and political organism capable of transcending the cultural and ideological divorce between *alta cultura* and *cultura popolare*. In effect, Gramsci's concern with the organization of permanent consent (hegemony) is comparable to Machiavelli's principal preoccupation with the "founding of great States" and the emergence of a sta-

148   ble and durable sociopolitical order based on "fixed principles"[20]—what Machiavelli calls a *vivere libero e politico*.

In Gramsci's thought, the political party becomes the modern equivalent of the Machiavellian prince who attempts to transform existing society into a new and superior one. Thus to Gramsci the party performs the same role as the prince does to Machiavelli: the prince was to have been the vehicle for the founding of a new and unified Italian state; the party is the force that will create the conditions for a superior socialist hegemony. Just as the new prince was to have been the new Centaur and armed prophet that would have created a national-popular, collective will by uniting the fragmented wills of the Italian people, so too the revolutionary party is to forge the collective will of the proletariat by bridging the gap between the *alta cultura* of the intellectuals and the *cultura popolare* of the masses.

The revolutionary party, then, is the "modern Prince,"[21] which, like Machiavelli's Centaur, will instruct "boldly and openly" "*chi non sa*"—the subordinate classes—and instill in them a new conception of the world and a new way of life; and, as a consequence, the party will create the basis for a socialist and proletarian hegemony in opposition to the prevailing culture and ideology of the bourgeois class. The party is thus envisioned as a hegemonic organism that articulates and disseminates a new form of knowledge and a new morality. It organizes the discrete, particular wills of the masses into a national-popular collective will by means of its intellectual and moral leadership (*direzione*). Consequently, it initiates a process of intellectual and moral reform (*riforma*), whose ultimate goal is the total transformation of bourgeois thought and culture.

An interesting comparison can be made between Gramsci's *riforma* and Machiavelli's *rinnovazione*. In the same way that Machiavelli's new prince was to have forged a political and cultural alliance with the people, and thus initiate a *rinnovazione* aiming at a new Italian state, Gramsci's modern prince is to wage an ideological and cultural struggle to attain a moral and intellectual reform of existing society. And as the new prince, to create the new state and the new form of rule, must use his *virtù* to destabilize and delegitimate the ensemble of cultural, customary, and traditional relations upon which the power of the *principe naturale* (the established, hereditary prince) is based, so too the revolutionary party conducts a hegemonic struggle to undermine the legitimating institutions of bourgeois society.

On this point, the relation that Machiavelli establishes between *virtù* and *fortuna* is revealing, and offers insight into the dynamics of revolution.[22]

Virtù can be considered as conscious and purposeful will, and *fortuna* is to Machiavelli the domain of unlegitimated force and violence, a highly unstable condition in which human beings are subject to unpredictable and random forces. The *principe naturale* is normally immune to the contingency of *fortuna* because his rule is based on generally accepted traditional values and patterns of behavior whose legitimacy is sanctified by religion and custom. The problem of *fortuna* arises with the *principe nuovo*: the innovating activity of his *virtù* will destabilize the traditional social structure and delegitimate the customary values. To avoid or to circumscribe the random forces thus unleashed, the innovator prince must develop new legitimating institutions that will reestablish on a higher level a sociopolitical space or topos from which the violent and unpredictable consequences of *fortuna* are excluded. What defines the new character of this topos is given by Machiavelli's project to initiate a moral and intellectual reform—that is, the founding of a politics defined by the self-reflection of the people and by a rational discourse.

In addition, such an admittedly neo-Ciceronian conception of political topos is implicit in, and suggested by, Machiavelli's use of *fortuna*. Machiavellian *fortuna* underlines the related perception that human beings have not found the world already ordered; the order in the world is the product of their own conscious ordering activity. But saying this is already to say that Machiavelli is not simply concerned with "how men live." To create a durable and stable political order—or what Machiavelli calls a *vivere libero e civile*—is, in fact, to be concerned with "how men ought to live." This is precisely Gramsci's point in his criticism of Russo's and Croce's interpretations of Machiavelli: Savonarola does not represent the *dover essere* (what ought to be) and Machiavelli the *essere* (what is); rather, Machiavelli, in investigating the *verità effettuale* of the given situation, attempts to point toward a superior sociopolitical order, which ought to be, not because it is judged by extrahistorical or apolitical morality, but because the *dover essere* is given by the *essere*. Indeed, the *essere* itself is an ensemble of sociopolitical and sociocultural relations that cannot be understood or made intelligible without the *dover essere*. As a consequence, to posit as the foundation of Machiavellian thought and of Machiavelli's political intention a radical and irremediable rupture between *kratos* and *ethos* is seriously to misconstrue the point and direction of Machiavelli's project.[23] Machiavelli, therefore, by positing human beings as a self-creating subject, is concerned with the formation and elaboration of a hegemonic conception of the world in opposition to the prevailing traditional ideology.

150   Gramsci envisions the proletarian revolution in terms of the Machiavellian model of innovation: as a simultaneous process of legitimation and delegitimation, as the articulation of a new conception of the world and the concurrent destruction of the established conception.

The revolutionary party must create legitimating institutions within the proletarian class and at the same time develop a strategy that will destabilize the prevailing structure of power. This is the moment of consent and *direzione*. The moment of force and *dominio* appears only after the consent of the masses has been achieved. Intellectual and moral reform thus implies that the party articulate and proliferate an all-encompassing conception of the world within the existing society before the seizure of power. A social group must first be leading (that is, hegemonic) before it can be dominant. Gramsci reverses the Leninist revolutionary pattern: whereas the Bolshevik party first seized state power and afterwards attempted to form legitimating institutions (the result of which the fate of the soviets is an eloquent testimony), Gramsci insists that a legitimating hegemony must first be established; without such a hegemony, the revolution is transformed into a mere coup d'état, which will simply reproduce the social and political pattern of existing power relations.[24]

In this respect, the political party in Gramsci (and in Marxist and socialist thought in general) addresses a fundamental point—namely, the question of knowledge (its nature and status) and its bearer.[25] In Marx, knowledge or consciousness is a product of the practical activity of a subject actively engaged in the world. Thus, to the question, how does consciousness arise? Marx would answer: through activity, through praxis; that is, consciousness is the result of a being in movement in the world. What this means is that in Marx the bearer of knowledge or consciousness is the working class as it struggles and as it practically engages the world. The party, to Marx, is an organ or institution instrumentally subordinated to the purposes and goals set by the conscious working class. In Kautsky and Lenin, however, knowledge and consciousness are no longer seen as the inherent concomitants of an active class. On the contrary, the subordinate classes are now inherently unable to acquire consciousness through their own activity, but can only acquire it as an alien importation from bourgeois intellectuals, who, in a manner reminiscent of Croce and Guicciardini, possess the knowledge, the science, and the culture necessary for political and organized activity. What is crucial here is that Lenin and Kautsky severed the Hegelian and Marxian connection between knowledge, activity, and becoming. Knowledge is now an object "possessed" by a group outside the life experience of a particular class, and, conversely, the way of life and the way of acting of this class are no longer necessary to this knowledge. Here the revolutionary party is no longer an instrument subordinated to the directive purposes of a determinate and conscious class. Here the party is the bearer of a knowledge that the subordinate classes can never reach or attain through their own life activity. In effect, the Marxian relation between class and party is reversed. It is now the party that is the conscious subject actively engaged in the world, and the subordinate classes are the instruments subordinated to the direction and purposes elaborated by the bearer of knowledge, the party. In this dialectic, the party acts, and thereby learns how to rule. But if the subordinate groups cannot attain consciousness through their own actions, and if the party is the subject that in its consciousness of the world acts in it and transforms it, the former will always remain passive objects, always unable to acquire the knowledge and culture necessary to rule.

It is possible to see Gramsci's project as an attempt to resolve the antithesis between the Marxian and the Kautsky-Lenin conceptions of the party. This attempt is carried forward by (1) an interpretation of Machiavelli's new prince as a hegemonic innovator, and (2) understanding Machiavelli himself as the democratic philosopher (or the organic intellectual) who wants to teach the people a new political knowledge; this knowledge, however, must now be understood as one always internal to the people, because the democratic philosopher (the teacher) is himself a product of the people he intends to educate. Thus Gramsci, in his analysis of the last chapter of *The Prince*, notes that Machiavelli's analysis is an "internal rational discourse" between Machiavelli and the people to whom the new knowledge is addressed. The innovative and novel character of this Machiavellian knowledge is precisely that it is "open" to the people. The key here is Gramsci's notion that "every teacher is also a student, and every student is also a teacher." Here knowledge is not an established body of data and ideas possessed by a culturally superior entity; rather, knowledge is itself the product of the "conversation" (the "rational discourse") between teacher and student, and "truth" is now understood as the "intersubjective" product of the interaction and common activity of the democratic philosopher and the people. It is in this context that a discussion of Gramsci's party as the modern prince ought to be conducted. What this context establishes is the boundaries that fix the general contours of what a revolutionary party ought to look like. These boundaries enable us to say what the Gramscian party is not, in the sense that any party whose charac-

152 teristics fall outside these limits is not hegemonic and "leading." For, however one might perceive the party as an organization, and whatever its practical and everyday ideology and programs, such a context can only mean that the party does not possess a knowledge to whose "truths" its followers and members must submit.

To Gramsci, the figure of Machiavelli, and the interpretation of his political theory, assumed political and theoretical significance because they presented questions and problems that underlined and focused within themselves what Gramsci, as a Marxist and a Hegelian, understood to be the major issue that a theory of political action must address. This is the problem of the political and historical subject: who, or what entity, is the agent that, through its practice and active engagement in the world ("*nel temporale*," as Machiavelli would put it), resolves the contradiction between thought and action, ethics and politics, "culture" and people?

Such an antinomy, as Marx pointed out, was expressed in thought by the elaboration of philosophical and metaphysical systems characterized by an inherent dualism that posited a total disjunction between the word (or the idea) and the deed; and it was embodied within history and society by the development of sociopolitical and sociocultural formations founded upon the antagonism between the ruling groups or classes who possess knowledge and the instruments of culture, and the subordinate groups whose "knowledge" and culture are both reflections and causes of their subordination. In a fundamental sense, the liberal thought and culture expressed by Crocean philosophy reproduce in modern and pseudo-Hegelian terms the Platonic and Augustinian dualism between thinking and acting that has permeated Western political thought since the fall of classical society and the advent of Christian (and later, medieval) society.

The Platonic opposition between the Idea (which is "truth" or reality) and the world (which is opinion and appearance) is taken by Christianity and retranslated into the religious and theological duality that Augustine posits between the *civitas dei* and the *civitas terrena*. In both instances the idea—the *logos* that expresses and embodies the truth and essence of reality—is a preexisting entity, given by either a philosophical or a spiritual form of activity that is divorced from the world of material and practical life. In both cases, moreover, the notion of the political, understood as a generative and creative activity that transforms reality, is eliminated, and is replaced with a conception of politics that locates the political within the world of appearance and error. The Christian Platonism of Augustine strips the political of all moral, intellectual, and cultural (and thus educational)

elements and reduces it to a negative instrument whose utility is made
necessary by the unredeemable and unchangeable nature of the earthly
city. The nature of man in the earthly city is corrupt; his will and his reason
are ruled by passions and appetites that result in war, struggle, misery, and
domination. The political, therefore, is both a product of the appetitive nature of man and a remedy that will insure peace and security in a world
governed by the competition of opposing interests and unlimited desires.
To Augustine, the essential constitutive element of the political is pure
force and coercion; the "state" is reduced to an instrument of domination
and repression.

The opposition between the *civitas dei* and the *civitas terrena* destroys
the classical, and basically Aristotelian, problematic that envisions the polis and the nature of the political as the concrete embodiment of the *logos*
within a social space that is itself created by the social and rational activity
of man. The Augustinian and Christian conception of the relation between
thought and action destroys the ethical and educational dimension of the
political, so that the "ought to be" is relegated to a sphere of being totally
separated from the material world of the "is." What this does is sever the
connection between action and rational purpose—the relation between
the positing of ends and their realization in society—and the *dover essere* is
no longer seen as emerging from within the structure of the *essere*, but
rather as a given whose realization and attainment are independent of human activity in the world.

The Machiavellian project, both theoretically and politically, attempts to discover—or rediscover—the elements and means by which the
disjunction between the "ought" and the "is," and the severing of human
ends from human activity, may be uncovered and overcome. Machiavelli's
thought stands in radical opposition to that of his predecessors and his
contemporaries: it is conscious of itself as the knowledge that attempts to
negate the prevailing conception of the world. Such a conception does not
merely see human beings as passive creatures subject to forces over which
they have no control. More important, human activity and practice are
themselves seen not as "remedies," but as the very source of the sociopolitical and sociocultural problems that confront human beings. In such a
conception, political action does not lead to overcoming the given reality
and creating a superior one; the political, embedded within this given, and
severed as it is from reason and from the ethical, can only reproduce and
reflect the given reality.

154   The Crocean interpretation of Machiavelli as the thinker who first discovered the "autonomy of politics," and who first developed a theory of the political that posited a complete and thoroughgoing antinomy between ethics and politics, presupposes a philosophical system that understands itself as the product of "pure" thought and "pure" reason. To Gramsci, liberal thought, and the philosophy of Croce in particular, have reproduced in metaphysical and speculative language the dualistic opposition between thought and action first posited by the Platonist and Christian conceptions of the world. In the philosophy of Croce, the Augustinian distinction between the *civitas dei* (the realm where "true" justice and universal right are located) and the *civitas terrena* (the realm where natural necessity and brute force reign) is transformed and translated into the secular and elitist opposition between the "aristocracy of the intellect" (the *alta cultura* of the intellectuals and the ruling groups) and the popular culture of the masses (the *volgo*).

What this means is that to posit a theory that asserts the primacy of "pure" thought—such that the preservation of its integrity and "dignity" requires the separation of "thinking" from "feeling," of philosophy from practice—is to posit simultaneously the political and social proposition that asserts the primacy of intellectuals over the rest of society, so that society is divided into spheres—into two *civitates*: one an aristocracy of those who possess knowledge; the other a subject and incoherent group composed of the majority of the population, whose culture, issuing from the uncontrolled "passions" and "desires" of the *semplici* (the common people), cannot attain to the level of the first. In effect, liberal thought is based on the fundamental divorce between the thought of intellectuals and the popular culture of the people. Such a sociocultural and sociopolitical contradiction expresses itself in a philosophy that can only envision itself as the product of thought itself—that is, thought emerges from the rational and philosophical activity of a stratum of intellectuals who identify and define themselves as a group separate and autonomous from society and from the masses.

Given such a perspective on the relation between philosophy and the people, what does it mean to say that the political is autonomous from the ethical, and that the political world is a realm separate and distinct from the world of thought and culture? If thought, as Croce says, becomes "corrupt" as it addresses itself to an interest or to a subject embedded within the world of action and practice (or to "all other human interests," as he puts it) and thereby is no longer able to think—"il pensiero non pensa"—then the locus of universal reason is to be found not within the life and practice of a sensuously active historical subject, but rather within the eternal categories of thought itself. And if this is so, then moral and ethical action, whose validity and universality can only be attained through philosophy and culture, is relegated to an extrasocial and extrapolitical realm: the problem of freedom (moral action) and the question of right (justice) are transferred to the personal and private realm of the individual. The separation of the ethical from the political leads to the separation of the *dover essere* from the *essere*; the realization of the former is no longer a question (as in the thought of Plato and Aristotle) of the transformation of the latter. Indeed, the *essere* is a given which cannot be changed, and the realization of the *dover essere* is located within thought—that is, within the mind of individuals (who are capable of rational and ethical thinking)—and not within the practical, everyday life of social and collective human beings.

In effect, the philosophy of Croce—and liberal thought in general—remains fixed within a problematic originally formulated by Kant, a frame of reference unable to transcend the contradiction between the world of nature (the realm of necessity) and the world of thought and culture (the realm of freedom). To assume such an antinomy as a given that cannot be overcome—or that can be transcended only within the "conscience" and thought of the individual—is to assume that action in the world (the practical relation of means to ends) will always remain subject to the "iron laws" of necessity. It is, furthermore, to assume that freedom—morally and intellectually autonomous action—is attained not through engagement with the world of nature and necessity in order to overcome and change it, but rather through the erection of an artificial sphere of thought and culture whose very existence presupposes the preservation of the contradiction between culture and nature (or between "thinking" and "feeling"). Thus the culture of the intellectuals—where intellectual and moral autonomy is possible—presupposes the existence of a realm of necessity, in which the "common people" are subject to the brute and "objective" laws of nature, and from which, as a people and as a collectivity, they cannot escape. In Hegel's words, the freedom of the few presupposes the necessity of the many.

Given such a way of posing the problem, the figure and thought of Machiavelli, when inserted into the context of Crocean liberal philosophy, are seen as the genesis of a knowledge that posits the political as an activity separate and distinct from ethics and culture. The autonomy of the

156 political implies that the contradiction between freedom and necessity, and between the *dover essere* and the *essere*, can never be resolved. For now the political is itself seen as an activity immersed in, and subject to, the necessary laws of nature. Thus arises the formulation that politics is pure technique, an instrumentality characterized by pure power and pure force, and political knowledge is a "science" that teaches the technique of the "lion and the fox." This means that domination, coercion, manipulation, and the generation of popular belief systems—what Croce would call "technical instruments of rule," and what in Marx would translate as "ideology" in the sense of "false consciousness"—exhaust the meaning of politics and political knowledge.

The liberal and bourgeois notion of politics reduces it to a mere appendage of the economic—to a mere utility: politics can never be directed to the creation of a universal realm where the freedom and moral-cultural autonomy of one does not necessitate the domination and subjection of the other. Where Machiavelli, Marx, and Gramsci begin—the problem of moving from the objective and given particularity of economic utility to the establishment of a conscious subject capable of transforming this particularity into a universal space where the natural objectivity of the particular is transcended into a self-determining and moral universal—the liberal-bourgeois thinkers end. Where the particular is viewed by the former as a problem that needs to be addressed, and thus it is made as their point of departure, the latter see the particular as the "natural" and "necessary" foundation of society and politics, and thus it becomes the latter's point of arrival.

If the political, therefore, is utility and instrumentality, and if political action is necessarily directed toward the particular, then this implies not only that domination is the defining characteristic of political activity, but also that political action can never transcend domination. Here rule is conceived as equivalent to the *dominium* that the *dominus* exercises over his *familia*, where the relation between ruler and ruled exists within the private and particular realm of necessity. In a real sense, to Croce and the liberal-bourgeois thought he represents, ruling is always a question of domination. It is so precisely because the political cannot be conceived as other than an instrumentality directed toward a particular interest and a particular end. But if this is so, then political knowledge is itself an instrument of domination, whose function is not just to elaborate the technical instruments of power, but, equally important, to direct such knowledge toward the masking and mystification of the *arcana imperii*.

Thus, to assert, as Croce does, that Marx is the Machiavelli of the proletariat, and to equate Marx and Machiavelli, is to attack the Marxian formulation that the realization of philosophy presupposes the development of the proletariat as a conscious and purposive subject. The equation Marx = Machiavelli, within the context of the Crocean interpretation of Machiavelli, reduces the Marxian critique of bourgeois society and bourgeois power relations to an ideology—to an instrument of rule—no different from other belief systems whose function is to mask the antithesis between those who rule and those who are ruled. What Croce is saying is that Marxism, as the ideology of the proletariat in its struggle against the bourgeoisie, is a technical knowledge that was originally discovered by Machiavelli. As such, as pure technique, this knowledge is socially and materially neutral; there is no necessary relation between the knowledge and the subject who knows it and acts upon it.

The Marxian formulation that revolutionary socialism is the active and practical consciousness of the proletariat, and that the activity of the proletariat creates a revolutionary consciousness, is based on a conception of knowledge, and a posture toward action in the world, that see knowledge as the product of a subject who is actively engaged in the world; knowledge and the subject that knows it mutually presuppose each other. Croce and the liberal bourgeois see Marxism—which wants, "boldly and openly," to teach a revolutionary theory to the proletariat and to the popular masses in general—as an ideology that merely reproduces, with a different terminology, the notion of politics as domination and utility. The revolutionary nature of the Marxian project is negated, and Marxism is reduced to another instrument of domination and of rule. In Croce, the equation Marx = Machiavelli asserts the futility of political and revolutionary action: the praxis of the proletariat cannot destroy the bourgeois forms of domination, and cannot lead to overcoming the contradiction between freedom (the realm of moral-intellectual and cultural autonomy) and necessity (the realm of nature and domination). The proletariat, to Croce, is merely a formless *volgo* that cannot constitute itself as an independent, self-directing entity capable of positing itself as a conscious subject and legislating for itself its own values and ends. The nature of the proletariat renders it incapable of creative and critical thought—it cannot "think"—so its political and social existence is reduced to that of a mere instrument, subject to the direction and control of a force or entity external to it. As such, its activity and its moral being are dependent upon the existence of an "aris-

158   tocracy of the intellect" embodied within an "aristo-democracy" of the ruling groups.

Gramsci's interpretation of Machiavelli is intended not only to negate the Crocean notion of Machiavelli's thought, but also to develop a theory of politics and political action that will resolve the liberal antinomy between those who know and those who merely "feel," between the *alta cultura* of the ruling groups and the *cultura popolare* of the masses. Gramsci opposes Machiavelli to Croce, and Machiavellian knowledge to Croce's philosophy: the former is the democratic philosopher whose thought is the knowledge of the people to which it is addressed, and the latter is the traditional intellectual whose thought represents the negation of the people. The knowledge of Machiavelli is generated by the reciprocal movement described by the process "I to you"/"you to me," which embodies the unity of Machiavelli's new knowledge and the subject to which it is addressed; the philosophy of Croce sees itself as the thought of intellectuals in opposition to the life of the people, a knowledge whose very existence requires that the people as subject be denied.

The Gramscian Machiavelli discovers a knowledge of politics whose realization in the world depends upon the formation of the people as a coherent and purposive subject, whereas the Crocean Machiavelli discovers a knowledge whose very nature as "knowledge" presupposes the existence of the masses as *volgo*, of the *moltitudine*, which is *"disgiunta," "sciolta,"* and disaggregated into a mass of competing particular interests. To Croce, the people is the *volgo* that does not seek the "truth," because this truth can only be given by the aristocracy of the intellect; to Machiavelli, the people is the subject and carrier of the new knowledge, because the truth—the *verità effettuale*—is the product of the interactive relation between this knowledge and the people it addresses, a relation based upon the mutual discourse delineated by the "io ... da voi ... come voi da me" construction Machiavelli establishes in The Art of War. The knowledge of Machiavelli, as the consciousness of the *populo "nel temporale,"* leads to the citizen democracy, which is, in turn, the realization of this knowledge in action and in practice; the knowledge of Croce, as the consciousness of intellectuals, leads to the aristo-democracy whose attainment and continued existence require that the *volgo* be and remain a passive, subordinate object. Indeed, in Croce the distinction between *alta cultura* and *cultura popolare*, culture and politics, which leads to the conception of the autonomy of politics, necessitates the reduction of the popular masses to the category and status of *volgo*, where the latter is defined by the opaque objectivity of inert matter.

This opaque quality of the culture and consciousness of the people **159** implies that political knowledge, when related to the life and practice of the masses, is a knowledge whose function is to mask—*velare*—the technique and science of politics. Since the *volgo* does not seek the truth, and since its consciousness cannot attain to the level of the moral-intellectual discipline that self-reflection gives to the intellectual and scientific aristocracy, knowledge, when it "descends" to the level of the popular and the mass, transforms itself into ideology, into an instrument whereby the *volgo* will remain *volgo*, and thus remain subordinate to those who know. Since knowledge cannot emerge from the life of the people, and since any contact with the people transforms it into a technical instrument of rule, knowledge, rather than educating and transforming the *volgo* into a collective entity that possesses a coherent consciousness of itself and its relation to the world, attempts to maintain them in their condition of sociopolitical domination and in their state of cultural and moral-intellectual incoherence. This means that there can be no discourse with the people, that speech and argumentation based on reciprocity and mutuality are possible only within the narrow and limited space defined by the structures of the aristo-democracy. There can be no discourse precisely because, in the words of Tacitus, the *volgo* is mute and speechless. The relation between those who know and those who do not know, therefore, is based on domination and manipulation.

Gramsci sees the Machiavellian enterprise as the attempt to render articulate and conscious those who are mute and speechless. But to transform the mute and speechless *volgo* into a morally and intellectually articulate subject is to initiate a process of reform and renovation that will lead to the constitution of the *moltitudine* into a disciplined and coherent people—a people whose self-definition and self-consciousness are equivalent to the introduction and proliferation of Machiavelli's new knowledge. The distinctive and original character of this new knowledge lies in its intention to address the people as an autonomous and independent entity. It must, therefore, present itself as an open and public knowledge that sparks the *moltitudine* to engage in the process of mutual and rational discourse. Such a process, which is carried forward by the relation between the teacher who "speaks" (*parlare*) and the student who responds and questions (*domandare*), is evidenced by Machiavelli's intention to present his knowledge without the use of force or of authority. To "disputare le cose sanza rispetto" (to argue and converse "freely"), and to "ragionare sanza volervi usare o l'autorità o la forza," would only be meaningful if the subject that is addressed is not, or no longer is, mute and speechless.

160   The constructions "io a voi"/"voi a me" and "io ... da voi ... come voi da me" are equivalent to the "disputare le cose sanza rispetto" and the "ragionare sanza volervi usare o l'autorità o la forza." Together they express the nature of the new knowledge that Machiavelli intends to introduce. It is these two sets of constructions, I have argued, that form the essential and original constituting elements of the Gramscian notion of *egemonia*. Hegemony is the formulation and elaboration of a moral-intellectual and cultural conception of the world, whose elaboration throughout society transforms it into a way of life and a form of practice characteristic of an entire people. Hegemony, in fact, is precisely the synthesis of the Crocean antitheses that posit a total divorce between thought and action, ethics and politics, culture and people. The development of hegemony, and its proliferation in society, represent the concretization of thought in action, and the realization of the ethical moment within the political moment.

The relation that Machiavelli establishes between the knowledge that he intends to introduce, and the subject to which this knowledge is addressed, parallels the relation that Gramsci establishes between the democratic philosopher and the popular masses within whom he emerges. The notion of hegemony, therefore, represents the unity of culture and people, philosophy and politics; the realization of philosophy in the world of action and of practice is equivalent to the proliferation of hegemony throughout society. Hegemony is the concretization of philosophy and knowledge within a sociopolitical and historical subject, and this concretization is itself the constitution and the becoming of this subject in action within the *verità effettuale* of the *essere*. The development of hegemony can be nothing other than the development of the *volgo* and the *moltitudine* into a determinate *populo*, and the constitution of this *volgo* into a people is nothing other than the development and elaboration of hegemony.

Hegemony establishes a direct and intimate connection between knowledge and the subject to which it is addressed. The nature of the knowledge is determined by both the act of addressing and the subject that is addressed. The knowledge against which Machiavelli was reacting, and the liberal and bourgeois thought that Gramsci intended to supersede, presuppose not simply the existence, but also the necessary continuation, of the popular masses as a mere collection of disaggregated individuals: both assume the necessary and inevitable subordination of the people to a culturally superior group, which alone is capable of moral-intellectual—and hence political—autonomy. The thought of Croce and Guicciardini, as well as the theological and metaphysical systems of the

Christian and medieval conception of the world, require that the *moltitudine* **161** remain *disgiunta* and *dissipata*—that is, their internal integrity and "dignity" demand that thought be distinct from action, and that culture maintain its distance from the popular masses. To posit thought and culture as the products of an "aristocracy of the intellect" is to posit the popular masses as morally and intellectually incompetent. Such thought, therefore, thinks of itself as emerging from itself, and thus addresses only itself—that is, it addresses *alta cultura* and the aristo-democracy of those who possess knowledge and who thereby rule. The integrity of thought, and the moral and intellectual freedom of those who know, necessitate that the masses be and remain mute and speechless. Since the masses are incompetent, since they are mute and speechless, the "ragionare senza usare o l'autorità o la forza" is an activity from which they are necessarily and "naturally" excluded, an activity that properly belongs to the aristo-democracy that describes the realm of freedom wherein are located those who know and those who rule. But to exclude the masses from this realm is to relegate them to the realm of necessity, where it is precisely their subordination to "force" and to "authority" that characterizes their life and practice; from which follows the necessity to posit the political as force, technique, and domination.

On the other hand, the subject to which Machiavelli addresses the product of his *"lunga pratica"* and *"continua lezione"*—action and thought— establishes a form of knowledge and a form of cultural life whose very existence presupposes the transformation of the people from moral-intellectual incompetents into a coherent and purposive entity capable of positing for itself ends and values that are independent of those given by the established and prevailing conception of the world. The subject that is addressed by this knowledge—the popular masses—determines the nature and role of the knowledge, just as the knowledge initiates the moral and intellectual reform of the *volgo* that will transform it into a self-determining subject. This form of knowledge does not see itself or think of itself as independent of practice and action, for its very emergence is contingent upon the development of the people it addresses into a subject capable of transforming the *essere* into a new sociopolitical and sociocultural reality, whose attainment is also the fulfillment of the new knowledge in the world. The knowledge acquires its particular and original character in the very act of addressing itself to the popular masses, and the popular masses acquire their moral and intellectual character as they become the active embodiment of this knowledge. To address the people is simultaneously to transform them from a *volgo* that is mute and speechless into a conscious

162   subject that determines itself through its own autonomous activity. To address the people is to initiate the process whereby they move from the realm of necessity, within which they are subject to the "force" and "authority" of the rulers who possess knowledge, toward the realm of freedom, where social and political life is grounded on the reciprocity and mutuality of equal speech and discourse.

If, however, the addressing of the people is equivalent to the introduction of the new knowledge, and if, in addition, this knowledge is the expression and the consciousness of the people as they act within the "effective reality" of the *essere*, then the relation between the knowledge and the people is at once an educational and a political one. Since both knowledge and people presuppose each other, and since the mutual interaction between the two is what establishes the movement toward free and equal discourse, then to address the people as an intellectual and moral subject is also to establish a political and social topos where such discourse is possible. It is to establish a space where universal speech prevails and from which force and domination are excluded. The transformation of the *volgo* into an entity that posits for itself its particular moral-intellectual ends and values is also the transformation of a subordinate group into a political subject whose conscious activity renders it an entity that can and will rule.

To posit ends and values for oneself—a consequence of moral-intellectual autonomy—is also to rule oneself in the sense of self-determination and self-becoming. Thus the development of the people as a political and determinate subject is the development of a political space where discourse "*sanza rispetto*" is possible and where force and authority are no longer the ground of social and political life. And to exclude domination from such a space implies the proliferation of the "io a voi"/"voi a me" relation throughout the body of the people, such that the particular and narrow boundaries of the *alta cultura* and of the aristo-democracy are transformed into a universality whose character is not given merely in thought, but in the life and practice of the people. Domination and force are necessary precisely because the space of speech and discourse is limited to the narrow circle of those who possess knowledge and rule (as defined and posited by the prevailing and established conception of the world). To rule oneself through the positing of ends for oneself is to negate domination and force, and such a negation is at the same time the destruction and overcoming of the present reality, where those who rule live within one space, and those who are ruled exist within another, which is subject to the authority and force of the former.

Notes

1. Introduction: Gramsci and Machiavelli

1. See Giorgio Nardone, *Il pensiero di Gramsci* (Bari: De Donato, 1971), pp. 72-94; Carl Boggs, *Gramsci's Marxism* (London: Pluto Press, 1978), pp. 90-94, 100; and Lucio Magri, "Problems of the Marxist Theory of the Revolutionary Party," *New Left Review* 60 (March-April 1970), p. 115. See also Gramsci, *Selections from the Prison Notebooks of Antonio Gramsci*, ed. and trans. Quintin Hoare and Geoffrey Nowell Smith (New York: International Publishers, 1973), henceforth cited as *SPN*, pp. 264-65, 268-69.

2. A. R. Buzzi, *La teoria politica di Gramsci* (Florence: La Nuova Italia, 1973), pp. 6, 167-71. See also Joseph V. Femia, *Gramsci's Political Thought: Hegemony, Consciousness, and the Revolutionary Process* (Oxford: Clarendon Press, 1981), pp. 113-15, 120-25.

3. See Gramsci, *Il Grido del popolo*, October 19, 1918, in *Scritti giovanili, 1914-1918* (Turin: Einaudi, 1974); Leopold Labedz, ed., *Revisionism: Essays in the History of Marxist Ideas* (New York: Praeger, 1962); and George Lichtheim, *Marxism: A Historical and Critical Study* (New York: Praeger, 1970). See also John Merrington, "Theory and Practice in Gramsci's Marxism," in *The Socialist Register* (London: Merlin Press, 1968), pp. 145-76, and R. Mondolfo, *Il pensiero politico nel Risorgimento italiano* (Milan: Nuova Accademia, n.d.), pp. 43-56, 123-44.

4. See Andrew Arato, "The Second International: A Reexamination," *Telos* 18 (Winter 1973-74), pp. 2-52; and Lucio Colletti, *From Rousseau to Lenin*, trans. John Merrington and Judith White (New York: Monthly Review Press, 1972). See also James Edward Miller, *From Elite to Mass Politics: Italian Socialism in the Giolittian Era, 1900-1914* (Kent, Ohio: Kent State University Press, 1990), pp. 11-29, 30-53, 54-73, for a historical and party-political analysis of the relation between the Italian Socialists and policies of the Italian state under the liberal government of Giolitti.

5. See Gramsci's article "The Revolution Against Capital," *Avanti*, December 24, 1917, in *Antonio Gramsci: Selections from Political Writings, 1910-1920*, ed. Quintin Hoare, trans. John Mathews (New York: International Publishers, 1977), pp. 34-37. See also Paul Piccone, "Gramsci's Marxism: Beyond Lenin and Togliatti," *Theory and Society* III, 4 (Winter 1976), pp. 485-512; Leonardo Salamini, "Gramsci and Marxist Sociology of Knowledge: An Analysis of Hegemony-Ideology-Knowledge," *The Sociological Quarterly* 15 (Summer 1974), pp. 359-80; John Cammett, *Antonio Gramsci and the Origins of Italian Communism* (Stanford: Stanford University Press, 1967), pp. 65-95, 190-92; Femia, *Gramsci's Political Thought*, pp. 92-94; Massimo Salvadori, *Gramsci e il problema storico della democrazia* (Turin: Einaudi, 1973); Giacomo Graziano, "Alcune considerazioni

164 intorno all'umanesimo di Gramsci," in *Studi gramsciani*, Proceedings of a conference held in Rome 11-13 January 1958, Istituto Gramsci (Rome: Riuniti, 1973), pp. 149-64; R. Mondolfo, "Intorno a Gramsci e alla filosofia della prassi," in his *Umanesimo di Marx: studi filosofici 1908-1966* (Turin: Einaudi, 1968); Giuseppe Tamburrano, "Fasi di sviluppo del pensiero di Gramsci," in *La città futura: Saggi sulla figura e sul pensiero di Antonio Gramsci*, ed. Alberto Caracciolo and Gianni Scalia (Milan: Feltrinelli, 1976), pp. 47-67; and Mario Tronti, "Tra materialismo dialettico e filosofia della prassi," in *La città futura*, pp. 71-92.

6. *Gramsci e la cultura contemporanea*, Proceedings of the international conference of Gramsci studies held in Cagliari 23-27 April 1967, ed. Pietro Rossi (Rome: Riuniti-Istituto Gramsci, 1975), vols. 1 and 2; Salvadori, *Gramsci e il problema storico della democrazia* (see the essay "Gramsci e il rapporto tra soggetività e oggetività nella prassi rivoluzionaria," pp. 208-61; Nardone, *Il pensiero di Gramsci*, pp. 21-36 and 261-87; Cammett, *Antonio Gramsci*, pp. 96-136; Piccone, "Gramsci's Marxism," as well as his "Gramsci's Hegelian Marxism," *Political Theory* 11 (January-Februrary 1974), pp. 32-45, and his *Italian Marxism* (Berkeley: University of California Press, 1983), pp. 111-26, 154-66, 165-200.

7. On the Crocean Gramsci, see Gramsci, *Sotto la Mole, 1916-1920* (Turin: Einaudi, 1974), pp. 145, 365; Benedetto Croce, "Gramsci era uno dei nostri," *Quaderni della critica* 3, 8 (July 1947), p. 86, in which Croce argues that Gramsci shared with him a basically similar philosophical and intellectual orientation; Croce's *Terze pagine sparse* (Bari: Laterza, 1955), vol. 2, pp. 252-53; Walter L. Adamson, *Hegemony and Revolution: A Study of Antonio Gramsci's Political and Cultural Theory* (Berkeley: University of California Press, 1980), pp. 26-36; Giancarlo Bergami, *Il giovane Gramsci e il marxismo 1911-1918* (Milan: Feltrinelli, 1977); Leonardo Paggi, *Antonio Gramsci e il moderno principe* (Rome: Riuniti, 1970), pp. 15-16; Eugenio Garin, "Gramsci nella cultura italiana," in *Studi gramsciani*, pp. 398-99; Emilio Agazzi, "Filosofia della prassi e filosofia dello spirito," in *La città futura*, pp. 95-175; Alastair B. Davidson, "Gramsci and Lenin, 1917-1922," in *The Socialist Register* (London: Merlin Press, 1974), pp. 125-50, especially pp. 125-28, and his *Antonio Gramsci: Towards an Intellectual Biography* (London: Merlin Press, 1977); Guido Morpurgo-Tagliabue, "Gramsci tra Croce e Marx," *Il Ponte* 4, 5 (May 1948), pp. 429-38; Maurice A. Finocchiaro, "Gramsci's Crocean Marxism," *Telos* 41 (Fall 1979), pp. 17-32; and Dante Germino, *Antonio Gramsci: Architect of a New Politics* (Baton Rouge: Louisiana State University Press, 1990). On the Hegelian Gramsci, see Piccone, "Gramsci's Hegelian Marxism," pp. 32-45; Norberto Bobbio, "Gramsci e la concezione della società civile," in *Gramsci e la cultura contemporanea*, vol. 1, pp. 75-100; Adamson, *Hegemony and Revolution*, pp. 4-6; and Leonardo Paggi, "Gramsci's General Theory of Marxism," *Telos* 33 (Fall 1977), pp. 27-70. On the Leninist Gramsci, see Giorgio Bonomi, *Partito e rivoluzione in Gramsci* (Milan: Feltrinelli, 1976), pp. 13-31, 33-50; C. L. Ottino, *Concetti fondamentali nella teoria politica di Antonio Gramsci* (Milan: Feltrinelli, 1956); and Palmiro Togliatti, *Gramsci* (Rome: Riuniti, 1967). On the Jacobin Gramsci, see Cammett, *Antonio Gramsci*, pp. 41-58, 209-12, 214-22; Buzzi, *La teoria politica di Gramsci*, pp. 149-54; Davidson, "Gramsci and Lenin, 1917-1922," pp. 140-45, especially p. 141; and Gramsci, *Scritti giovanili* (Turin: Einaudi, 1974), pp. 271-73. On the democratic-spontaneist Gramsci, see Giuseppe Tamburrano, *Antonio Gramsci: la vita, il pensiero, l'azione* (Manduria: Lacaita, 1963); R. Orfei, *Antonio Gramsci: coscienza critica del marxismo* (Milan: Relazioni sociali, 1965); Nicola Matteucci, *Antonio Gramsci e la filosofia della prassi* (Milan: Giuffrè, 1951); Aldo Garosci, *Pensiero politico e storiografia moderna: saggi di storia contemporanea* (Pisa: Nistri-Lischi, 1954), pp. 193-257. See also Tamburrano's "Gramsci e l'egemonia del proletariato," in *Studi gramsciani*, pp. 277-86, and his "Fasi di sviluppo nel pensiero di Gramsci," in *La città futura*, pp. 117-36, especially p. 131; and Serafino Cambareri, "Il concetto di egemonia nel pensiero di A. Gramsci," in *Studi gramsciani*, pp. 87-94. On the voluntarist Gramsci, see Neil McInnes, "From Marx to Marcuse," *Survey* 16, 1 (1971), pp. 147-67; Adamson, *Hegemony and Revolution*, pp. 202-7; Salamini, "Gramsci and Marxist Sociology of Knowledge," pp. 359-80, and Salamini's *The Sociology of Political Praxis: An Introduction to Gramsci's Theory* (London: Routledge & Kegan Paul, 1981).

8. See Togliatti, *Gramsci*; Gian Carlo Jocteau, *Leggere Gramsci* (Milan: Feltrinelli, 1975); Eric J. Hobsbawm, "The Great Gramsci," *New York Review of Books* (4 April 1974), pp. 39-41; Paolo Spriano, *Storia del Partito comunista italiano* (Turin: Einaudi, 1967), vol. 1; Maria Antonietta Macciocchi, *Per Gramsci* (Bologna: Il Mulino, 1974); Christine Buci-Glucksman, *Gramsci et l'Etat: pour une théorie matérialiste de la philosophie* (Paris: Fayard, 1975) (this work, certainly a major and significant contribution to the study of Gramsci's thought, sees Lenin through a Gramscian prism, by means of which it becomes possible to see a close affinity between the two thinkers); Perry Anderson, "The Antinomies of Antonio Gramsci," *New Left Review* 100 (November 1976-January 1977), pp. 5-78; Cammett, *Antonio Gramsci*, pp. 196-97. In addition, see Anne Showstack Sassoon, *Gramsci's Politics* (Minneapolis: University of Minnesota Press, 1987), pp. 11-19, 109-19, 150-61; but also Gwyn A. Williams, "The Concept of 'Egemonia' in the Thought of Antonio Gramsci: Some Notes on Interpretation," *Journal of the History of Ideas* 21, 4 (October-December, 1960), pp. 586-99. Carl Boggs, in *Gramsci's Marxism* (London: Pluto Press, 1978), understands Gramsci as an "Italian Lenin," a position he no longer holds; see his *The Two Revolutions: Gramsci and the Dilemma of Western Marxism* (Boston: South End Press, 1984).

9. Nardone, *Il pensiero di Gramsci*; H. Stuart Hughes, *Consciousness and Society: The Reorientation of European Social Thought 1890-1930* (New York: Vintage Books, 1961), pp. 96-104; Lichtheim, *Marxism*, pp. 368-69. In addition, see Carmelo Vigna, "Gramsci e l'egemonia. Una interpretazione metapolitica," in *Antonio Gramsci: il pensiero teorico e politico, la "questione leninista"*, 2 vols., ed. Virgilio Melchiorre, Carmelo Vigna, and Gabriele de Rosa (Rome: Città Nuova Editrice, 1979), vol. 1, pp. 11-69, especially p. 60; and Sidney Hook, *Marxism and Beyond* (Totowa, N.J.: Rowman & Littlefield, 1983), p. 81.

10. Alastair B. Davidson, "Gramsci and Reading Machiavelli," *Science and Society* 37, 1 (Spring 1973), pp. 56-80; Buzzi, *La teoria politica*, pp. 149-65; Gennaro Sasso, "Antonio Gramsci, interprete di Machiavelli," *Lo spettatore italiano* 3, 4 (April 1950), pp. 91-93; and Felice Alderisio, "Ripresa machiavelliana. Considerazioni critiche sulle idee di A. Gramsci, di B. Croce e di L. Russo intorno a Machiavelli," *Annali dell'Istituto universitario di Magistero di Salerno* 1 (1949-50), pp. 203-66. See also Matteucci, *Antonio Gramsci e la filosofia della prassi*, pp. 58-65; Saveria Chemotti, *Umanesimo, Rinascimento, Machiavelli nella critica gramsciana* (Rome: Bulzoni, 1975), pp. 87-110; Leonardo Paggi, "Machiavelli e Gramsci," *Studi storici* 10, 4 (1969), pp. 856-66; Franco Catalano, "Le note sul Machiavelli di Antonio Gramsci," *Quarto Stato* 4, 22-23 (1-15 December 1949), pp. 37-40; Luciano Gruppi, "Machiavelli e Gramsci," *Critica marxista* 7, 3 (May-June 1969), pp. 81-91; and V. Gerratana, "Gramsci e Machiavelli," *Il Calendario del popolo* 25, 299-300 (September-October 1969), pp. 2779-82. Maurice Finocchiaro, in his *Gramsci and the History of Dialectical Thought* (Cambridge: Cambridge University Press, 1988), has a chapter on Gramsci and Machiavelli (pp. 123-46). Federico Sanguineti (*Gramsci e Machiavelli* [Rome: Laterza, 1982]) understands Gramsci as using Machiavelli to "deepen" the Leninist and Bolshevik positions regarding the nature of political leadership and its relation to the masses. The book suffers, however, from a lack of textual and conceptual analysis of the works of Gramsci and Machiavelli (see pp. 55-66, 67-71).

The most recent works on Machiavelli I have been able to consult are by Rita Medici, *La Metafora Machiavelli: Mosca Pareto Michels Gramsci* (Modena: Mucchi Editore, 1990), and Evelyne Buissière, "Il Machiavelli di Gramsci," *Critica marxista* 29, 6 (November-December 1991), pp. 70-83.

11. On this, see Cammett, *Antonio Gramsci*, pp. 209-11; Nardone, *Il pensiero di Gramsci*, pp. 20-24; Adamson, *Hegemony and Revolution*, pp. 47, 184, 203-4; Femia, *Gramsci's Political Thought*, pp. 133-34, 254-56; Merrington, "Theory and Practice," pp. 152-53; Eugenio Garin, "Antonio Gramsci nella cultura italiana (Appunti)," in *Studi gramsciani*, pp. 9-10, and his "Gramsci nella cultura italiana," *ibid.*, pp. 404-5, 413-16. See also Buzzi, *La teoria politica*, pp. 149-65; Matteucci, *Antonio Gramsci e la filosofia della prassi*, pp. 56-57; and Boggs, *Gramsci's Marxism*, pp. 106-9.

166   In addition to the critical edition of Gramsci's work cited in the text (*Quaderni del carcere,* ed. Valentino Gerratana [Turin: Einaudi, 1975]), there are editions of two complete notebooks, one on Machiavelli and politics (*Quaderno* 13. *Noterelle sulla politica di Machiavelli,* intro. and notes by Carmine Donzelli [Turin: Einaudi, 1981]), the other on Italian unification and the Risorgimento (*Quaderno* 19. *Risorgimento italiano,* intro. and notes by Corrado Vivanti [Turin: Einaudi, 1977]), as well as the volumes of the thematically organized original Einaudi edition of the *Prison Notebooks,* of which *Gli Intellettuali e l'organizzazione della cultura, Il Risorgimento,* and *Note sul Machiavelli, sulla politica e sullo Stato moderno* deal directly with Machiavelli.

Joseph A. Buttigieg is in the process of editing and translating for Columbia University Press Valentino Gerratana's critical edition of the *Quaderni del carcere,* of which the first volume has just been published (1992). For a bibliography of Gramsci's works in Italian and English, see Buttigieg's preface, pp. x-xiv.

12. See Boggs, *Gramsci's Marxism,* pp. 163-65; Adamson, *Hegemony and Revolution,* pp. 202-28; Anderson, "Antinomies," pp. 67-72; Salvadori, *Gramsci e il problema storico;* and Togliatti, "Gramsci e il leninismo," in *Studi gramsciani* pp. 419-44.

13. See Lichtheim, *Marxism,* and Hughes, *Consciousness and Society.*

14. See the essays by Togliatti in *Studi gramsciani* and Ernesto Ragionieri, "Gramsci e il dibattito teorico nel movimento operaio internazionale," in *Gramsci e la cultura contemporanea,* pp. 101-47; and Bonomi, *Partito e rivoluzione.*

15. See Boggs, *Gramsci's Marxism,* pp. 11-20; and Nicola Matteucci, "Partito e Consigli di fabbrica nel pensiero di Gramsci," *Il Mulino* 4, 4 (April 1955), pp. 350-59. See also Adamson, *Hegemony and Revolution,* pp. 229-46; Femia, *Gramsci's Political Thought,* pp. 245-50; and Davidson, *Antonio Gramsci,* pp. 197-203.

16. Adamson, *Hegemony and Revolution,* pp. 170-79; Williams, "Concept of 'Egemonia,' " pp. 586-99; Femia, *Gramsci's Political Thought,* pp. 22-60; Tamburrano, *Antonio Gramsci,* pp. 266-67; Cammett, *Antonio Gramsci,* pp. 204-6; Bobbio, "Gramsci e la concezione della società civile"; Eugenio Garin, "Politica e cultura in Gramsci (il problema degli intellettuali)," in *Gramsci e la cultura contemporanea* 1, pp. 37-74; Buzzi, *La teoria politica,* pp. 309-23; Boggs, *Gramsci's Marxism,* pp. 37-42. But see H. Stuart Hughes, *Consciousness and Society,* pp. 101-2.

17. On this point, the sources and commentators, though engaged in different intellectual and theoretical endeavors and though departing from different political and philosophical orientations, are in substantial agreement. See Buzzi, *La teoria politica,* pp. 172-78; Nardone, *Il pensiero di Gramsci,* pp. 11-36; Bonomi, *Partito e rivoluzione,* pp. 13-31; Agazzi, "Filosofia della prassi," in *La città futura,* pp. 104-7; and Carlo Cicerchia, "Il rapporto col leninismo e il problema della rivoluzione italiana," in *La città futura,* pp. 19-43.

18. Gramsci, *Lettere dal carcere,* ed. Sergio Caprioglio and Elsa Fubini (Turin: Einaudi, 1955), pp. 132, 186, 466.

19. Gramsci, *Sotto la mole,* pp. 145, 365; and *Selections from Political Writings,* 1921-1926, ed. and trans. Quintin Hoare (New York: International Publishers, 1978), pp. 447-62. See also *Quaderni del carcere* 2:10, pp. 1232-34.

20. Garin, "Gramsci nella cultura italiana," pp. 395-418, and his "Antonio Gramsci nella cultura italiana (Appunti)," in *Studi Gramsci,* pp. 6-11; Boggs, *Gramsci's Marxism,* pp. 43-44; Nardone, *Il pensiero di Gramsci,* pp. 261-87; and H. Stuart Hughes, *Consciousness and Society,* pp. 103-4.

21. See Garin, "Gramsci nella cultura italiana," and Piccone, *Italian Marxism,* pp. 194-97; Buzzi, *La teoria politica,* pp. 323-35; Abbate, *La filosofia di Benedetto Croce,* pp. 8-13; and Agazzi, in *La città futura.* See also Gramsci, *Lettere dal carcere,* pp. 132, 192; Edmund E. Jacobitti, "Labriola, Croce, and Italian Marxism 1895-1910," *Journal of the History of Ideas* 36, 2 (April-May 1975), p. 298; Salamini, "Gramsci and Marxist Sociology of Knowledge," pp. 364-67; and Finocchiaro, "Gramsci's Crocean Marxism," and his *Gramsci and the History of Dialectical Thought,* pp. 8-27; and Salvadori, *Gramsci e il problema storico,* pp. 259-60.

22. See Benedetto Croce, "Machiavelli e Vico. La politica e l'etica," in *Etica e politica* (Bari: Laterza, 1931), pp. 251-55; "Ciò che il Machiavelli fece e ciò che lasciò fare," in *Terze pagine sparse* (Bari: Laterza, 1955), vol. I, pp. 217-18; "Teoria e politica" and "Un giuoco che ormai dura troppo," in *Terze pagine sparse*, vol. 2, pp. 129-40, 252-53; "Il Machiavelli volta al morale" and "Un detto di Machiavelli," in *Conversazioni critiche* (Bari: Laterza, 1951), vol. 4, pp. 14-15, 17-20; "La quistione del Machiavelli," in *Indagini su Hegel e schiarimenti filosofici* (Bari: Laterza, 1952), pp. 164-76; and "Moralità del Machiavelli," in *Nuove pagine sparse* (Naples: Ricciardi, 1949), vol. I, pp. 238-39.

23. See Garin, "Gramsci nella cultura italiana," pp. 416-18; Buzzi, *La teoria politica*, pp. 334-35. See also Felice Alderisio, "Ripresa machiavelliana," pp. 231-46; Alderisio asserts (pp. 205-6) that Gramsci's notes on Machiavelli added nothing new, original, or substantial to Machiavelli studies. See Croce, "Un giuoco che ormai dura troppo," pp. 252-53.

24. Nardone, *Il pensiero di Gramsci*, p. 21. See also Sheldon S. Wolin, *Politics and Vision: Continuity and Innovation in Western Political Thought* (Boston: Little, Brown and Company, 1960), pp. 228-35; J. G. A. Pocock, *The Machiavellian Moment: Florentine Political Thought and the Atlantic Republican Tradition* (Princeton: Princeton University Press, 1975), pp. 181-82, 212-13; and Croce, *Etica e politica*, pp. 224-27.

25. See Croce's *Etica e politica*; his *My Philosophy: Essays on the Moral and Political Problems of Our Time*, selected by R. Klibansky, trans. E. F. Carritt (New York: Collier Books, 1962); and his *History as the Story of Liberty*, trans. Sylvia Sprigge (Chicago: Gateway Editions, 1970). See also Wilden Carr, *The Philosophy of Benedetto Croce* (New York: Russell and Russell, 1969); David D. Roberts, *Benedetto Croce and the Uses of Historicism* (Berkeley: University of California Press, 1987); and Benedetto Croce, *Philosophy, Poetry, History: An Anthology of Essays*, trans. with an introduction by Cecil Sprigge (London: Oxford University Press, 1966), the Introduction by Sprigge, pp. ix-lxx.

26. Croce, "Machiavelli e Vico," in *Etica e politica*, pp. 250-56.

27. Ibid., p. 251.

28. Croce, *My Philosophy*, p. 93.

29. Croce, *Etica e politica*; *My Philosophy*, the section entitled "Philosophy of Politics," and *Terze pagine sparse*.

30. Gramsci, *Quaderni del carcere* 1:3, pp. 353-57, 3:12, pp. 1513-30. And SPN, pp. 5-23, 323-36, 389-99.

31. Gramsci, *Quaderni del carcere* 2:11, p. 1385; SPN, p. 350.

2. Croce and Gramsci: From Philosophy to Politics

1. For Gramsci's evaluation of the intellectual and cultural influence of Croce's philosophy in Italian history and society, see Antonio Gramsci, *Quaderni del carcere*, critical edition, ed. Valentino Gerratana (Turin: Einaudi, 1975), henceforth cited as QC, 2:10, pp. 1352-53, 1232-33, 1326, 1267-68, 1306-7, 1259. See also QC 2:6, pp. 782-83 and his *Lettere dal carcere*, ed. Sergio Caprioglio and Elsa Fubini (Turin: Einaudi, 1965), henceforth cited as LC, pp. 132, 186.

Gramsci's statement, in QC 2:10, p. 1233, should be noted ("Fundamentally I was rather a Crocean"), as well as his letter to Tatiana, 17 August 1931, where he writes, "It seemed to me that I as well as Cosmo [Gramsci's professor at the University of Turin] and many other intellectuals of that time (one could say during the first fifteen years of the century) stood on common intellectual ground, and participated entirely or in part in the moral and intellectual reform promoted in Italy by Benedetto Croce" (LC, p. 466). One should also note Gramsci's belief, in *La città futura 1917-1918*, ed. Sergio Caprioglio (Turin: Einaudi, 1982), that Croce is "at the present time the greatest thinker in Europe" (p. 21). But in 1926—that is, during the period that fascism was consolidating its power and dismantling the parliamentary system—Gramsci sees Croce as "the most important figure of Italian reaction," and as "the most significant reactionary in the peninsula," in "Alcuni temi della quistione meridionale," in *La costruzione del Partito*

168   *communista*, 1923-1926 (Turin: Einaudi, 1972), pp. 151, 155-56, and in Gramsci, *Selections from Political Writings*, 1921-1926, ed. and trans. Quintin Hoare (New York: International Publishers, 1978), pp. 447-62. Finally, in his *Prison Notebooks*, Gramsci returns to his original position and distinguishes Croce from the fascists, writing that Croce is "the national leader of liberal democratic culture" (QC 2:10, pp. 1352-53). See H. Stuart Hughes, *Consciousness and Society: The Reorientation of European Social Thought 1890-1930* (New York: Vintage Books, 1958), pp. 19, 60-65; and Giancarlo Bergami, *Il giovane Gramsci e il marxismo 1911-1918* (Milan: Feltrinelli, 1977), p. 81. See also Attilio Momigliano, "La critica," *La rassegna d'Italia* 1 (February-March 1946), where Momigliano reports that since 1903 "philosophy . . . aesthetics, literary criticism, history and historical criticism, the criticism of art, linguistics, law, have all come under the influence |of Croce|" (p. 275).

For a discussion of Gramsci and Croce, see Eugenio Garin, "Antonio Gramsci nella cultura italiana," in *Studi gramsciani*, Proceedings of a conference held in Rome 11-13 January 1958, Istituto Gramsci (Rome: Riuniti, 1973), pp. 3-14; and Garin's "Politica e cultura in Gramsci (il problema degli intellettuali)," in *Gramsci e la cultura contemporanea*, Proceedings of the international conference of Gramsci studies held in Cagliari 23-27 April 1967, ed. Pietro Rossi, (Rome: Riuniti-Istituto Gramsci, 1975), vol. 1, pp. 37-74. See also Maurice A. Finocchiaro, "Gramsci's Crocean Marxism," *Telos* 41 (Fall 1979), pp. 17-32, and his *Gramsci and the History of Dialectical Thought* (Cambridge: Cambridge University Press, 1988), pp. 8-27; Paul Piccone, *Italian Marxism* (Berkeley: University of California Press, 1983), parts 3 and 4; and Leonardo Salamini, "Gramsci and Marxist Sociology of Knowledge: An Analysis of Hegemony-Ideology-Knowledge," *The Sociological Quarterly* 15 (Summer 1974), pp. 359-80.

On the distinction between *alta cultura* and *cultura popolare*, see Gramsci, QC 2:11, pp. 1375-95.

2. Gramsci, QC 2:10, pp. 1219-22, 1324-26, and Benedetto Croce, *Etica e politica* (Bari: Laterza, 1931), "Elementi di politica," pp. 213-29. See also H. Stuart Hughes, *Consciousness and Society*, pp. 215-29.

3. Gramsci, *Selections from the Prison Notebooks*, ed. and trans. Quintin Hoare and Geoffrey Nowell Smith (New York: International Publishers, 1973), henceforth cited as SPN, pp. 130-32, 421-22. See also *Antonio Gramsci: Selections from Cultural Writings*, ed. and intro. David Forgacs and Geoffrey Nowell Smith, trans. William Boelhower (Cambridge, Mass.: Harvard University Press, 1985), pp. 206-12.

4. Gramsci, QC 2:11, pp. 1406-8, 2:10, pp. 1259-61, 1212-13, 1221-22; and QC 3:13, pp. 1567-68.

5. Benedetto Croce, *Terze pagine sparse* (Bari: Laterza, 1955), vol. 2, pp. 132-39. Croce's terminology and use of language in characterizing Gramscian thought echo and parallel Gramsci's theoretical and political critique of Crocean thought: see QC 2:6, pp. 688-92, 2:10, pp. 1229-32.

6. Croce, *Terze pagine sparse*, p. 139. Croce's understanding of Gramsci is comparable to his statement on Marx: "Marx was an active and intelligent *politico*, or rather he was a revolutionary genius whose work gave coherence and importance to the workers' movement, arming it with an historiographical and economic doctrine" in *Materialismo storico ed economia marxistica* (Bari: Laterza, 1951), p. 302. On this, see Giuseppe Tamburrano, *Antonio Gramsci: la vita, il pensiero, l'azione* (Manduria: Lacaita, 1963), p. 195; H. Stuart Hughes, *Consciousness and Society*, pp. 82-90; and Serge Hughes, *The Fall and Rise of Modern Italy* (Minerva Press, 1967), pp. 37-58.

7. Gramsci notes that Croce's historical writings describe those periods of Italian and European history characterized by the absence of revolutionary change or structural transformations. Thus, the *Storia d'Italia nell'età barocca* (Bari: Laterza, 1957) discusses developments occurring during the Counter-Reformation, the *Storia d'Italia dal 1871 al 1915* (Bari: Laterza, 1967) analyzes Italian events after the struggle for unification is completed, and the *Storia dell'Europa nel secolo decimonono* (Bari: Laterza, 1932) looks at European history after 1815, that is, after the

defeat of Napoleon and his revolutionary armies. See QC 2:11, pp. 1219-21, 2:10, p. 1316. See also David Roberts, *Benedetto Croce and the Uses of Historicism* (Berkeley: University of California Press, 1987), pp. 267-315, and Federico Chabod, "Croce storico," in *Lezioni di metodo storico: con saggi su Egidi, Croce, Meinecke,* ed. Luigi Firpo (Bari: Laterza, 1969), pp. 211-15.

8. Croce, "Elementi di politica." See Gramsci, QC 3:13, pp. 1572-74; 2:11, pp. 1505-6.

9. Karl Marx, "On the Jewish Question," *Karl Marx: Early Writings,* ed. T. B. Bottomore (New York: McGraw-Hill, 1964), pp. 1-40. Note also Marx's "Contribution to a Critique of Hegel's Philosophy of Right: Introduction," in the same volume, pp. 43-59, especially pp. 58-59.

10. Karl Marx, *The German Ideology* (New York: International Publishers, 1968), part 1, and the "Theses on Feuerbach," pp. 197-99; and *The Poverty of Philosophy* (New York: International Publishers, 1967), pp. 190-91. See also Herbert Marcuse, *Reason and Revolution: Hegel and the Rise of Social Theory* (Boston: Beacon Press, 1968), pp. 287-95, 314-19; Sidney Hook, *From Hegel to Marx: Studies in the Intellectual Development of Karl Marx* (Ann Arbor: University of Michigan Press, 1968).

11. See Georg Lukács, *The Young Hegel: Studies in the Relations between Dialectics and Economics,* trans. Rodney Livingstone (Cambridge: The MIT Press, 1976), pp. 501-7; Shlomo Avineri, *Hegel's Theory of the Modern State* (Cambridge: Cambridge University Press, 1974), pp. 3, 7-8, 47-52, 74; and Marcuse, *Reason and Revolution,* pp. 3-16. See also G. W. F. Hegel, *Political Writings,* trans. T. M. Knox (Oxford: Oxford University Press, 1964), pp. 159-64, 281, and his *Hegel's Lectures on the History of Philosophy,* trans. E. S. Haldane and Frances H. Simson (New York: Humanities Press, 1974), vol. 3, p. 409. Gramsci, in QC, cites this work, and quotes Hegel's statement that "the philosophy of Kant, Fichte, and Schelling expresses and contains in thought the revolution," whereas the "new principle" theorized abstractly in Germany is expressed in France "as effective reality," 2:11, pp. 1505-6.

12. Croce, *Terze pagine sparse,* p. 252.

13. Ibid., pp. 91-92, 137-38. See H. Stuart Hughes, *Consciousness and Society,* pp. 210-11; and Emilio Agazzi, "Filosofia della prassi e filosofia dello spirito," in *La città futura: Saggi sulla figura e sul pensiero di Antonio Gramsci,* ed. Alberto Caracciolo and Gianni Scalia (Milan: Feltrinelli, 1976), pp. 95-175, especially pp. 99-107.

14. Gramsci, QC 3:12, pp. 1518-30, and Agazzi, "Filosofia della prassi," in *La città futura,* pp. 111-13.

15. Gramsci, QC 2:10, pp. 1266-67, 2:11, pp. 1481-82, 1476-77, 2:10, pp. 1225-26. See also Croce, *Terze pagine sparse,* pp. 83-84.

16. Croce, *Etica e politica,* pp. 207-10, and *History as the Story of Liberty,* part 4, "Historiography and Morals," pp. 207-26, and especially pp. 227-34.

17. Machiavelli, *Il Principe,* chapter 15, in *Opere,* vol. 1, ed. Sergio Bertelli (Milan: Feltrinelli, 1960). The question of *velare* and *svelare* recurs throughout Gramsci's critique of Croce. It is precisely this relation *velare/svelare* that determines the nature and character of a given philosophy or a given form of knowledge: whether it reveals and uncovers the foundations of established reality, or whether it masks and mystifies them. This, of course, is the burden of Marx's assertions in *The German Ideology* and in the "Theses on Feuerbach." See also Gramsci, QC 3:13, pp. 1572-75.

18. Gramsci, QC 2:11, pp. 1485-86, 2:10, pp. 1335-38, 3:15, pp. 1784-85.

19. Ibid., 2:10, pp. 1240-41. And Benedetto Croce, *Saggio sullo Hegel* (Bari: Laterza, 1948), p. 60.

20. Gramsci, QC 2:10, pp. 1241-42. See also Giorgio Nardone, *Il pensiero di Gramsci* (Bari: De Donato, 1971), pp. 127-45, 165-70, 173-79.

21. Gramsci, QC 2:10, pp. 1241-42, 1324-27, 1291-1301, 1328-29, 1354-56. See also Agazzi, "Filosofia della prassi"; Mario Tronti, "Tra materialismo dialettico e filosofia della prassi,"

170 in *La città futura*, pp. 71-92; and A. R. Buzzi, *La teoria politica di Gramsci* (Florence: La Nuova Italia, 1973), pp. 304-5.

22. See T. A. Sinclair, *A History of Greek Political Thought* (Cleveland: Meridien Books, 1968); Sir Ernest Barker, *The Political Thought of Plato and Aristotle* (New York: Dover, 1949); and Victor Ehrenberg, *From Solon to Socrates: Greek History and Civilization During the 6th and 5th Centuries BC* (London: Methuen, 1973).

23. Sinclair, *History of Greek Political Thought*; Ehrenberg, *From Solon to Socrates*; and Friedrich Nietzsche, *Beyond Good and Evil* (New York: Vintage Books, 1966), for the concept of philosopher-actor, one who creates and generates values, and embodies them within a given social and cultural space.

24. Gramsci, QC 2:7, p. 886, 2:10, p. 1250; 3:13, pp. 1565-67.

25. Gramsci, QC 2:11, pp. 1378-86.

26. Tronti, "Tra materialismo dialettico." See also Marx, "Contribution to a Critique of Political Economy," in *The Marx-Engels Reader*, ed. Robert Tucker (New York: W. W. Norton, 1972), and the "Theses on Feuerbach." In addition, see R. Mondolfo, *Il pensiero politico nel Risorgimento italiano* (Milan: Nuova Accademia, n.d.), pp. 133-44.

27. Buzzi, *La teoria politica*, pp. 316-17. See Gramsci, QC 2:11, pp. 1380-85, and 3:12, pp. 1516-21.

28. Gramsci, QC 2:10, pp. 1241-42; Marcuse, *Reason and Revolution*, pp. xii-xiii, 258-62.

29. Marx, "Theses on Feuerbach," in *The German Ideology*, and Hook, *From Hegel to Marx*, pp. 272-307.

30. Gramsci, QC 2:10, p. 1242.

31. Ibid., pp. 1354-55; and QC 3:15, p. 1815.

32. Gramsci, QC 3:13, pp. 1577-78.

33. Gramsci, QC 2:7, p. 886, 2:11, pp. 1492-93, 1487-90.

34. Gramsci, QC 2:10, pp. 1326-28. See also Nardone, *Il pensiero di Gramsci*.

35. Gramsci, QC 2:7, p. 886, 2:10, pp. 1241-42.

36. Nardone, *Il pensiero di Gramsci*. See QC 2:10, p. 1319, where Gramsci approvingly quotes Croce that "la filosofia della prassi è storia fatta e in fieri." The citation is from Croce's *Materialismo storico ed economia marxistica* (Bari: Laterza, 1951), p. 118.

37. Gramsci, QC 2:11, pp. 1485-86.

38. On "restoration" and *diplomazia* (or what Gramsci also calls *piccola politica*), see QC 3:15, pp. 1832-33, 1563-64, 1, 8, p. 970; QC 2:10, pp. 1326-28; SPN, section on "The Modern Prince"; and Buzzi, *La teoria politica*, pp. 128-30. Gramsci establishes an opposition between *diplomazia* and *politica*, and *piccola politica* and *grande politica*, where the former terms represent the conserving, restorative activity that occurs within a given historical structure, and the latter signify transformative, creative activity that leads to a new structure.

39. On the notion of moral and intellectual reform, see Gramsci, QC 1:4, pp. 430-32, 3:13, pp. 1598-1601; and QC 3:16, pp. 1854-63, 2:10, pp. 1293-99. See Nardone, *Il pensiero di Gramsci*, and Croce, *Etica e politica*, pp. 192-96. See also chapter 3 below.

40. Gramsci, QC 3:16, pp. 1858-61.

41. Ibid., pp. 1859-60.

42. Ibid., pp. 1859-61.

43. Ibid., pp. 1854-55.

44. See Walter L. Adamson, *Hegemony and Revolution: A Study of Antonio Gramsci's Political and Cultural Theory* (Berkeley: University of California Press, 1980); Joseph V. Femia, *Gramsci's Political Thought: Hegemony, Consciousness, and the Revolutionary Process* (Oxford: Clarendon Press, 1981); Alastair B. Davidson, *Antonio Gramsci: An Intellectual and Political Biography* (London: Merlin Press, 1977); Garin, "Politica e cultura in Gramsci," pp. 65-67; Wilden Carr, *The Philosophy of Benedetto Croce* (New York: Russell and Russell, 1969); and Piccone, *Italian Marxism*, pp. 1-43, 117-26.

45. Gramsci, QC 3:12, pp. 1514-16, 3:24, pp. 2264-66; and QC 2:11, pp. 1487-90, 1492-93.
46. Ibid., QC 2:11, pp. 1380-82, 2:10, p. 1354.
47. Ibid., QC 2:10, pp. 1330-31.
48. Ibid.
49. SPN, p. 350 n; and Marx, Third Thesis on Feuerbach, in *The German Ideology*, pp. 197-98.
50. Gramsci, QC 2:10, pp. 1330-31; and SPN, p. 350.
51. Ibid.; LC, p. 620. See also Adamson, *Hegemony and Revolution*; Lamberto Borghi, "Educazione e scuola in Gramsci," in *Gramsci e la cultura contemporanea*, vol. 1, pp. 212-14; and Antonio Labriola, *Scritti di pedagogia e di politica scolastica*, ed. D. Bertoni Jovine (Rome: Riuniti, 1961), "Della scuola popolare," pp. 231-60.

In addition, a discussion of Gramsci's understanding of the relation between hegemony, education, and politics is found in Angelo Broccoli, *Antonio Gramsci e l'educazione come egemonia* (Florence: La Nuova Italia, 1972). See also Gramsci, *La formazione dell'uomo: Scritti di pedagogia*, ed. Giovanni Urbani (Rome: Riuniti, 1974).

52. Gramsci, QC 2:10, pp. 1331-32, 1343-44; and SPN, p. 350.
53. Croce, *Etica e politica*, p. 171, for his views on the relation between the philosopher and the *volgo*. See also Gramsci, QC 2:11, pp. 1375-75, 1381-82, 2:10, pp. 1217-18, 1230-32, 1294-95. Croce, in his *Conversazioni critiche* (Bari: Laterza, 1950), vol. 2, p. 61, writes, regarding the "dissemination of culture" and the education of the masses, that "the appropriate and concrete method to disseminate and to proliferate culture . . . may sometimes be governed by the formula *Odi profanum vulgus*, |as well as by| the violent and forceful barring of the people from the temple of science, compelling them to remain outside its gates until they become worthy |of entering|." Cited in Borghi, "Educazione e scuola in Gramsci," p. 216.
54. Gramsci, QC 3:12, pp. 1514-18, 1:3, pp. 353-57, 2:7, pp. 904-7, 1:3, p. 401, 2:6, p. 809, 2:9, p. 1118; SPN, p. 7.
55. Gramsci, QC 2:11, pp. 1381-82, 1384-86.
56. Ibid., pp. 1375-76, 1382-83. See SPN, p. 344: "the majority of mankind are philosophers insofar as they engage in practical activity and in their practical activity (or in their guiding lines of conduct) there is implicitly contained a conception of the world, a philosophy."
57. Gramsci, QC 2:11, pp. 1384-85.
58. Ibid., pp. 1380-81.
59. Ibid., pp. 1383-84.
60. Ibid., pp. 1384-86.
61. Ibid., pp. 1391-92.
62. Ibid., pp. 1391-93.
63. For Gramsci on Vico, see QC 2:11, pp. 1480-82. For an interesting and informative discussion of Vico's thought, see Sir Isaiah Berlin, *Vico and Herder: Two Studies in the History of Ideas* (New York: Vintage Books, 1977), pp. 12-21, 25-29, 37-41; and Berlin's *Against the Current: Essays in the History of Ideas*, ed. and with a bibliography by Henry Hardy, intro. Roger Hausheer (Harmondsworth: Penguin Books, 1982), the essay on Vico, "Vico's Concept of Knowledge," pp. 111-19.
64. Gramsci, QC 2:10, pp. 1277-78.
65. On the concept of *direzione*, see Adamson, *Hegemony and Revolution*, and Carl Boggs, *Gramsci's Marxism* (London: Pluto Press, 1978), pp. 36-54. See also Gramsci, SPN, introduction; LC, pp. 481, 616; and QC 3:19, pp. 2010-11, 3:13, pp. 1558-61. Gramsci opposes *direzione* to *dominio*; see QC 1:3, pp. 311-12, 3:12, pp. 1516-20, and LC, p. 481.

Also, see Norberto Bobbio, "Gramsci e la concezione della società civile," in *Gramsci e la cultura contemporanea*, pp. 88, 90, 95-96. Bobbio's article is translated into English in *Gramsci*

172 *and Marxist Theory*, ed. Chantal Mouffe (Boston: Routledge & Kegan Paul, 1979), pp. 21-47. In this volume see also the essays by Chantal Mouffe, "Hegemony and ideology in Gramsci," pp. 168-204; Massimo Salvadori, "Gramsci and the PCI: Two Conceptions of Hegemony," pp. 237-58; Jacques Texier, "Gramsci, theoretician of the superstructures," pp. 48-79; and Biagio de Giovanni, "Lenin and Gramsci: state, politics, and party," pp. 259-88.

66. Gramsci, QC 3:12, pp. 1550-51.

67. Gramsci, SPN, pp. 40, 332-33, 334-35. See also Adamson, *Hegemony and Revolution*, pp. 144-45.

68. Gramsci, QC 2:11, pp. 1384-86.

69. Ibid.

70. Ibid. See also QC 2:11, pp. 1381-83, 2:10, pp. 1249-50, 2:8, pp. 1051-52, 2:10, p. 1244; and 3:12, pp. 1530-31, 2:11, pp. 1366-68, 1370.

71. Gramsci, QC 2:11, pp. 1386-87.

72. Ibid., pp. 1434-35. See also 2:11, pp. 1491-92, 2:10, pp. 1225-26, 1269-71; and LC, pp. 313-14, 585, 619.

73. Gramsci, QC 2:10, pp. 1330-31.

74. Gramsci, QC 2:11, pp. 1407-8.

75. Gramsci, QC 2:10, pp. 1241-42; see also 2:10, pp. 1249-50, 2:11, pp. 1424-26.

76. Gramsci, QC 3:16, pp. 1860-61; see also 2:10, pp. 1232-33; and Nardone, *Il pensiero di Gramsci*, p. 209.

3. Renaissance and Reformation

1. See Antonio Gramsci, *Selections from the Prison Notebooks of Antonio Gramsci*, ed. and trans. Quintin Hoare and Geoffrey Nowell Smith (New York: International Publishers, 1973), henceforth cited as SPN, pp. 132, 395 n. 14. and Gramsci, *Quaderni del carcere*, critical edition, ed. Valentino Gerratana (Turin: Einaudi, 1975), henceforth cited as QC 3:16, p. 1860. See also QC 3:14, pp. 1682-84. See also Rita Medici, *La Metafora Machiavelli: Mosca Pareto Michels Gramsci* (Modena: Mucchi Editore, 1990), pp. 221, 266 n. 20.

2. On this point, see A. R. Buzzi, *La teoria politica di Gramsci* (Florence: La Nuova Italia, 1973); Walter L. Adamson, *Hegemony and Revolution: A Study of Antonio Gramsci's Political and Cultural Theory* (Berkeley: University of California Press, 1980) pp. 162-63; Joseph V. Femia, *Gramsci's Political Thought: Hegemony, Consciousness, and the Revolutionary Process* (Oxford: Clarendon Press, 1981) pp. 122, 277 n. 58; and Paul Piccone, "From Spaventa to Gramsci," *Telos* 31 (Spring 1977), pp. 35-65, especially p. 52. Note also Giorgio Nardone, *Il pensiero di Gramsci* (Bari: De Donato, 1971), the chapter "massa e cultura," especially pp. 206-15. See also Gramsci, QC 3:16, pp. 1860-63; and SPN, pp. 395-98.

3. Gramsci, QC 2:7, pp. 905-6; Buzzi, *La teoria politica*, pp. 81-85. See also Michael Mullett, *Radical Religious Movements in Early Modern Europe* (Boston: George Allen and Unwin, 1980), chapter 1, and the section "Documents and Commentary"; and Lewis W. Spitz, *The Protestant Reformation* (New York: Harper and Row, 1985), pp. 352-53, 362-63. For an excellent discussion of the political and theoretical orientations of Lutheranism and Calvinism (as well as the Catholic Tridentine reaction to them in the form of a Thomistic revival in the Counter-Reformation), see Quentin Skinner, *The Foundations of Modern Political Thought* (Cambridge: Cambridge University Press, 1978), vol. 2: The Age of Reformation. See also J. N. Figgis, *Political Thought from Gerson to Grotius: 1414-1625* (New York: Harper Torchbooks, 1960), the essays "The Conciliar Movement and the Papalist Reaction," pp. 41-70, and "Luther and Machiavelli," pp. 71-121.

4. Skinner, *Foundations*, vol. 2, pp. 3-19, 35-47, 189-205. And Spitz, *Protestant Reformation*, pp. 158-62. In addition, see Karl Marx's observations in "Contribution to a Critique of Hegel's Philosophy of Right," in *Karl Marx: Early Writings*, ed. T. B. Bottomore (New York: McGraw-Hill, 1964), p. 53.

5. Gramsci, QC 2:11, pp. 1381-84; Spitz, *Protestant Reformation*, pp. 313-14; Mullett, *Radical Religious Movements*, pp. 59-60, 71; Skinner, *Foundations*, vol. 2, pp. 3-19, 34-41; and Sheldon S. Wolin, *Politics and Vision: Continuity and Innovation in Western Political Thought* (Boston: Little, Brown and Company, 1960), "Luther: The Theological and the Political," pp. 95-140, and "Calvin: The Political Education of Protestantism," pp. 165-94, especially pp. 143-50 and 169-76.

6. Mullett, *Radical Religious Movements*, p. 69. See also Gramsci, QC 3:29, pp. 2342-44, 2350; as well as QC 1:3, pp. 353-57.

7. Gramsci, QC 1:3, pp. 353-55; 3:27, pp. 2313-14; and 2:11, pp. 1375-78, 1468-70, 2:10, pp. 1330-32. Gramsci notes that "Language means also culture and philosophy (if only at the level of common sense) and therefore the fact of 'language' is in reality a multiplicity of facts more or less organically coherent and coordinated: at the limit it could be said that every speaking being has a personal language of his own, that is, his own particular way of thinking and feeling" (QC 2:10, p. 1330). See SPN, p. 359, and editors' notes and introduction.

8. Gramsci, QC 1:3, p. 352; "The relation between intellectuals and the people-nation |should be| studied under the aspect of language as written by intellectuals and as used in their mutual relationships, and |also| under the aspect of the function performed by Italian intellectuals in the medieval Cosmopolis due to the fact that the papacy had its |temporal| seat in Italy (the use of Latin as the learned and cultured tongue is linked to the cosmopolitanism of Catholicism). . . . literary Latin becomes crystallized in the Latin of the learned and educated |dotti|, of the intellectuals—the so-called 'middle Latin'—which can in no way be compared to a spoken language, historically living."

And: " 'In any case there is a break |frattura| between the people and the intellectuals, between the people and culture. |Even| religious books are written in middle Latin, so that even religious discussions |and debates| become incomprehensible to the people, although religion is the prevailing form of culture. What the people receives from religion are the rites and rituals it can see and the homiletic sermons it can hear, but it cannot follow debates and ideological developments because they are the monopoly of a caste' " (Gramsci's citation of Filippo Ermini, 1:3, p. 353-54).

And note Gramsci's statement: "the vernacular |i volgari| is written when the people regains importance" (QC 1:3, p. 354); but also his comments in 1:3, pp. 354-55 regarding the reabsorption of the vernacular into the traditional language of the *dotti* and the clerical-intellectual caste, a phenomenon that parallels the decline and collapse of the communal republics—that is, of the people—in northern Italy. In this regard, see Giuliano Procacci, *Studi sulla fortuna del Machiavelli* (Rome: Istituto storico italiano, 1965), pp. 27-28, on Antonio Brucioli, a friend and admirer of Machiavelli, who was condemned by the church, and who was "a translator of the Bible into the vernacular, |and| had been a frequent participant in the literary and political conversations in the Orti Oricellari, during which he often had occasion to listen and to reflect upon the observations and discourses of the Florentine ex-secretary." See chapter 6 of this book.

On the relation between various forms of language (vernacular, Latin, dialect), intellectuals, and the formation of a sociopolitical order, an interesting and informative work is Franco Lo Piparo, *Lingua, intellettuali, egemonia in Gramsci* (Bari: Laterza, 1979), pp. 153-58, 160-66.

9. Gramsci, QC 2:10, p. 1330. On the relation between reform, hegemony, and language, see Lo Piparo, *Lingua, intellettuali, egemonia*, pp. 103-8, 113-16, 118-26, 135-45. See also Leonardo Salamini, *The Sociology of Political Praxis: An Introduction to Gramsci's Theory* (London: Routledge & Kegan Paul, 1981), pp. 181-96.

10. Gramsci, QC 2:11, pp. 1375-77, 2:10, p. 1330.

11. Ibid., pp. 1377-78, 1330; and Adamson, *Hegemony and Revolution*, pp. 149-51.

12. Gramsci, QC 3:16, pp. 1858-59.

174   13. Ibid., pp. 1859-60; and QC 3:29, p. 2350. See also Herbert Marcuse, *Studies in Critical Philosophy* (Boston: Beacon Press, 1972), the essay "Luther and Calvin," pp. 56-78; Skinner, *Foundations*, vol. 2, pp. 81-89, 254-73; and Figgis, "Luther and Machiavelli," in *Political Thought*, pp. 71-121.

14. Gramsci, QC 2:10, pp. 1330-32.

15. Emilio Agazzi, "Filosofia della prassi e filosofia dello spirito," in *La città futura: Saggi sulla figura e sul pensiero di Antonio Gramsci*, ed. Alberto Caracciolo and Gianni Scalia (Milan: Feltrinelli, 1976), p. 110; Buzzi, *La teoria politica*, p. 118. See Gramsci, QC 3:16, pp. 1856-58, 2:10, pp. 1235-38.

16. Benedetto Croce, *Storia dell'età barocca in Italia* (Bari: Laterza, 1957), cited by Gramsci in QC 3:16, pp. 1858-59. See also Giorgio Nardone, *Il pensiero di Gramsci* (Bari: De Donato, 1971), pp. 36, 49; Saveria Chemotti, *Umanesimo, Rinascimento, Machiavelli nella critica gramsciana* (Rome: Bulzoni, 1975), pp. 60-69; Figgis, "Luther and Machiavelli," in *Political Thought*, pp. 71-79.

17. Benedetto Croce, *Storia dell'età barocca in Italia* (Bari: Laterza, 1957), p. 8; see also Gramsci, QC 3:16, pp. 1858-59; and Lamberto Borghi, "Educazione e scuola in Gramsci," in *Gramsci e la cultura contemporanea*, Proceedings of the international conference on Gramsci studies held in Cagliari 23-27 April 1967, ed. Pietro Rossi (Rome: Riuniti-Istituto Gramsci, 1975), vol. 1, pp. 214-16.

Interesting and informative is a comparison of Croce's position on the relation between the Renaissance and the Reformation to that of Friedrich Nietzsche: "The Italian Renaissance contained within itself all the positive forces to which we owe modern culture: namely, liberation of thought, disdain for authority, the triumph of education over the arrogance of lineage, enthusiasm for science and men's scientific past, the unshackling of the individual, an ardor for veracity and aversion to appearance and mere effect (which ardor blazed forth in a whole abundance of artistic natures who, with the highest moral purity, demanded perfection in their works and nothing but perfection). . . . Despite all its flaws and vices, it was the Golden Age of this millennium. By contrast, the German Reformation stands out as an energetic protest of backward minds who had not yet had their fill of the medieval world view and perceived the signs of its dissolution—the extraordinary shallowness and externalization of religious life—not with appropriate rejoicing, but with deep displeasure. With their northern strength and obstinacy, they set men back, forced the Counter-Reformation, that is, a defensive Catholic Christianity, with the violence of a state of siege, delaying the complete awakening and rule of the sciences for two or three centuries, as well as making impossible, perhaps forever, the complete fusion of the ancient and modern spirit. The great task of the Renaissance could not be carried to its completion; this was hindered by the protest of the now backward German character (which in the Middle Ages had had enough sense to redeem itself by climbing over the Alps again and again)" (*Human, All Too Human*, trans. Marion Farber with Stephen Lehmann, introduction and notes by Marion Farber [Lincoln: University of Nebraska Press, 1984]), pp. 146-47. For this interpretation Nietzsche relies on the work of Jacob Burckhardt; see his *Civilization of the Renaissance in Italy: An Essay*, trans. S. G. C. Middlemere (London: George Allen and Unwin, 1965).

In addition, compare the statement from Nietzsche to that of de Sanctis in the latter's *Storia della letteratura italiana*, ed. Benedetto Croce (Bari: Laterza, 1965), vol. 1, p. 420, in which he says that Luther would have been regarded in the Italy of the Renaissance as simply another "medieval scholastic," and thus the Reformation could not have taken root there because Italy "now no longer believed in anything except science." And note Gramsci's comments on the differences and similarities between de Sanctis and Burckhardt on the Renaissance: "De Sanctis paints in dark colors the political and moral corruption of the Renaissance; notwithstanding all the merits that may be attributed to the Renaissance, it destroyed Italy and rendered it subject to the foreigner. . . . |And| Burckhardt sees the Renaissance as the point of departure for a new epoch in European civilization—progressive, and the cradle of modern man. |On the other hand|, for de Sanctis, from the point of view of Italian history and Italy itself the Renaissance was the point of departure for a regressive movement. . . . Nevertheless, Burckhardt and de Sanctis present a similar analysis regarding the particulars of the Renaissance, and are in agreement in showing as characteristic elements of the Renaissance the formation of a new *mentalità*, and the divorce of religion, authority, *patria*, and family from all medieval ties" (QC 3:17, p. 1919).

18. Gramsci, QC 2:10, pp. 1293, 1219-22; Nardone, *Il pensiero di Gramsci*, pp. 170-73. See also Eugenio Garin, "Antonio Gramsci nella cultura italiana," in *Studi gramsciani*, Proceedings of a conference held in Rome 11-13 January 1958, Istituto Gramsci (Rome: Riuniti, 1973), p. 410 n. 3.

19. Gramsci, QC 2:10, p. 1293. See Wolin's comments on the legacy of the Reformation, *Politics and Vision*, pp. 192-93. See also Figgis, "Luther and Machiavelli," in *Political Thought*, pp. 80-82, 86-91.

20. Gramsci, QC 2:10, pp. 1292-93, 1226-29. On Croce's position in Italy during the Mussolini era, and his relationship to fascism, see Serge Hughes, *The Fall and Rise of Modern Italy* (New York: Minerva Press, 1967).

21. Gramsci, QC 2:10, pp. 1303-4; and QC 3:21, pp. 2118-19.

22. See Gramsci's citation of Filippo Ermimi, QC 1:3, pp. 353-54, and his references to Giuseppe Toffanin, *Che cosa fu l'Umanesimo* (Florence: Sansoni, 1929), QC 2:7, pp. 904-6, and QC 3:17, p. 1910. See also Buzzi, *La teoria politica*, p. 67; Nardone, *Il pensiero di Gramsci*, pp. 95-100, 111 n. 50.

23. Nardone, *Il pensiero di Gramsci*, pp. 95-106; Femia, *Gramsci's Political Thought*, pp. 130-33, 273-74; Adamson, *Hegemony and Revolution*, 93-94, 142-46; and Carl Boggs, *Gramsci's Marxism* (London: Pluto Press, 1978), pp. 75-79.

24. Gramsci, QC 1:5, pp. 614-15, 2:7, pp. 904-7, 1:3, p. 401, 2:6, p. 807 (Int, pp. 34-38), and QC 3:15, pp. 1801-2. See also Buzzi, *La teoria politica*, pp. 66-67.

25. Gramsci, I:3, p. 401, 1:5, pp. 614-15, 2:6, p. 807, 2:7, pp. 904-7 (Int, pp. 34-38); and QC 2:11, pp. 1380-84, 3:16, pp. 1857-59. See also Spitz, *Protestant Reformation*, pp. 300-308, on the efforts of the Catholic Church to regain the initiative and on the Counter-Reformation.

26. Gramsci, QC 3:17, p. 1913.

27. Gramsci, QC 1:5, pp. 657-58.

28. Gramsci, QC 2:11, p. 1378.

29. Ibid., pp. 1233-34. See also QC 2:10, pp. 1225-26, 1240, 1315-17.

30. Nardone, *Il pensiero di Gramsci*, p. 172. See Gramsci, QC 3:16, pp. 1858-59, 2:10, p. 1222.

31. Gramsci, QC 2:11, pp. 1331-32, 1485-86.

32. Gramsci, QC 3:17, p. 1936: "Può esser vero che l'Umanesimo nacque in Italia come studio della romanità e non del mondo classico in generale (Atene e Roma); ma occorre allora distinguere. L'Umanesimo fu 'politico-etico', non artistico, fu la ricerca delle basi di uno 'Stato italiano' che sarebbe dovuto nascere insieme e parallelamente alla Francia, alla Spagna, all'-Inghilterra: in questo senso l'Umanesimo e il Rinascimento hanno come esponente più espressivo il Machiavelli. Fu 'ciceroniano', come sostiene il Toffanin, cioè ricercò le sue basi nel periodo che precedette l'Impero, la cosmopolis imperiale (e in tal senso Cicerone può essere un buon punto di riferimento per suo opporsi a Catalina prima, a Cesare poi, cioè all'emergere delle nuove forze anti-italiche, di classe cosmopolita)."

On the Ciceronian concept *res publica res populi est*, see George H. Sabine's introduction to Cicero, *On the Commonwealth* (Indianapolis: Bobbs-Merrill, 1970); and Neal Wood, *Cicero's So-*

176 cial and Political Thought (Berkeley: University of California Press, 1988). See also Quentin Skinner, Machiavelli (New York: Hill and Wang, 1981).

Note that Gramsci equates the rise of the military dictators with the destruction of the Italian societas created by the Roman republic. See Gramsci, QC 3:17, pp. 1935-36, and QC 3:19, pp. 1959-60. It is evident that Gramsci is attacking both Russo and Burckhardt, the former for his vision of Machiavelli as an "artist-hero," and the latter for his aesthetic interpretation of the Renaissance (see Luigi Russo, Machiavelli [Bari: Laterza, 1975], p. 24, and Burckhardt, Civilization of the Renaissance, part 1, "The State as a Work of Art," and part 3, "The Revival of Antiquity"). See also the comments of J. H. Whitfield, Machiavelli (New York: Russell and Russell, 1965), pp. 117-18, and especially Hans Baron, The Crisis of the Early Italian Renaissance: Civic Humanism and Republican Liberty in an Age of Classicism and Tyranny (Princeton: Princeton University Press, 1955), pp. 47-54, 121-29, 146-67.

Baron's analysis, which establishes an antinomy between Caesar and Brutus, Caesar and Cicero, imperium and res publica, as well as between Dante and Petrarch on the one hand (who praise Caesar and condemn Brutus and Cicero), and Salutati and Bruni on the other, is similar to, and parallels, the discussion Francesco de Sanctis presents in his Storia della letteratura italiana (ed. Benedetto Croce [Bari: Laterza, 1965]) and in his "Machiavelli Conferenze" (in Saggi critici, ed. Luigi Russo [Bari: Laterza, 1965], vol. 2, pp. 329-38), in which he establishes an opposition between Dante and Machiavelli, where the former represents the medieval idealization of the Empire (expressed both in the apotheosis of Caesar and in the struggle between emperors and popes), and where the latter represents the advent of a new conception of political space, one no longer bound and defined by the traditional poles of Empire and church, but rather where this new topos (both in thought and in action), emerging from the ongoing, local struggles of the Florentine state, redirects the traditional categories and the established ways of life into channels that will eventually lead into what Gramsci calls the "absolute laicism" of the modern world.

Thus Dante-Caesar express the cosmopolitan, antipopular character of the imperium and the cosmopolis, whereas Machiavelli-Cicero represent the national-popular, "pro-Italic" orientation of the res publica. As Gramsci observes in the Prison Notebooks, in his comments on the intellectuals and on medieval Italian history, the social and political struggles in Florence were expressed in Dante in a language and discourse defined by the imperial-papal antagonism, an antithesis that placed one kind of cosmopolis against another. On the other hand, in Machiavelli there is a movement away from these medieval antinomies, such that the opposition between Caesar and Brutus, Caesar and Cicero, is no longer presented in universal and cosmopolitan terms; rather, the opposition is transformed into one between empire and republic, lords and people, populo grasso and populo minuto, and vivere politico e libero and vivere privato. On Dante and Machiavelli, see QC 1:6, pp. 758-59.

See also Felix Gilbert, "The Concept of Nationalism in Machiavelli's Prince," Studies in the Renaissance 1 (1954), pp. 38-48; and Franco Gaeta, "Machiavelli storico," in Machiavelli nel V centenario della nascita (Bologna: Boni, 1973), pp. 139-53, especially 141-42.

33. Gramsci, QC 3:17, p. 1913. It should be noted that Gramsci's view of Machiavelli, which is also a critique of the Italian Renaissance and of modern politics and society in Italy, is similar to Marx's view of German philosophy: what Hegel achieved in thought the French Revolution realized in action, and what Machiavelli had theorized in Italy was realized in Europe, but not in Italy. Thus, compare Gramsci's statement to that of Marx, in "Contribution to a Critique of Hegel's Philosophy of Right" (1843): "In politics the Germans thought what other nations did. Germany was their theoretical consciousness. . . . If therefore the status quo of German statehood expresses the perfection of the ancien regime, the perfection of the thorn in the flesh, the modern state, the status quo of German political theory expresses the imperfection of the modern state, the defectiveness of its flesh itself" (Karl Marx and Frederick Engels, Collected Works [New

York: International Publishers, 1975|, vol. 3, p. 181; also found in Bottomore, ed., *Karl Marx: Early Writings*, pp. 51-52).

And in *The Holy Family*, Marx writes: "If Herr Edgar compares French *equality* with German 'self-consciousness' for an instant, he will see that the latter principle expresses *in German*, i.e., in abstract thought, what the former says *in French*, that is, in the language of politics and of thoughtful observation" (Marx and Engels, *Collected Works*, vol. 4, p. 39).

Finally, it is instructive to compare both Gramsci and Marx to Hegel: "In this great epoch of the world's history |the last quarter of the eighteenth century|, two nations only have played a part, the German and the French, and this in spite of their absolute opposition, or rather because they are so opposite. . . . In Germany this principle |the principle of will, the principle of liberty| has burst forth as thought, spirit, Notion; in France, in the form of actuality" (G. W. F. Hegel, *Hegel's Lectures on the History of Philosophy*, trans. E. S. Haldane and Frances H. Simson |New York: Humanities Press, 1974|, vol. 3, p. 409). See also the *Philosophy of History*, trans. T. M. Knox (Oxford: Oxford University Press, 1960), where Hegel says that in Germany the principle of abstract liberty remained a tranquil theory, whereas in France the attempt was made to translate the principle into practice, to act upon it, and realize it in history. See Gramsci, QC 2:11, pp. 1471-72, where he cites both Marx and Hegel, and where he connects these statements to Marx's Eleventh Thesis.

34. De Sanctis, *Storia della letteratura italiana*, vol 2, p. 72.

35. Ibid. See also de Sanctis, "Machiavelli Conferenze," in *Saggi critici*, vol. 2, pp. 329-38.

36. See Ronald Symes, *The Roman Revolution* (Oxford: Oxford University Press, 1939), for an incisive and detailed account of the social, political, and cultural transformation that occurred during the Marius-Sulla and Caesar-Pompey struggles for supreme power that marked the fall of the Roman republic and its transformation into the Augustan Principate. In addition, for an analysis of class conflict and political institutions in the ancient world, see M. I. Finley, *Politics in the Ancient World* (Cambridge: Cambridge University Press, 1983). For an analysis of political institutions and political technique during the rise of Caesar, see Lily Ross Taylor, *Party Politics in the Age of Caesar* (Berkeley: University of California Press, 1961).

37. The nature of this life is discussed in chapter 6.

38. See especially QC 3:19, pp 1959-60. See also the introduction of the editors to the *Selections from the Prison Notebooks*.

39. For a discussion of Machiavelli's use of the ancient writers and his "retranslation" of Ciceronian Stoicism, see Skinner, *Foundations*, vol. 1, pp. 118-38, 152-85, and his *Machiavelli*. See also Hans Baron, "Cicero and the Roman Civic Spirit in the Middle Ages and Early Renaissance," *Bulletin of the John Rylands Library* 22 (1938), pp. 72-97. See also Jerrold Seigel, *Rhetoric and Philosophy in Renaissance Humanism* (Princeton: Princeton University Press, 1968), pp. 17-21, 25-30.

40. See Felix Gilbert, *Machiavelli and Guicciardini: Politics and History in Sixteenth Century Florence* (Princeton: Princeton University Press, 1965); J. G. A. Pocock, *The Machiavellian Moment: Florentine Political Thought and the Atlantic Republican Tradition* (Princeton: Princeton University Press, 1975), part I; and Nicolai Rubinstein, "Politics and Constitution in Florence at the End of the Fifteenth Century," in *Italian Renaissance Studies*, ed. E. F. Jacob (London: Faber and Faber, 1960), pp. 148-83, especially pp. 151-52, 158-60, 172-73, 178-81.

41. Nardone, *Il pensiero di Gramsci*, pp. 256-59; and Chemotti, *Umanesimo, Rinascimento, Machiavelli*, pp. 42-45.

42. Gramsci, QC 2:10, p. 1250, 2:7, pp. 885-86.

43. De Sanctis, "Machiavelli Conferenze," in *Saggi critici*, vol. 2, pp. 329-38, and de Sanctis's essay on Machiavelli in his *Storia della letteratura italiana*; see also Gramsci, QC 3:13, pp. 1598-99, 1572-73.

4. Power and the State:
Croce and Gramsci on the Nature of Machiavelli's Politics

1. For Machiavelli as the discoverer of an objective political science, see Benedetto Croce, *Etica e politica* (Bari: Laterza, 1931), "Machiavelli e Vico. La politica e l'etica," pp. 251-55. See also Croce, "Ciò che il Machiavelli fece e ciò che lasciò fare," in *Terze pagine sparse* (Bari: Laterza, 1955), vol. 1, pp. 217-28,; "Teoria politica" and "Un giuoco che ormai dura troppo," in *Terze pagine sparse*, vol. 2, pp. 129-40, 252-53; "Moralità del Machiavelli," in *Nuove pagine sparse* (Naples: Ricciardi, 1949), vol. 1, pp. 238-39; "La quistione del Machiavelli," in *Indagini su Hegel e schiarimenti filosofici* (Bari: Laterza, 1952), pp. 164-76; and his *Storia dell'età barocca in Italia* (Bari: Laterza, 1957), pp. 80, 83. In addition, see Carlo Curcio, *Machiavelli nel Risorgimento* (Milan: Giuffrè, 1953), pp. 97-131.

And note Croce's polemic against Alderisio, in Benedetto Croce, *Conversazioni critiche* (Bari: Laterza, 1951), vol. 4, "Il Machiavelli volta al morale," pp. 14-17, where Croce attacks the moralistic and "theological" interpretation of Machiavelli advanced by Alderisio, who argues that Machiavelli does not stand outside the accepted and traditional (read Christian) conceptions of politics and morality (*Machiavelli: l'arte dello nell'azione e negli scritti* [Bologna: Zuffi, 1950]). Gramsci agrees with Croce on Alderisio, see Gramsci, *Quaderni del carcere*, critical edition, ed. Valentino Gerratana (Turin: Einaudi, 1975), henceforth cited as QC 3:17, pp. 1927-29.

It is interesting and ironic that on this point a thinker such as Leo Strauss would agree with both Croce and Gramsci; see Strauss, *Thoughts on Machiavelli* (Chicago: University of Chicago Press, 1978). See also the essay by Croce "Un detto di Machiavelli," in his *Conversazioni critiche*, vol. 4, pp. 17-20, where he remarks upon Machiavelli's famous statement in his letter to Vettori, "amo la patria più che l'anima." On Machiavelli and Croce, see Gramsci, QC 3:17, pp. 1927-29, and Gennaro Sasso, *Il pensiero politico di Niccolò Machiavelli* (Turin: ERI, 1964), pp. 47-61; on Croce's importance and position within the field of Machiavellian studies, see Sasso, pp. 53-56. See also Hans Baron, "Machiavelli: the Republican Citizen and the Author of 'The Prince,' " *English Historical Review* 76 (1961), pp. 207-53, in which Baron argues against Croce's interpretation of Machiavelli. See also Felice Alderisio's "Ripresa machiavelliana. Considerazioni critiche sulle idee di A. Gramsci, di B. Croce e di L. Russo intorno a Machiavelli," *Annali dell'Istituto universitario di Magistero di Salerno* 1 (1949-50), pp. 231-46, in which Alderisio polemicizes against Croce's reading of Machiavelli as the theorist who presents the notion of the political as *pura politica*, independent of *etica*.

For a discussion and analysis of Croce's thought and its relation to his political philosophy, see Norberto Bobbio *Politica e cultura* (Turin: Einaudi, 1955), chapters 7 and 13, Giovanni Sartori, *Stato e politica nel pensiero di Benedetto Croce* (Naples: Morano, 1966), and David D. Roberts, *Benedetto Croce and the Uses of Historicism* (Berkeley: University of California Press, 1987), pp. 210-65, 267-315.

2. Francesco de Sanctis, *Storia della letteratura italiana*, ed. Benedetto Croce (Bari: Laterza, 1965), 2 vols. (hereafter SLI). See also his "La letteratura italiana nel secolo XIX," in *Opere*, ed. Niccolò Gallo (Milan: Ricciardi, 1961), pp. 1115-25. Gramsci relies heavily on de Sanctis, whose literary criticism and methods he believes are superior to and more historically and politically grounded than are those of Croce. See Gramsci, QC 2:6, p. 720, 3:17, pp. 1940-41, 3:23, pp. 2185-88, in which Gramsci calls for a "ritorno a de Sanctis," by which he means the development of a culture, a literature, and a language—and thus a politics—centered within the life and practice of the Italian people (see QC 2:11, pp. 1374-95).

Gramsci understands de Sanctis as a thinker and critic whose work could lead Italian intellectuals toward a new relation with the people, who himself worked to achieve a reform of the attitudes and the culture that established the intellectual/*semplici* relation into a frozen structure of domination and subordination. The "return to de Sanctis" is thus equivalent to a "struggle for a new culture, that is, for a new humanism, the critique of custom, of sentiments, **179** and of conceptions of the world" (QC 3:23, p. 2188).

See Giorgio Nardone, *Il pensiero di Gramsci* (Bari: De Donato, 1971), pp. 251-56, where it is stated that "Gramsci finds in de Sanctis |confirmation| of his own notion of culture . . . |where| culture means a 'conception of life that is at once coherent, integrated, and disseminated throughout the nation.' To him such a total and complete dissemination includes within itself the unity of theory and practice. . . . |a philosophy is transformed into culture| when it has generated an ethic, a way of life." On the relation between culture and people, see de Sanctis, "La scuola democratica," in *Opere*, pp. 1115-25. See also Giancarlo Bergami, *Il giovane Gramsci e il marxismo 1911-1918* (Milan: Feltrinelli, 1977), pp. 55-56, 63-69.

3. De Sanctis, SLI, vol. 2, pp. 60-68; quotation on p. 63. The notion of disharmony in de Sanctis, where it is viewed as the political and cultural condition that is equivalent to the disintegration of the old order and of the traditional conception of the world, parallels Gramsci's critique of the Crocean "fracture" or "break" (*frattura*) between thought and action, culture and politics, and between language and life. In both, the antinomies are product and herald of the crisis within the established order.

4. Ibid., p. 63.

5. De Sanctis, SLI, vol. 1, p. 420. See Gramsci, QC 2:3, pp. 1129-30.

6. De Sanctis, SLI, vol. 1, p. 421.

7. Ibid., p. 420.

8. Ibid. See Saveria Chemotti, *Umanesimo, Rinascimento, Machiavelli nella critica gramsciana* (Rome: Bulzoni, 1975), pp. 94, 107. And note Croce's critique of Gramsci's "return" to a de Sanctian Machiavelli: "There is nothing new in Gramsci's argument |concerning the interpretation of Machiavelli|. But he has diminished the great idea of Machiavelli and Vico because he makes them, in a way worse than the mere denial of morality, basely conceptualize it as dependent upon a social class" ("Un giuoco che ormai dura troppo," in *Terze pagine sparse*, p. 253). See also Raymond Aron, "Machiavel et Marx," in *Machiavelli nel V centenario della nascita* (Bologna: Boni, 1973), pp. 11-30, especially pp. 27-28.

9. Gramsci, QC 2:6, p. 761. Gramsci envisions de Sanctian criticism and thought as a fertile seed that contains within itself the potential to develop into a national-popular culture and a national-popular reform. See Gramsci, QC 3:23, pp. 2187-88; QC 3:23, pp. 2185-86; and de Sanctis, "La scuola democratica," in *Opere*, pp. 1115-25, as well as his "Machiavelli Conferenze," in *Saggi critici*, ed. Luigi Russo (Bari: Laterza, 1965), vol. 2, pp. 309-38.

10. De Sanctis, "Machiavelli Conferenze," in *Saggi critici*, p. 324.

11. Gramsci, QC 3:13, p. 1572.

12. See Eric Cochrane, "Machiavelli: 1940-1960," *The Journal of Modern History* 33 (1961), pp. 113-36. Cochrane presents a discussion of the origins and the widespread acceptance of the interpretation that Machiavelli is the discoverer and elaborator of the now-famous formula "the autonomy of politics." Cochrane is correct when he says that Croce is the most influential and original source of the interpretation that Machiavelli's fundamental purpose was to present a political science centered on the autonomy of politics. Thus, for example, Chabod and Russo, as well as Gramsci (not to mention Wolin) are indebted, though in different ways and for different purposes, to Croce on this point. See Federico Chabod, *Machiavelli and the Renaissance* (New York: Harper Torchbooks, 1965), as well as Chabod's *Scritti su Machiavelli* (Turin: Einaudi, 1964); Luigi Russo, *Machiavelli* (Bari: Laterza, 1975); and Sheldon S. Wolin, *Politics and Vision: Continuity and Innovation in Western Political Thought* (Boston: Little, Brown and Company, 1960). See also Sasso, *Il pensiero politico di Niccolò Machiavelli*; and Felix Gilbert, "Machiavelli in modern historical scholarship," in *Machiavelli nel V centenario della nascita*, pp. 157-71.

For an interpretation of politics as human activity, as action, and Machiavelli as an "impassioned" theorist of political action—"self-conscious, purposeful motion"—(a notion quite

180 similar to Gramsci's), as well as the notion of politics as an autonomous form of human activity, see Neal Wood, "Machiavelli's Humanism of Action," in *The Political Calculus: Essays on Machiavelli's Philosophy*, ed. Anthony Parel (Toronto: University of Toronto Press, 1972), pp. 31-57, especially pp. 34-40, 43-57. The term "humanism of action" recalls Gramsci's "return" to de Sanctis, and his notion that philosophy = history = politics, such that *politica = storia in atto + filosofia in atto = riforma morale e intellettuale = egemonia.*

For Marxism and humanism, see Norberto Bobbio's introduction to R. Mondolfo, *Umanesimo di Marx: studi filosofici, 1908-1966* (Turin: Einaudi, 1968), p. xlv, where Bobbio writes: "In the various couplets of opposing elements—economic moment and ethico-political moment, objective moment-subjective moment, necessity-liberty—the second element is always the primary moment." And see Sir Isaiah Berlin, "The Originality of Machiavelli," in *Against the Current: Essays in the History of Ideas*, ed. and with a bibliography by Henry Hardy, intro. Roger Hausheer (Harmondsworth: Penguin Books, 1982).

For a Bolshevik (or Stalinist) interpretation, see Kamenev's introduction to the Russian edition (Moscow, 1934) of Machiavelli's *The Prince*, in which he sees Machiavelli as a "publicist" who analyzes the "mechanism of the struggle for power" during the Renaissance. In Kamenev, Machiavelli becomes a "sociologist" who brilliantly analyzes the "sociological" *bellum omnium contra omnes* before the creation of a "powerful, national, and basically bourgeois" Italian state. Machiavelli has an almost "dialectical" understanding of power structures and power relations, such that his thought is free from metaphysical and theological impedimenta. Kamenev notes that Machiavelli may be seen as a forerunner of Marx, Engels, Lenin, and Stalin. See L. B. Kamenev, "Preface to Machiavelli," *New Left Review* 15 (May-June 1962), pp. 39-42. Compare this to Gramsci, QC 3:13, pp. 1577-78, 3:20, pp. 1600-1601; and to Benedetto Croce, *Historical Materialism and the Economics of Karl Marx*, trans. C. M. Meredith, intro. A. D. Lindsay (New York: Russell and Russell, 1966), pp. 110, 118.

Note also Karl Marx and Frederick Engels, *Selected Correspondence*, trans. I. Lasker, ed. S. Ryazanskaya (Moscow, 1965), letter no. 37, Marx to Engels, 25 September 1857, p. 98, in which Marx recognizes Machiavelli as the precursor of a modern politics and a modern view of life, and sees his work as a secular humanism.

For an excellent and sharp analysis of Marx and Machiavelli, see Sami Naïr, *Machiavel et Marx: fétichisme du pouvoir et passion du social* (Paris: Presses Universitaires de France, 1984), pp. 20-23, 56-57, 99-100.

13. Croce, *Etica e politica*, henceforth cited as EP, p. 251, and *Terze pagine sparse*, vol. 2, p. 253. Contrast this to de Sanctis, SLI, vol. 2, p. 74. See also Croce's *Storia dell'età barocca in Italia*, p. 80, where, referring to Machiavelli's status during the Counter-Reformation, Croce says: "but though Machiavelli and reason of state were condemned, there yet remained [the doctrine of] Machiavellianism, that is, a scheme of considerations and a body of precepts without which one could not manage, because they are dictated by the necessary nature of things and [thus] conform to a universal practicality."

On machiavellianism and anti-Machiavellianism, see Gramsci, QC 3:13, pp. 1572-75, 1598, 1617-18, 3:14, pp. 1689-91.

See also Anthony Parel's essay, "Introduction: Machiavelli's Method and His Interpreters," in *The Political Calculus*, pp. 3-32; Giuliano Procacci, *Studi sulla fortuna del Machiavelli* (Rome: Istituto storico italiano, 1965); and Chabod, *Scritti su Machiavelli*, pp. 108-35.

The most well known work on Machiavelli as the founder of *Staatsräson* and *Realpolitik* is Friedrich Meinecke, *Machiavellism: The Doctrine of Raison d'Etat and Its Place in Modern History*, trans. Douglas Scott (New York: Praeger, 1965), an interpretation that manages to be both Hegelian and Crocean, and that combines elements of German romanticism and Italian realism. For a discussion of Croce and Meinecke, see Gennaro Sasso, *Niccolò Machiavelli: storia del suo pensiero*

(Napoli: Nella sede dell'Istituto, 1958), as well as Sasso's *Il pensiero politico di Niccolò Machiavelli*, **181**
pp. 47-61.
On Croce, Gramsci, and the autonomy of politics, see Maurice A. Finocchiaro, *Gramsci and the History of Dialectical Thought* (Cambridge: Cambridge University Press, 1988), pp. 133-40.
14. De Sanctis, SLI, vol. 2, pp. 62, 68. See Eugenio Garin, *La cultura italiana tra '800 e '900* (Bari: Laterza, 1963), pp. 175-209, for a discussion of de Sanctis and Croce in relation to Machiavelli. See also Nardone, *Il pensiero di Gramsci*, pp. 255-58. On de Sanctis and Machiavelli, see Giuliano Procacci, *Studi sulla fortuna del Machiavelli*, pp. 442-47.
15. Croce, EP, p. 251.
16. De Sanctis, SLI, vol. 2, p. 76.
17. A. R. Buzzi, *La teoria politica di Gramsci* (Florence: La Nuova Italia, 1973), pp. 116-20. In addition, see H. Stuart Hughes, *Consciousness and Society: The Reorientation of European Social Thought 1890-1930* (New York: Vintage Books, 1961), pp. 206-29.
18. Croce, EP, p. 253. Croce here refers to Machiavelli's *The Prince*, chapter 12.
19. Ibid., "Politica in nuce," pp. 213-49. For the classic statement on the dualism of the modern state, see Karl Marx, "On the Jewish Question," in *Karl Marx: Early Writings*, ed. T. B. Bottomore (New York: McGraw-Hill, 1964), pp. 1-40, especially pp. 13-15, 26-31.
20. Croce, *Historical Materialism*, p. 110 n. 1. See also A. D. Lindsay's introduction to this edition, pp. xiv-xvi; and "Politica in nuce," in *Etica e politica*.
21. Gramsci, QC 2:10, pp. 1213, 1352-53. By "Giolittian" is meant a politics whose techniques and methods (*trasformismo*) are directed toward the maintenance and preservation of a preexisting order or balance of sociopolitical forces, within which the political performs the stabilizing and integrating functions necessary to maintain the break or *frattura* between the *colti* and the *semplici*, the intellectuals and the people. On Giolitti and Croce, see QC 2:6, pp. 779-80, 2:8, pp. 997-98. See also William Salomone, *Italy in the Giolittian Age* (Philadelphia: University of Philadelphia Press, 1960), pp. 14, 16-17, 107-13, and the chapter "The Great Debate on the Giolittian Era," pp. 133-53; and James Edward Miller, *From Elite to Mass Politics: Italian Socialism in the Giolittian Era 1900-1914* (Kent, Ohio: Kent State University Press, 1990), pp. 30-53.
22. Croce, EP, pp. 215-18, 241-45. See Guido de Ruggiero, *The History of European Liberalism*, trans. R. G. Collingwood (Boston: Beacon Press, 1967), pp. 347-69.
23. Croce, EP, p. 182.
24. Ibid., p. 181.
25. Ibid. See also Croce's *Materialismo storico ed economia marxistica* (Bari: Laterza, 1951), where he says that Marx brought him back "to the best traditions of Italian political *science*, thanks to the firm assertion of the principle of force, of struggle, of power, and satirical and caustic opposition to the anti-historical and democratic insipidities of natural law doctrine—to the so-called ideals of 1789" (pp. xii-xiii; Croce's italics). See Hegel on Machiavelli, in Georg Lukács, *The Young Hegel: Studies in the Relations between Dialectics and Economics*, trans. Rodney Livingstone (Cambridge: MIT Press, 1976), pp. 303-5, 307-10, where Lukács refers to Hegel's *The German Constitution*. See also G. W. F. Hegel, *The Philosophy of History*, trans. T. M. Knox (Oxford: Oxford University Press, 1960), and his *Political Writings*, trans. T. M. Knox (Oxford: Oxford University Press, 1964), *The German Constitution*, pp. 217-23, especially, pp. 220-21; Procacci, *Studi sulla fortuna del Machiavelli*, pp. 393-94, for Hegel and Machiavelli; Aron, "Machiavel et Marx," in *Machiavelli nel V centenario della nascita*, pp. 16-17, 19-20.
26. Croce, *Historical Materialism*, p. 118, in which Croce states, "I am surprised that no one has thought of calling him |Marx| 'the most notable *successor* of the Italian Niccolò Machiavelli'; a Machiavelli of the labour movement" (Croce's italics). See also Croce, *Filosofia e storiografia* (Bari: Laterza, 1949), p. 277, in which he notes: "Ammirai la sua |Marx's| genialità politica di rivoluzionario e lo salutai col nome di 'Machiavelli del proletariato', quasi parallelo di quel Machiavelli che fu consigliere ed esortatore del principato a prò dell'unità e dell'in-

182 dipendenza italiana." This is found in English in *Philosophy, Poetry, History: An Anthology of Essays*, trans. with an introduction by Cecil Sprigge (London: Oxford University Press, 1966): "I admired his political gifts as a revolutionary and saluted him by the appellation 'Machiavelli of the proletariat,' implying a parallelism with Machiavelli the counsellor and stimulator of the princes in the cause of the unity and independence of Italy" (p. 626). Croce's parallel between Machiavelli and Marx is cited by Gramsci, QC 2:10, p. 1315. In addition, see Croce, *Filosofia, poesia, storia* (Milan: Ricciardi, n.d.), p. 556; and cf. note 25. On the relation between Machiavelli and Marx as posited by Croce, see Eugenio Garin, "Gramsci nella cultura italiana," in *Studi gramsciani*, Proceedings of a conference held in Rome 11-13 January 1958, Istituto Gramsci (Rome: Riuniti, 1973), pp. 413 n. 3, 414.

See also Felice Alderisio, "Ripresa machiavelliana," in *Annali dell'Istituto Universitario di Magistero di Salerno* I, pp. 231-46; Nicola Matteucci, *Antonio Gramsci e la filosofia della prassi* (Milan: Giuffrè, 1951), p. 58; and Buzzi, *La teoria politica*, pp. 152-53.

27. Gramsci, QC 3:13, 1568-70, 1577-78; and QC 2:10, p. 1315, 2:11, p. 1480.

28. Croce, EP, pp. 250-52; his *Conversazioni critiche*, vol. 4, pp. 14-17; and his "Il problema della politica e il machiavellismo," in *Filosofia della pratica. Economica ed etica* (Bari: Laterza, 1957). See also Russo, *Machiavelli*, and Russo's notes and commentary to his edition of Machiavelli's *Il Principe e pagine dei discorsi e delle I storie*, ed. Luigi Russo (Florence: Sansoni, n.d.). See also Chabod's *Machiavelli and the Renaissance*, Neal Wood's introduction to Machiavelli's *Art of War*, trans. Ellis Farnesworth (Indianapolis: Bobbs-Merrill, 1978), de Sanctis's "Machiavelli Conferenze," in *Saggi critici*, and Giuseppe Saitta, *Il pensiero italiano nell'Umanesimo e nel Rinascimento* (Florence: Sansoni, 1961), vol. 3, pp. 376-78.

29. Croce, EP, p. 254.

30. See Saitta, *Il pensiero italiano*, pp. 375-81; de Sanctis, SLI, vol. 2, pp. 58-112; and Gramsci's critique of Russo on this point, in QC 3:5, pp. 1563-64, 3:13, p. 1578. See also Buzzi, *La teoria politica*, pp. 154-56.

31. Croce, EP, p. 182.

32. See especially "Politica in nuce" and "Storia economica-politica e storia etica-politica," in EP, pp. 213-49, 273-83, respectively.

33. Croce, EP, p. 170.

34. See Croce, EP, pp. 250-51, and especially pp. 207-10. In addition, see Croce's "Why we cannot help calling ourselves Christian" and "The Identity of Philosophy and Moral Life," in *My Philosophy: Essays on the Moral and Political Problems of Our Time*, selected by R. Klibansky, trans. E. F. Carritt (New York: Collier Books, 1962), pp. 38-48, 240-46, respectively. For an excellent analysis of Augustinian social and political thought, see Herbert A. Deane, *The Political and Social Ideas of St. Augustine* (New York: Columbia University Press, 1963).

35. Croce, *Historical Materialism*, pp. 110-13. For Gramsci on Kant, see QC 2:11, pp. 1472-73, 1484-85; QC 3:13, pp. 1561-62; QC, 3:16, pp. 1876-77; and Garin, *La cultura italiana tra '800 e '900*, pp. 408-9. On Kant, see Herbert Marcuse, *Studies in Critical Philosophy* (Boston: Beacon Press, 1972), pp. 79-94. See also Sidney Hook, *From Hegel to Marx: Studies in the Intellectual Development of Karl Marx* (Ann Arbor: University of Michigan Press, 1968), pp. 17-76, 308-12.

36. Gramsci, QC 2:10, pp. 1221-24, 1326-27; and *Lettere dal carcere*, ed. Sergio Caprioglio and Elsa Fubini (Turin: Einaudi, 1965), p. 186. See also Emilio Agazzi, "Filosofia della prassi e filosofia dello spirito, in *La città futura: Saggi sulla figura e sul pensiero di Antonio Gramsci*, ed. Alberto Caracciolo and Gianni Scalia (Milan: Feltrinelli, 1976), pp. 110-12; Croce, EP, p. 220; Gramsci, QC 2:10, pp. 1240-42.

37. Croce, EP, pp. 182-83; see also Gramsci, QC 2:10, pp. 1217-18, 1231.

38. Agazzi, "Filosofia della prassi," in *La città futura*, pp. 103-4. See Gramsci, QC 2:6, pp. 779-80, 782-83, 3:15, pp. 1790-91; QC 2:10, pp. 1219-20, 1227-32, 1310-11; *Lettere dal carcere*, p. 193; and QC 3:12, pp. 1515-16.

39. Croce, EP, p. 180.

40. See, for example, Croce's *Storia dell'età barocca in Italia*; and Gramsci, QC 2:10, pp. 1220-22, 1324-25.

41. Gramsci, QC 2:10, pp. 1220-22.

42. See Benedetto Croce, *History as the Story of Liberty*, trans. Sylvia Sprigge (Chicago: Gateway Editions, 1970), pp. 59-62, especially pp. 55-58. See also H. Stuart Hughes, *Consciousness and Society*, pp. 217-29.

43. Croce, EP, p. 175.

44. Ibid.

45. See Serge Hughes, *The Fall and Rise of Modern Italy* (New York: Minerva Press, 1968), part 1, "Sand Castle 1890-1925"; de Ruggiero, *History of European Liberalism*, pp. 298-343; and Roberts, *Benedetto Croce and the Uses of Historicism*, pp. 210-65.

46. Croce, EP, pp. 228-29.

47. Ibid., p. 175.

48. Ibid., p. 230.

49. Croce, *My Philosophy*, p. 93.

50. Croce, EP, pp. 171-72.

51. See Croce's essay on "*Religiosità*," where it becomes quite clear that the modern form of "religion"—that is, the philosophy of liberty and of the ethico-political of the Spirit as propounded by Croce—is antithetical to the "*volgo*": "the masses . . . live in a condition of disharmony. With them thought and desire, wanting and doing, contradict each other." But "la religiosità"—now transformed into the conscious, "demythologized," and demystified "religion of liberty"—"in quanto armonia, è aristocrazia" (EP, p. 208). Thus the popular masses are defined by an intrinsic disharmony between what they will and what they do, such that the *frattura* between thought and action is embodied in the irrationality of the mass as a purely emotional and reactive entity. On the other hand, harmony exists within the level of the *colti* and those who know how to rule, who together possess the culture and the knowledge to relate *vagheggiare* to *fare*, and thus understand the relation between means and ends, thinking and doing, willing and acting. Contrast Croce's *disarmonia* to de Sanctis's (SLI, vol. 1, pp. 63-66).

52. See Sir Ernest Barker, *The Political Thought of Plato and Aristotle* (New York: Dover, 1949), and T. A. Sinclair, *A History of Greek Political Thought* (Cleveland: Meridien Books, 1968).

53. Croce, *My Philosophy*, pp. 91-92; contrast this to Gramsci, QC 2:11, pp. 1504-5. See also H. S. Hughes, *Consciousness and Society*, pp. 249-50; Rita Medici, *La Metafora Machiavelli: Mosca Pareto Michels Gramsci* (Modena: Mucchi Editore, 1990), pp. 7-20.

54. See Barker, *Political Thought of Plato and Aristotle*; and Sinclair, *History of Greek Political Thought*; and Croce, EP, the essay on "*Religiosità*."

55. On the Hegelian notion of freedom, see Herbert Marcuse, *Reason and Revolution: Hegel and the Rise of Social Theory* (Boston: Beacon Press, 1968), pp. 184-94; Shlomo Avineri, *Hegel's Theory of the Modern State* (Cambridge: Cambridge University Press, 1974), pp. 179-84, 221-38; Marcuse, *Studies in Critical Philosophy*, pp. 95-110; and Lukács, *The Young Hegel*.

56. Croce, *My Philosophy*, p. 93.

57. The theorists of modern-day pluralism are noteworthy in this regard. See David M. Ricci, *Community Power and Democratic Theory: The Logic of Political Analysis* (New York: Random House, 1971); Gaetano Mosca, *The Ruling Class*, ed. and rev. A. Livingston, trans. Hannah D. Kahn (New York: McGraw-Hill, 1939); Medici, *La Metafora Machiavelli*, chapter 1.

58. Croce, *Il carattere della filosofia moderna* (Bari: Laterza, 1945), pp. 117-18.

59. Croce, *My Philosophy*, p. 93.

60. Mosca, *Ruling Class*, pp. 409-29. See also H. Stuart Hughes, *Consciousness and Society*, pp. 249-77.

61. See Robert A. Dahl, "A Critique of the Ruling Elite Model," *American Political Science Review* 52 (1958), pp. 369-463; and Joseph A. Schumpeter, *Capitalism, Socialism and Democracy* (New York: Harper, 1942). T. B. Bottomore, *Elites and Society* (London: Watt, 1964), provides a good discussion of pluralism and elitism. See also Croce, *My Philosophy*, p. 93, and EP, pp. 302-15; and Federico Chabod, "Croce storico," in *Lezioni di metodo storico: con saggi su Egidi, Croce, Meinecke,* ed. Luigi Firpo (Bari: Laterza, 1969), pp. 213-14.

62. Gramsci, QC 2:11, pp. 1504-5.

63. Gramsci, QC 3:13, pp. 1599-1600.

64. Ibid., p. 1599; and QC 2:10, p. 1242.

65. Gramsci, QC 3:13, p. 1599.

66. Ibid., pp. 1617-18; QC 3:17, p. 1928.

67. Gramsci, QC 3:13, pp. 1599-1600.

68. Ibid.

69. See Russo, *Machiavelli,* and Chabod, *Machiavelli and the Renaissance.*

70. Gramsci, QC 3:13, pp. 1599-1600.

71. Ibid., p. 1561.

72. De Sanctis, SLI, vol. 1, pp. 419-20.

73. Croce, EP, p. 171.

74. Gramsci, QC 2:7, pp. 885-86, 2:11, pp. 1485-86.

75. Gramsci, QC 3:13, pp. 1617-18, 3:14, pp. 1689-91, 3:17, pp. 1927-28.

76. Gramsci, QC 2:10, pp. 1234-35, 1330-32, 1342, 2:11, pp. 1384-85.

77. Gramsci, QC 3:13, p. 1600. See Alastair B. Davidson, "Gramsci and Reading Machiavelli," *Science and Society* 37, 1 (Spring 1973), pp. 77, 79; and Alderisio, "Ripresa machiavelliana," in *Annali dell'Istituto universitario di Magistero di Salerno* 1, pp. 218-19, 223-30.

78. Gramsci, QC 2:11, pp. 1375-77, 1480.

79. Gramsci, QC 1:4, pp. 430-31.

5. Hegemony and *Virtù*:
Moral and Intellectual Reform in Gramsci and Machiavelli

1. Antonio Gramsci, *Quaderni del carcere,* critical edition, ed. Valentino Gerratana (Turin: Einaudi, 1975), henceforth cited as QC, 1:5, p. 657; and *Selections from the Prison Notebooks,* ed. and trans. Quintin Hoare and Geoffrey Nowell Smith (New York: International Publishers, 1973), p. 248. See also QC 2:10, pp. 1255-56, 1263, 1344-45, 2:11, pp. 1485-86; and A. R. Buzzi, *La teoria politica di Gramsci* (Florence: La Nuova Italia, 1973), pp. 167-69.

2. On Machiavelli's "intention," see Gramsci, QC 2:6, p. 724, 3:13, pp. 1563-64, 1572-73, 1599-1601, 3:14, pp. 1689-91, 3:15, pp. 1832-33.

For a traditionalist—that is, moral law and "medieval"—attempt to arrive at Machiavelli's intention, see Leo Strauss, *Thoughts on Machiavelli* (Chicago: University of Chicago Press, 1978). It is interesting that Strauss's antimodernist—that is, pre-Machiavellian—interpretation of Machiavelli, which is seen through a philosophical prism clearly fashioned in a Judeo-Christian conception of the world, arrives at a conclusion not dissimilar to that of de Sanctis and Gramsci—namely, that Machiavelli presents a politics whose aim is to transform the moral, intellectual, and cultural system of the established order. The significant difference, of course, is that Strauss on the one hand, and Gramsci and de Sanctis on the other, assign opposite values to Machiavelli's enterprise, such that the "morality" or "immorality" of Machiavelli depends upon the interpreter's attitude toward the popular masses. For an excellent discussion of this and other interpretations of Machiavelli, see Sir Isaiah Berlin, "The Originality of Machiavelli," in *Against the Current: Essays in the History of Ideas,* ed. and with a bibliography by Henry Hardy, intro. by Roger Hausheer (Harmondsworth: Penguin Books, 1982), pp. 25-79. In addition, see Sebastian de Grazia, *Machiavelli in Hell* (Princeton: Princeton University Press, **185** 1989), chapters 8, 9, 10.

3. Niccolò Machiavelli, *The Prince*, chapter 15, in *The Prince and the Discourses* (New York: Modern Library, 1950). For a discussion of Machiavelli's "predecessors," see Allan H. Gilbert, *Machiavelli's "Prince" and Its Forerunners: "The Prince" as a Typical Book de regimine principium* (Durham, N.C.: Duke University Press, 1938). Gilbert discusses the relation of *The Prince* to other works whose subject is princely rule, especially the literature of the *speculum principii* type. He says that Machiavelli follows the tradition of previous authors who had written on princeship, and that these earlier works serve as a pattern or model for Machiavelli.

See also Felix Gilbert, "The Humanist Concept of the Prince and the 'Prince' of Machiavelli," *Journal of Modern History* 11 (1939), pp. 449-83, in which he analyzes the relation of *The Prince* to its predecessors and to the speculum tradition, but argues that although this literature may indeed have served as a pattern or guide, Machiavelli's real purpose is to satirize and attack a literature that idealizes rulers and princes. See also Quentin Skinner's important contribution, *The Foundations of Modern Political Thought* (Cambridge: Cambridge University Press, 1978), vol. 1, pp. 118-28, and his *Machiavelli* (New York: Hill and Wang, 1981), pp. 25-47.

4. Niccolò Machiavelli, *Discourses*, Book 1, chapter 58, in *The Prince and the Discourses*.

5. Benedetto Croce, "La questione del Machiavelli," in *Indagini su Hegel e schiarimenti filosofici* (Bari: Laterza, 1952), pp. 164-76; and "Moralità del Machiavelli," in *Nuove pagine sparse* (Naples: Ricciardi, 1949), vol. 1. See also Francesco Ercole, *La politica di Machiavelli* (Rome: A. R. E., 1926), in which the distinction between ethics and politics is denied, and in which an interpretation of Machiavelli as a theorist of the "ethical state" is put forward. On this question, both Federico Chabod, *Machiavelli and the Renaissance* (New York: Harper Torchbooks, 1965), and Luigi Russo, *Machiavelli* (Bari: Laterza, 1975), follow Croce.

6. Gramsci, QC 1:2, pp. 215-16, 1:5, pp. 555-56, 3:13, pp. 1573-75, 1598, 1617-18, 3:14, pp. 1689-91; QC 2:9, pp. 1129-30, 3:15, p. 1919; and QC 2:9, pp. 1301-2. See also Skinner, *Foundations*, vol. 1, pp. 248-54.

7. See Strauss, *Thoughts on Machiavelli*, and Harry C. Mansfield, Jr., "Introduction" to his translation of Machiavelli's *The Prince* (Chicago: University of Chicago Press, 1985), pp. vii-xxiv. And Croce, "Machiavelli e Vico," in *Etica e politica* (Bari: Laterza, 1931).

Croce emphasizes the amorality of Machiavelli, and sees his special contribution to thought as being the formulation of a truly scientific knowledge of politics. On the other hand, Strauss and his school stress the immorality of Machiavelli; they understand Machiavelli as one who intends to overthrow the traditional moral law that forms the basis (according to Strauss) of the classical and medieval conceptions of the world. In the first case, Machiavelli is a thinker of the Crocean type, aloof and "Olympian" in his orientation toward *le cose del mondo*; in the second case, he is a thinker who presents a teaching that negates the established order of the moral universe (the "teacher of evil"). What is scientific neutrality and amorality to Croce is passionate and committed immorality to Strauss, an opposition that is translated in Gramsci into a reading of Machiavelli as the thinker who dissolves traditional categories of morality and immorality (and thus of amorality as well), and who attempts to develop new criteria for a new moral interpretation of the world, that is, for a redefinition of moral and intellectual categories.

8. For a discussion of the moral question in Machiavelli, see Gennaro Sasso, *Niccolò Machiavelli: storia del suo pensiero* (Naples: Nella sede dell'Istituto, 1958), pp. 290-303, and Russo, *Machiavelli*, "Prolegomeni a Machiavelli," pp. 11-87. See also J. H. Whitfield, *Machiavelli* (New York: Russell and Russell, 1965), pp. 114-17.

9. Croce, *Etica e politica*, Strauss, *Thoughts on Machiavelli*, Francesco de Sanctis, "Machiavelli Conferenze," in *Saggi critici*, ed. Luigi Russo (Bari: Laterza, 1965), vol. 2, pp. 329-38), and Russo, *Machiavelli*, pp. 38-46. See also Chabod, "The Prince: Myth and Reality," in *Machiavelli and*

186 *the Renaissance*, pp. 95-96, especially pp. 98-99, p. 99 n. 2 and pp. 104-9; Felix Gilbert, *Machiavelli and Guicciardini: Politics and History in Sixteenth Century Florence* (Princeton: Princeton University Press, 1965), pp. 239-40, 278-80; Sasso, *Niccolò Machiavelli*; Luigi Firpo, "Machiavelli politico," in *Machiavelli nel V centenario della nascita* (Bologna: Boni, 1973), pp. 113-36, especially pp. 114-19; and Raymond Aron, "Machiavel et Marx," in *Machiavelli nel V centenario della nascita*, pp. 11-30, especially pp. 16-20.

In a curious parallel of Strauss's position, Sami Naïr, in his *Machiavel et Marx: fétichisme du pouvoir et passion du social* (Paris: Presses Universitaires de France, 1984), sees Machiavelli as the "teacher of evil" and Machiavellian thought as asserting both the autonomy of politics (p. 56) and the necessity of a prince as an *"homme démonique"*: "In order to resolve the contradictory interests that are openly in conflict with each other, the prince must be a demonic man, à la Goethe, or he must be a Weberian prophet legislator. And the political method |*méthode du pouvoir*| employed can only be rational calculation and concrete analysis of the relation of forces" (p. 98).

10. See Francesco de Sanctis, *Storia della letteratura italiana*, ed. Benedetto Croce (Bari: Laterza, 1965), henceforth cited as SLI, vol. 2, the essay on Machiavelli. See Georg Lukács, *The Young Hegel: Studies in the Relations between Dialectics and Economics*, trans. Rodney Livingstone (Cambridge: MIT Press, 1976), for Hegel's use of the term "prose." Note, in addition, Labriola's use of "prose" in connection with the rise of communism: "The secret of history has become simplified. We have arrived at prose |*Siamo alla prosa*| . . . . And even communism has become prose, or rather it is now science" (Antonio Labriola, "In memoria del Manifesto dei comunisti," in *Scritti filosofici e politici*, ed. Franco Sbarberi |Turin: Einaudi, 1973|, vol. 2, p. 518). And see Gramsci, QC 2:10, pp. 1215-16, for the phrase "prosa scientifica italiana."

11. Gramsci, QC 3:16, pp. 1577-78; see also QC 2:8, pp. 990-91.

12. Gramsci, QC 3:16, p. 1578.

13. De Sanctis, SLI, vol. 2; Chabod, "The Prince: Myth and Reality," in *Machiavelli and the Renaissance*; and Felix Gilbert, *Machiavelli and Guicciardini*, pp. 195-200. See also Giuseppe Saitta, *Il pensiero italiano nell'Umanesimo e nel Rinascimento*, vol. 3, pp. 411-13; Gramsci, QC 2:10, pp. 1880-81; QC 2:6, p. 756.

14. Gramsci, QC 3:17, p. 1919; QC 2:6, p. 809; and QC 1:3, p. 401, 2:6, p. 809. See also Saitta, *Il pensiero italiano*, vol. 3, pp. 312-18.

Galileo's attempt to retranslate the scriptural texts by establishing two distinct, but equal, levels of discourse was doomed to failure because, as Saitta points outs, the separation of *Scrittura* from *Scienza* was equivalent to the subordination of the former to the latter: the authority of the scriptural texts was questioned, for now these texts would be perceived as human texts, as the products of a human intelligence and a human purpose, and, as such, necessarily and inherently subject to the critical scrutiny of human reason.

On this point, one should compare Machiavelli's apparent separation of sacred history from secular history (and thus sacred text from secular text) in *The Prince*, chapters 6 and 11—an opposition that is eventually resolved into the supremacy and primacy of secular action, of profane history over sacred history, and profane texts over sacred texts; as Machiavelli points out, the deeds of Romulus, Cyrus, and Theseus, in founding their respective states, are no different in kind or in method than the deeds of Moses in founding the Hebrew people; that is, Machiavelli's new knowledge destroys the integrity of the distinction between sacred and secular, and recognizes all human activity and thought as products of human beings engaged within the *verità effettuale*.

On Galileo, see Eugenio Garin, *Science and Civic Life in the Italian Renaissance*, trans. Peter Munz (New York: Anchor Books, 1969), pp. 113-16. See also Leonardo Olschki, *Machiavelli the Scientist* (Berkeley: The Gillick Press, 1945), pp. 22-33, in which Olschki compares Machiavelli's new knowledge to Galileo's new science.

15. Machiavelli, *Discourses*, dedication; and *The Prince*, dedication.
16. Machiavelli, *Discourses*, Book 2, introduction.
17. Gramsci, QC 2:10, pp. 1294-96, 2:11, 1455-57. On Galileo's "primary objects," see A. R. Hall, *The Scientific Revolution 1500-1800: The Formation of the Modern Scientific Attitude* (Boston: Beacon Press, 1972), pp. 168-85. In addition, see Garin, *Science and Civic Life*, pp. 117-44.

It seems that there is a long tradition in the attempt to establish a parallel between the natural science of Galileo and the political science of Machiavelli, one that extends from Cassirer as far back as Gioberti in the early nineteenth century. See Firpo, "Machiavelli politico," in *Machiavelli nel V centenario della nascita*, pp. 118-19.

18. Machiavelli, *Discourses*, Book 2, introduction.
19. Machiavelli, *The Prince*, chapter 15; *Discourses*, Book 2, introduction.
20. Machiavelli, *Discourses*, Book 2, chapter 2. See Gramsci, QC 3:13, pp. 1572-73.
21. Croce, "Machiavelli e Vico," in *Etica e politica*; de Sanctis, SLI, pp. 105-9; Chabod, *Machiavelli and the Renaissance*, pp. 109-15; and Gramsci, QC 2:6, pp. 760-61. See also de Sanctis, "L'uomo del Guicciardini," in *Saggi critici*, vol. 3, pp. 1-23.
22. Gramsci, QC 3:17, pp. 1913-14.
23. On *virtù* see John Plamenatz, "In Search of Machiavellian Virtù," in *The Political Calculus: Essays on Machiavelli's Philosophy*, ed. Anthony Parel (Toronto: University of Toronto Press, 1972), pp. 157-78; Skinner, *Foundations*, pp. 129, 138, and *Machiavelli*, pp. 34-38; de Sanctis, "L'uomo del Guicciardini," in *Saggi critici*, vol. 3, pp. 1-23; J. G. A. Pocock, *The Machiavellian Moment: Florentine Political Thought and the Atlantic Republican Tradition* (Princeton: Princeton University Press, 1975), part 1; and Felix Gilbert, *Machiavelli and Guicciardini*, pp. 178-192; Friedrich Meinecke, *Machiavellism: The Doctrine of Raison d'Etat and Its Place in Modern History*, trans. Douglas Scott (New York: Praeger, 1965), pp. 25-41, who sees *virtù* as the key to understanding Machiavelli; J. H. Whitfield, *Machiavelli*, especially "The Anatomy of Virtù," pp. 93-98; and Pasquale Villari's famous biography of Machiavelli, *The Life and Times of Niccolò Machiavelli*, trans. Linda Villari (London: T. F. Unwin, 1892), in which he contrasts pagan *virtù* against Christian *bontà*. See also Russo, "Prolegomeni a Machiavelli" and "Postille a Machiavelli," in *Machiavelli*, pp. 11-87 and 167-75, respectively; and Naïr, *Machiavel et Marx*, pp. 58-69, especially pp. 58-63.
24. See Felix Gilbert's analysis of the relative merits of Machiavelli's and Guicciardini's historiographical methods, in *Machiavelli and Guicciardini*, pp. 236-40, 296-301. Guicciardini's historiography "approached the modern," that is, his method is more "scientific," "objective," and empirical (more respectful of the "facts" and "events" of history) than Machiavelli's. Gilbert makes the important point—noted by Gramsci—that Machiavelli's project and intention led him to subordinate history to politics, whereas, on the other hand, Guicciardini's political position (both theoretical and practical), and his belief that *virtù* was powerless against *fortuna*, resulted in a body of work that subordinated politics to history, and led Guicciardini and his historical method to the passive study and contemplation of events. See also pp. 243-44 and 245-46, as well as Franco Gaeta, "Machiavelli storico," in *Machiavelli nel V centenario della nascita*, pp. 141-42.
25. Felxi Gilbert, *Machiavelli and Guicciardini*, pp. 241-42; and Skinner, *Foundations*, vol. 1, pp. 186-87.
26. Gramsci, QC 2:10, p. 1354.
27. Francesco Guicciardini, "Considerazioni intorno ai Discorsi del Machiavelli," in *Scritti politici e Ricordi*, ed. R. Palmarocchi (Bari: Laterza, 1932). Machiavelli, writes Guicciardini, is too "absolute" in his statements, and analyzes "too absolutely" ("Considerazioni," p. 8). And, "How they deceive themselves who always praise the Romans! One would need to have a city similar to theirs, with the same experiences under the same circumstances, and then govern it according to their example—a situation so unlike present conditions that it would be like

188   wanting a donkey to race like a horse" (Ricordo 110, in Guicciardini, *Ricordi*, critical edition, ed. Raffaele Spongano [Florence: Sansoni, 1951], p. 121).

28. Gramsci, QC 1:6, pp. 640-53; and QC 2:7, pp. 904-7. See also Chabod, *Machiavelli and the Renaissance*, the chapter entitled "The Concept of the Renaissance"; Eugenio Garin, *Italian Humanism: Philosophy and Civic Life in the Renaissance*, trans. Peter Munz (New York: Harper and Row, 1965); and Hans Baron, *From Petrarch to Leonardo Bruni: Studies in Humanistic and Political Literature* (Chicago: University of Chicago Press, 1961).

29. Guicciardini, "Considerazioni," pp. 11-12. And, "Discussing things in an absolute and indiscriminate manner, and, so to speak, according to a general rule, is a great error. The manifold variety of circumstances renders almost all events uniquely distinctive and exceptional, and thus cannot be captured or fixed by one general standard. And these distinctions and exceptions cannot be found written in books, but can only be taught by discretion" (Ricordo 6, in *Ricordi*, p. 11).

Thus Guicciardini posits a fundamental distinction between theoretical discourse and practical action, between a theoretical construction of worldly events that artificially inserts them within a rational and coherent pattern, and the events themselves, which are resistant to the coherence and ordered discipline imposed upon them by *regola*. As Guicciardini writes, "How different practice is from theory." ("Quanto è diversa la pratica dalla teorica!" [Ricordo 35, in *Ricordi*, p. 42]), an antinomy—a *disarmonia* in de Sanctis's words—that cannot be overcome, and that must therefore be accepted in order to devise methods by which one will be able, by the use of prudence and *discrezione*, to employ it toward the advantage of one's *particulare*. See de Sanctis, "L'uomo del Guicciardini," in *Saggi critici*, vol. 3, pp. 1-23; Felix Gilbert, *Machiavelli and Guicciardini*, pp. 272-82; Chabod, "The Concept of the Renaissance," in *Machiavelli and the Renaissance*, pp. 195-97; and Saitta's chapter on Guicciardini in *Il pensiero italiano*, vol. 3, pp. 415-49.

See also Gramsci, QC 3:14, pp. 1688-89, where he notes Bandello's criticism of Machiavelli's fascination with Roman military organization and tactics.

One should also note Martin Fleisher's comments on Machiavelli and Guicciardini in his "A Passion for Politics: The Vital Core of the World of Machiavelli," in *Machiavelli and the Nature of Political Thought*, ed. Martin Fleisher (New York: Atheneum, 1972): "To accept Guicciardini's position is to deny the possibility of an art of politics since there are no general rules that may be taught. . . . Guicciardini's radical skepticism undermines the possibility of learning from the past—not, of course, in every area, but certainly in politics" (p. 144). If this is correct, as I believe it is, then such a skepticism would also deny the possibility of any form of political action directed toward the transformation of the present; for, if we relate Fleisher's observation to Gramsci's statement that "to interpret the past" is "to act in the present," then "interpreting the past" for Guicciardini is merely a form of historiographical activity—a kind of contemplation pursued through the prism of "detached" observation—that regards events from the isolated position of the *discrezione* of the observer's *particulare*. Such an orientation is quite different from that of Machiavelli, who, basing himself on *continua lezione* and *lunga pratica*, attempts to impose *regola* on worldly and temporal events in order to transform them. See Gramsci, QC 3:13, pp. 1577-78, 2:6, pp. 760-62; and Gaeta, "Machiavelli storico," in *Machiavelli nel V centenario della nascita*, pp. 140-43.

30. Gramsci, QC 2:10, p. 1242. The "crisis" of the Italian Renaissance, as Machiavelli saw it, was in part due to the *distacco* and the *frattura* between thought and action, culture and politics, that occurred in the later history of Florence. The political and the cultural had been united in the figures of great Italian humanists such as Leonardo Bruni, Salviati, Pomponazzi, and Coluccio Salutati—figures who excelled in both letters and political activity. Bruni and Salutati, leaders of the Florentine republic, may be seen as typical of the ideal *politicus*, who united philosophy and politics: they were concerned equally with culture and letters, as well

as with political freedom, civic obligation, and the affairs of their *patria*. These figures stand in marked opposition to figures such as Bracciolini and Scala, in whom the divorce between cultural activity and political activity becomes evident. As Garin points out, the break—the *frattura*—becomes complete with the rise of the Medici: Ficino and Poliziano are types directly opposed to those of Salutati and Bruni; the former are writers and thinkers who have retreated from politics, and who no longer see purpose and meaning through participation in public and political life. Indeed, it may be said that to Machiavelli this very *distacco* expressed the political degeneration and the civil corruption against which he polemicized. The absence of a *vivere politico*, the disintegration of the *vivere publico*, are together related by Machiavelli to the rise of a type of letters and culture that he believed contributed to the *ozio* (indolence) and the *corruttela* (corruption) of the times. See Machiavelli, *The Art of War*, trans. Ellis Farnesworth, intro. Neal Wood (Indianapolis: Bobbs-Merrill, 1978), Books 1 and 7.

See also Garin, *Science and Civic Life*, pp. 20-22, as well as his *Italian Humanism*, pp. 27-29, 38-46; Nicolai Rubinstein, "Machiavelli and the World of Florentine Politics," in *Studies on Machiavelli*, ed. Myron P. Gilmore (Florence: Sansoni, 1972), pp. 3-28; Hans Baron, *The Crisis of the Early Italian Renaissance: Civic Humanism and Republican Liberty in an Age of Classicism and Tyranny* (Princeton: Princeton University Press, 1955), pp. 104-20, 121-29, 315-31; and Jerrold Seigel, *Rhetoric and Philosophy in Renaissance Humanism* (Princeton: Princeton University Press, 1968), pp. 63-98, 99-136, 249-54.

In addition, see C. C. Bayley, *War and Society in Renaissance Florence: The "De Militia" of Leonardo Bruni* (Toronto: University of Toronto Press, 1961), where a comparison is made between Bruni and Machiavelli.

31. This question will be addressed in chapters 6 and 7.

32. Machiavelli, *The Prince*, chapter 25. On Machiavelli's *virtù*, see Whitfield, *Machiavelli*, pp. 93-98; Plamenatz, "In Search of Machiavellian Virtù," and Thomas Flanagan, "The Concept of *Fortuna* in Machiavelli," in Parel, ed., *Political Calculus*, pp. 157-77 and 127-56, respectively; and Pocock, *Machiavellian Moment*, pp. 161-282. See Fleisher, "A Passion for Politics," for a discussion of Machiavelli's language. See also Skinner, *Foundations*, vol. 1, pp. 33-34, 184-89; and Olschki, *Machiavelli the Scientist*, p. 38. Additional sources were listed in note 23.

33. Machiavelli, *Discourses*, Book 2, p. 1.

34. Machiavelli, *The Prince*, chapter 25. Machiavelli's discussion of *virtù* is somewhat similar to Marx's comments regarding the relation between human action and history: "Men make their own history but they do not make it just as they please; they do not make it under circumstances chosen by themselves, but under circumstances directly found, given and transmitted from the past. The tradition of all the dead generations weighs like a nightmare on the brain of the living" (*The Eighteenth Brumaire of Louis Bonaparte* [New York: International Publishers, 1963], p. 15).

35. See Skinner, *Machiavelli*, pp. 33-34; Fleisher, "A Passion for Politics," pp. 118-24; Neal Wood, "Machiavelli's Humanism of Action," in Parel, *Political Calculus*, pp. 33-57; and Emile Namer, "Machiavel et l'humanisme politique," in *Machiavelli nel V centenario della nascita*, pp. 175-89.

36. Gramsci, QC 2:10, pp. 1241-42.

37. Skinner, *Machiavelli*, pp. 35-39; Flanagan, "The Concept of Fortuna in Machiavelli," in Parel, *Political Calculus*, pp. 127-35; Chabod, *Machiavelli and the Renaissance*, p. 189; Olschki, *Machiavelli the Scientist*, pp. 37-38.

38. Gramsci, QC 2:11, p. 1480.

39. Gramsci, QC 3:13, p. 1577; and see QC 2:6, pp. 760-61, 781-82, 3:14, p. 1688, for Gramsci's use of *diplomazia*. The dichotomy *politica/diplomazia*, where the first term refers to transformative action, and the second to restorative and preservative activity, parallels the distinction *grande politica/piccola politica*. See QC 2:11, pp. 1415-16.

190

40. See Guicciardini, *Ricordi*: "To say 'people' is truly to say a mad animal, full of a thousand errors and confusions, without taste, pleasureless, and unstable" (Ricordo 140, p. 152). See Guicciardini, *Maxims and Reflections*, trans. Mario Domandi, intro. Nicolai Rubinstein (Philadelphia: University of Pennsylvania Press, 1972), pp. 76, 134, 140, 156.

In "Dal modo di ordinare il governo popolare," in *Dialogo e Discorsi del reggimento di Firenze*, ed. R. Palmarocchi (Bari: Laterza, 1932), Guicciardini observes: "Both experience and reason show that the people [*la moltitudine*] can never act as an autonomous agent [*non si regge mai per se medesima*], but because of its weakness is always dependent and subordinate" (p. 227). To Guicciardini the "moltitudine" is ignorant, and therefore does not possess the means necessary to recognize and to establish *libertà*. Thus the few who possess reason—*i savi, i boni, i nobili*—possess the knowledge and the will to establish a government—*un governo stretto*—based on *libertà* and on *ragione* (p. 227).

Moreover, Guicciardini says that "throughout history, in every well ordered republic it is always the case that the basis of rule is the *virtù* of the few. Glorious deeds and great endeavors are the work of the few because political leadership in a free state, and the management of important projects, require many varied and virtuous qualities [*moltissime parte e virtù*] that only come together within the few" (pp. 238-39).

See also Guicciardini's *Dialogo e Discorsi*, Book 2, p. 93, and Book 1, pp. 44-61. The *populo* is ignorant and irrational, and ignorance "blinds, confuses, and is intemperate and unruly" (Book 1, p. 46). The people "is coarse; it does not discern, nor does it weigh things subtly" (Book 1, p. 44). And finally, "This pertains specifically to a government based upon the rule of one or of the few, because only these have the time, the diligence, and the mind trained and attuned to the problems of government. When they recognize what needs to be done, they have the ability to take the necessary and rational measures—all of which is alien to a government of the people, because the many do not think and do not understand" and "the many . . . cannot reason" (Book 1, p. 61).

These statements should be compared to Croce's, in *My Philosophy: Essays on the Moral and Political Problems of Our Time*, selected by R. Klibansky, trans. E. F. Carritt (New York: Collier Books, 1962), and in *Etica e politica*. See also Machiavelli, *The Prince*, chapter 9, and the *Discourses*, Book 2, chapters 55, 58; and Fredi Chiappelli, "Machiavelli segretario," in *Machiavelli nel V centenario della nascita*, pp. 45-60, especially pp. 52-54.

41. Felix Gilbert, *Machiavelli and Guicciardini*, pp. 19-28, 48-57, 60-70, 73-76, 78-104.

42. See Guicciardini, *Maxims and Reflections*; Felix Gilbert, *Machiavelli and Guicciardini*, pp. 271-301; and Saitta, *Il pensiero italiano*, vol. 3, pp. 440-47.

43. Gramsci, QC 2:10, p. 1261; and QC 2:6, pp. 760-61. On the *particulare* of Guicciardini, see Saitta, *Il pensiero italiano*, vol. 3, pp. 426-34; Felix Gilbert, *Machiavelli and Guicciardini*, the chapter on Guicciardini; de Sanctis, "L'uomo del Guicciardini," in *Saggi critici*, and SLI, vol. 2, pp. 102-10; Pocock, *Machiavellian Moment*, pp. 219-71; and Skinner, *Foundations*, vol. 1, pp. 187-88.

44. Machiavelli, *The Prince*, chapter 25.

45. On Guicciardini on the restoration of the Medici, see Felix Gilbert, *Machiavelli and Guicciardini*, pp. 280-82. On Croce and his relation to fascism, see Serge Hughes, *The Fall and Rise of Modern Italy* (New York: Minerva Press, 1967), part 1. See also Aldo Garosci, "Croce e la politica," *Rivista storica italiana* 95, 2 (1983), pp. 282-313; and Ulisse Benedetti, *Benedetto Croce e il fascismo* (Rome: G. Volpe, 1967).

46. Machiavelli, *Discourses*, dedication, and Book 2, introduction.

47. Machiavelli, *The Prince*, chapter 18.

48. Machiavelli, *Discourses*, Book 2, chapter 2.

49. Ibid.

50. De Sanctis, SLI, vol. 2, pp. 60-68.

51. Machiavelli, *Discourses*, Book 2, chapter 2.

52. De Sanctis, SLI, vol. 2, pp. 67-74: "It is at bottom the idea of a national church, dependent upon the state and subordinated to the interests and ends of the nation" (p. 74). See Gramsci, QC 1:2, pp. 257-58; 1:3, pp. 361-63, 401; 1:5, pp. 615-17, 677-78; 2:5, pp. 587-90; 2:6, pp. 809, 839-40; 2:7, pp. 904-7; 2:8, pp. 937-38; and 2:9, p. 1118.

53. Such a reinterpretation is directly related to Gramsci's notion of *interpretando il passato* (interpreting the past) in order to, or by means of which, *operare nel presente* (act in the present); see QC 2:10, p. 1242. See also de Sanctis, "Machiavelli Conferenze," in *Saggi critici*, vol. 2, pp. 309-38.

54. On *vita activa* and *vita contemplativa* (*negotium* and *otium*), see de Sanctis, SLI, vol. 1; Skinner, *Foundations*, pp. 108-9, 115-17, 217-19. See also Baron, *Crisis of the Early Italian Renaissance*, pp. 104-20, 121-29, as well as Baron's "Cicero and the Roman Civic Spirit in the Middle Ages and Early Renaissance," *Bulletin of the John Rylands Library* 22 (1938), pp. 72-97, especially pp. 84-85.

On the futility of human action, and on the need for an external power to transform and direct the *vita terrena*—that is, on the necessity for *gratia* to transform human action and to overcome the corruption and resistance of the *cose del mondo*—see Saint Augustine, *The Political Writings of St. Augustine*, ed. Henry Paolucci (Chicago: Gateway Editions, 1970); and Herbert A. Deane, *The Political and Social Ideas of St. Augustine* (New York: Columbia University Press, 1963).

55. Machiavelli, *Discourses*, Book 2, chapter 2.

56. Machiavelli, *The Prince*, chapter 12; *Discourses*, Book 1, chapters 1, 11, 12, 16, 17, 18, 55, 58, Book 2, introduction, pp. 2, 5, 26, 27, and Book 3, chapters 1, 36, 46; as well as the minor political writings, such as the *Parole da dirle* and the *Discursus*, in *Opere*, vol. 2, ed. Sergio Bertelli (Turin: Feltrinelli, 1960-65). In addition, note *The Art of War* (Wood edition), *proemio*, pp. 3-5, Book 1, pp. 17-19, 24-26, 61, 64, 151, 159, 202, 209-11.

57. Machiavelli, *Discourses*, Book 2, chapter 2.

58. Machiavelli, *The Prince*, chapter 26.

59. Ibid., and the *Discourses*, Book 2, introduction.

60. Machiavelli, *Discourses*, dedication; see *The Prince*, chapter 15.

61. Machiavelli, *Discourses*, dedication; and *The Prince*, chapters 12, 13.

62. Machiavelli, *The Prince*, chapter 26; and *Discourses*, Book 1, introduction, and Book 2, introduction.

63. Giorgio Nardone, *Il pensiero di Gramsci* (Bari: De Donato, 1971), pp. 72-73.

64. Machiavelli, *Discourses*, dedication.

65. Gramsci, QC 3:13, p. 1601.

66. Machiavelli, *Discourses*, dedication, and Book 1, introduction. See also *The Art of War*, Book 1, p. 11.

67. Machiavelli, *Discourses*, dedication.

68. Machiavelli, *The Prince*, chapter 9. See also Nardone, *Il pensiero di Gramsci*, pp. 20-24; Gramsci, QC 2:6, pp. 760-62, 3:13, pp. 1555-56, 1558-59, 1600-1601; Eugenio Garin, "Gramsci nella cultura italiana," in *Studi gramsciani*, Proceedings of a conference held in Rome 11-13 January 1958, compiled by the Istituto Gramsci (Rome: Riuniti, 1973), pp. 415-16; and Sasso, *Niccolò Machiavelli*, p. 229.

6. Machiavelli and the Democratic Philosopher: The Relation between Machiavelli's "New Modes and Orders" and Gramsci's Hegemony

1. Antonio Gramsci, *Quaderni del carcere*, edizione critica a cura di Valentino Gerratana (Turin: Einaudi, 1975), henceforth cited as QC, 3:13, p. 1601. See also QC 2:11, pp. 1384-86.

2. Niccolò Machiavelli, *Discourses*, dedication: "I may seem to have departed from the ordinary usage of writers, who generally dedicate their works to some prince; and, blinded by ambition or avarice, praise him for all the virtuous qualities he has not, instead of censuring

192 him for his real vices, whilst I, to avoid this fault, do not address myself to such as are princes, but to those who by their infinite good qualities are worthy to be such; not to those who could load me with honors, rank, and wealth, but rather to those who have the desire to do so, but have not the power. For to judge rightly, men should esteem rather those who are, and not those who can be generous; and those who would know how to govern states, rather than those who have the right to govern, but lack the knowledge |quelli che sanno, non quelli che, sanza sapere, possono governare uno regno|.

"For this reason historians have praised Hiero of Syracuse, a mere private citizen, more than Perseus of Macedon, monarch though he was; for Hiero only lacked a principality to be a prince, whilst the other had nothing of the king except the diadem |altro che il regno|. Be it good or bad, however, you wanted this work, and such as it is I send it to you" |New York: Modern Library, 1950|.

Compare this quotation to *Discourses*, Book 2, introduction, and to Niccolò Machiavelli, *The Art of War*, trans. Ellis Farnesworth, intro. Neal Wood (Indianapolis: Bobbs-Merrill, 1978), Book 7, the last remarks of Fabrizio. It is important to note that Machiavelli reverses the distinction between *chi sa* (those who know) and *chi non sa* (those who do not know); he goes outside the *uso comune* of previous authors and locates the new political subject—that is, the new ruler that possesses the new knowledge—outside the established structure of power. This new knowledge asserts that those who in fact rule do not know how to rule, and those who do not rule do indeed know how to rule. At the very beginning of the *Discourses*, therefore, Machiavelli alerts the reader that "*quanto io so*" and "*quanto io ho imparato*" stand outside the established social and political order, and are generated in opposition to the established conception of the world. What this means is that the very notion of "rule" as it is commonly accepted is being questioned. See note 32.

3. On the Orti Oricellari, see Felix Gilbert, *Machiavelli and Guicciardini: Politics and History in Sixteenth Century Florence* (Princeton: Princeton University Press, 1965), pp. 140-41, as well as his "Bernardo Rucellai and the Orti Oricellari: A Study on the Origins of Modern Political Thought," *The Journal of the Warburg and Courtauld Institutes* 12 (1949), pp. 101-31, and his "Machiavelli in modern historical scholarship," in *Machiavelli nel V centenario della nascita* (Bologna: Boni, 1973), pp. 165-67.

It is interesting that Machiavelli dedicates "*questi mia scritti*" on republican institutions and on the conditions necessary for the development of the "*virtù* of the masses" to Cosimo Rucellai, the grandson of the Bernardo who had originally initiated the discussion circles in his Orti, around which, according to Guicciardini, the opposition to the republican government of Florence was organized and blossomed: "From that garden there came forth like a Trojan horse conspiracies, the return of the Medici, and the fire that swept this city" (cited in Gilbert, *Machiavelli and Guicciardini*, p. 81). See Machiavelli's *Discourses*, Book 3, chapter 6, in which he discusses conspiracies.

See also Felix Gilbert, "The Composition and Structure of Machiavelli's *Discorsi*," *The Journal of the History of Ideas* 14, 1 (1953), pp. 136-56, and his "Venetian Constitution and Florentine Political Thought," in *Florentine Studies: Politics and Society in Renaissance Florence*, ed. Nicolai Rubinstein (Evanston, Ill.: Northwestern University Press, 1968), pp. 463-500; Nicolai Rubinstein, "Politics and Constitution in Florence at the End of the Fifteenth Century," in *Italian Renaissance Studies*, ed. E. F. Jacob (London: Faber and Faber, 1960), pp. 148-83; and J. G. A. Pocock, *The Machiavellian Moment: Florentine Political Thought and the Atlantic Republican Tradition* (Princeton: Princeton University Press, 1975), pp. 120-21, 154, 185-86, 240.

The fact that Machiavelli, who had been a secretary and an active supporter of the republican government in Florence, addresses the *Discourses* to a grandson of the Bernardo who had been active in the aristocratic movement against the *governo* of the republic, is laden with political and theoretical significance. Machiavelli intends to present a republican and "popular" work, and he addresses it to a descendant of one who represents the aristocratic and "Venetian" alternative to the establishing of republican institutions—that is, a *governo stretto* based on the *savi* and the *boni* as opposed to a *governo largo* based on the *popolo minuto*—and such an addressing is done in the very place and setting that had initially served as the focus of the opposition to a *governo largo*. See Hans Baron, "Machiavelli: The Republican Citizen and the Author of The Prince," *English Historical Review* 76 (1961), pp. 217-53.

In addition, see Machiavelli, *Discourses*, Book 1, chapters 2, 5, 6, 36, 55; Book 2, chapters 3, 24, 31, in which Machiavelli compares the Roman republic to the aristocratic republic of Venice and the oligarchic politics of Sparta (that is, a *governo largo* to a *governo stretto*): the Roman republic achieved greatness and greater liberty because its sociopolitical institutions—and hence its military power—rested upon a popular foundation that supported a *governo largo*. See Machiavelli's *Istorie fiorentine*, Book 1, chapter 29, *Opere*, vol. 7, ed. Franco Gaeta (Milan: Feltrinelli, 1962).

4. Leo Strauss, *Thoughts on Machiavelli* (Chicago: University of Chicago Press, 1978), pp. 115-50, especially pp. 115-16, 141-42, and 143-44. Strauss's position, that Machiavelli intended to formulate a body of thought that would serve as a countersystem of beliefs to that prevailing at the time—is reminiscent of the de Sanctian and Gramscian positions, which view Machiavellian thought not merely or purely as a "scientific" body of knowledge, but also as a novel conception of the world that tends toward the moral and intellectual reform of the established political and cultural *verità effettuale*. Such a parallel between Gramsci and Strauss must be viewed in a precise and circumscribed manner: to Strauss, such a reform delineates the "immoral" character of Machiavellian thought, whereas to Gramsci and de Sanctis it exemplifies the "moral" engagement and "passionate" stance of Machiavelli toward his project and toward the world. On the one hand, in Strauss, philosophy is "beyond" the grasp and scope of the demos; on the other, in Gramsci, demos and *theoria* presuppose and define each other. See Strauss, pp. 296-97, and Benedetto Croce, *Etica e politica* (Bari: Laterza, 1931), on the demos and its relationship to thought and culture. But see Sir Isaiah Berlin, "The Originality of Machiavelli," in *Against the Current: Essays in the History of Ideas*, ed. and with a bibliography by Henry Hardy, intro. Roger Hausheer (Harmondsworth: Penguin Books, 1982), for a discussion of Machiavelli's "morality" and Berlin's argument that Machiavelli wanted to introduce a new conception of politics and ethics.

5. Machiavelli, *Discourses*, dedication.

The difference between the new knowledge and the old is immediately established, and it does not issue from an extrahistorical source, nor does it rely upon the gratuitous and unmerited *gratias* of the Word Incarnate. In addition, it should be pointed out that the subject to which the new knowledge is addressed, and the subject to which the old and established thought has (or had) been addressed, are quite different in character: the latter is passive, the former is active—that is, the new subject does not "receive" this knowledge; rather the knowledge is one that comes into existence because the subject itself desires it, and therefore because the new subject itself initiates the interaction from which results the formulation of the new knowledge.

6. Machiavelli, *Discourses*, Book 1, chapter 58.

7. Ibid. See also *Discourses*, Book 1, chapters 2, 5, 6, 16, 37, 44; *The Prince*, chapters 8, 9; the *Florentine Histories*, the speech given by plebians to the assembled plebs of Florence in 1378 (Book 3, chapter 3); and Strauss, *Thoughts on Machiavelli*, pp. 128-33.

Machiavelli criticizes Livy and the classical writers, but the critique is also a polemic against the aristocratic humanists of the Orti Oricellari. In *Discourses*, Book 1, chapter 58 Machiavelli places himself, and his new knowledge, in opposition to "tutti gli altri istorici" and to "tutti gli scrittori"—a position that encompasses a critique of past and present writings and thinkers. In addition, Machiavelli is saying that the accepted position, and the established

194 knowledge, exist as a force and as a power in the world because they do not rest on the "difendere alcuna opinione con le ragioni," but, on the contrary, the established conception of the world and the established way of life endure, and have endured, because of the "usare la autorità e la forza." Compare this to the dedication—"mi pare essere uscito fuora dell'uso comune di colore che scrivono"—as well as to Book I, introduction.

8. See Quentin Skinner, *The Foundations of Modern Political Thought* (Cambridge: Cambridge University Press, 1978), vol. I, pp. 87-88, 126, 161-64; And Pocock, *Machiavellian Moment*, chapter 4, especially pp. 60-65, 96-99; and Eugenio Garin, *Italian Humanism: Philosophy and Civic Life in the Renaissance*, trans. Peter Munz (New York: Harper and Row, 1965), chapter 3 and pp. 31-36.

9. Machiavelli, letter to Francesco Vettori, 10 December 1513, no. 137, in *The Letters of Machiavelli*, ed. and trans. Allan H. Gilbert (New York: Capricorn Books, 1961), pp. 139-44: "I enter the ancient courts of ancient men, where, received by them with affection, I feed on that food which only is mine and which I was born for, where I am not ashamed to speak with them and to ask them the reason for their actions; and they in their kindness answer me. . . . And because Dante says it does not produce knowledge when we hear but do not remember, I have noted everything in their conversation which has profited me, and have composed a little work On Princedoms. . . . and by a prince and especially a new prince, it ought to be welcomed" (pp. 142-43).

Machiavelli's conversation with the past is also a conversation with the present, for his attempt to ask the ancient writers the reason for their actions is immediately related to his attempt to discover the *verità effettuale* of the *cose del mondo*. (See Gramsci, QC 2:10, p. 1242, where the point is made that to interpret the past is to act in the present.) In addition, this letter should be related to the dedication in *The Prince*, where Machiavelli, a man of "humble and obscure condition," establishes a reciprocal movement between the action of the prince and action of the people. Also, compare this to letter no. 120, to Francesco Vettori, 9 April 1513, where Machiavelli states that "I have to talk about the government, and I must either make a vow of silence or discuss that" (in Allan H. Gilbert, *Letters of Machiavelli*, p. 104).

10. Machiavelli, *Discourses*, dedication.

11. Machiavelli, *The Art of War*, Book I, pp. 7-9.

12. *The Art of War*, Book I, p. 10 (Neal Wood edition).

13. *Arte della guerra* p. 331 (p. 10 in Neal Wood edition). Note the use of "*sanza rispetto*" in the *Discourses*, dedication, and here in *The Art of War*. See also Machiavelli's letter to Vettori, 9 April 1513, Allan H. Gilbert, *Letters of Machiavelli*, p. 104.

14. *Arte della guerra* (p. 11 in Neal Wood edition). Compare this to the dedication in the *Discourses*.

15. On humanistic literary usages and conventions, see Skinner, *Foundations*, vol. I, chapter 2, "Rhetoric and liberty;" Jerrold Seigel, *Rhetoric and Philosophy in Renaissance Humanism* (Princeton: Princeton University Press, 1968), as well as his "'Civic Humanism' or Ciceronian Rhetoric? The Culture of Petrarch and Bruni," *Past and Present* 34 (1966), pp. 7-78. See also, Allan H. Gilbert, *Machiavelli's "Prince" and Its Forerunners: "The Prince" as a Typical Book de regimine principium* (Durham, N.C.: Duke University Press, 1938); Felix Gilbert, *Machiavelli and Guicciardini*; and Eugenio Garin, *Italian Humanism*, pp. 19-20.

16. Machiavelli, *Il Principe*, dedication, *Opere*. It should be noted that Machiavelli refers to himself as a "uomo di basso et infimo stato"—that is, he is of the *infimo populo*, or *infima plebe*—one who nevertheless strives and desires ("*ardisce*") to "*discorrere*" on the nature of politics and of ruling. See Felix Gilbert, *Machiavelli and Guicciardini*, p. 24, on the political vocabulary used in Machiavelli's Florence.

17. Machiavelli, *The Art of War*, Book I (Neal Wood edition), p. 11.

18. Gramsci, QC 3:13, pp. 1568-70, 1600-1601. See also *The Prince*, chapter 18; and Strauss, *Thoughts on Machiavelli*, chapter 2.

19. Gramsci, QC 2:10, p. 1331. On Gramsci's concept of education, see Mario Alighiero Manacorda, "La formazione del pensiero pedagogico di Gramsci 1915-1926," in *Gramsci e la cultura contemporanea*, Proceedings of the conference held in Cagliari 23-27 April 1967, ed. Pietro Rossi (Riuniti-Istituto Gramsci, 1975), vol. 2, pp. 227-61, especially pp. 234-38, 240-41.

And see Lamberto Borghi, "Educazione e scuola in Gramsci," in *Gramsci e la cultura contemporanea*, vol. 1, pp. 207-38; and Giancarlo Bergami, *Il giovane Gramsci e il marxismo 1911-1918* (Milan: Feltrinelli, 1977), pp. 50-62, 156-59. Note Gramsci, in *Scritti giovanili* (Turin: Einaudi, 1975): "Education, culture, the organization of knowledge and of experience, mean the independence of the masses from the intellectuals. . . . It is the struggle against the despotism of career intellectuals |*intellettuali di carriera*|" (p. 301). To Gramsci, of course, it is axiomatic that, as he puts it, "all men are philosophers"—philosopher here understood not in the academic and literary sense but rather in the more concrete and fundamental sense that "living" and "acting" are historical experiences that presuppose a determinate and coherent conception of life, such that "acting" implies at the same time "thinking." See Gramsci, *Selections from the Prison Notebooks of Antonio Gramsci*, ed. and trans. Quintin Hoare and Geoffrey Nowell Smith (New York: International Publishers, 1973), pp. 323, 325, 326, 344, 354.

Moreover, in *Socialismo e fascismo* (Turin: Einaudi, 1974), Gramsci says that the worker is a "philosopher without knowing it" (p. 13). See Gramsci, QC 2:11, pp. 1373-80, 1384-95, and QC 3:12, pp. 1550-51. See also *L'Ordine Nuovo, 1919-1920* (Turin: Einaudi, 1955), p. 470, where Gramsci asserts "Do you want to transform into a man someone who until yesterday has been a slave? Begin by treating him always as a man."

In a letter of 1918 Gramsci stresses the need to develop and promote among the young the "disinterested discussion of ethical and moral problems, the formation of a habit of research, of disciplined and methodical reading, of the simple and clear expression of one's convictions" (Mario Alighiero Manacorda, *Il principio educativo in Gramsci: Americanismo e fordismo* |Rome: Riuniti, 1974|, pp. 24-25). Moreover, Gramsci wanted the Italian Socialist Party to establish "cultural associations" in order to educate the lower classes, to proliferate throughout the Italian people a form of education that would instill in them "the love of free discussion, |and| the desire to search for truth rationally and intelligently" (in Gramsci, *La formazione dell'- uomo: Scritti di pedagogia*, ed. Giovanni Urbani |Rome: Riuniti, 1974|, p. 95, and in *Antonio Gramsci: Selections from Cultural Writings*, ed. and intro. David Forgacs and Geoffrey Nowell-Smith, trans. William Boelhower |Cambridge, Mass.: Harvard University Press, 1985|, pp. 23, 25). Finally, Gramsci observes that what "is necessary to the proletariat is a disinterested school"—in other words, "a humanistic school such as was intended by the ancients and more recently by the men of the Renaissance," *Scritti giovanili*, p. 59.

On Gramsci and his concept of education and its relation to hegemony, see Angelo Broccoli, *Antonio Gramsci e l'educazione come egemonia* (Florence: La Nuova Italia, 1972); Harold Entwistle, *Antonio Gramsci: Conservative Schooling for Radical Politics* (London: Routledge & Kegan Paul, 1979); Franco Lombardi, *Idee pedagogiche di Antonio Gramsci* (Brescia: La Scuola Editrice, 1969); and Lucio Lombardo Radice, *Educazione e rivoluzione* (Rome: Riuniti, 1976).

20. Gramsci, QC 2:10, p. 1331.

21. Ibid.

22. Machiavelli, *The Art of War*, Book 1, p. 9 (Neal Wood edition). And note Gramsci's observation, in QC 3:13, p. 1556, in which he asserts that *The Prince* is the self-reflection of the people and an internal rational discourse—that is, the conversation between Machiavelli and the subject he addresses is in itself the new knowledge that Machiavelli is introducing; and this new knowledge, in turn, is the consciousness of the people dynamically generated by a rational discourse that is internal to the relation established between the *domandare* and the *rispondere*, and between the "io a voi" and the "voi a me."

On "constrains," see Gramsci, QC 2:10, pp. 1330-31.

196

23. Gramsci, QC 2:10, pp. 1331-32. Emphasis added.

24. Ibid.

25. Machiavelli, *The Art of War*, Book 1, p. 10 (Neal Wood edition).

26. Gramsci, QC 2:10, pp. 1330-32, 2:11, p. 1485.

27. Gramsci, QC 2:11, p. 1486.

28. Machiavelli, *The Prince*, chapter 15; the *Discourses*, Book 2, introduction; and *The Art of War*, Book 1, p. 10.

29. Machiavelli, *The Prince*, dedication, chapter 18; the *Discourses*, dedication, Books 1 and 2, introductions; and *The Art of War*, proemio, and Book 1, pp. 3-5, 12-13.

30. Machiavelli, *The Prince*, chapter 18; *Discourses*, Book 1, chapter 4; and *The Art of War*, Book 7, pp. 207-9. See also the *Florentine Histories*.
It should be noted that Machiavelli's proposals for the reform of military institutions of the Florentine republic presuppose a close relation between the establishment of a particular sociopolitical order and the specific organization of its military institutions. See Machiavelli, the *Discorso dell'ordinare lo stato di Firenze alle armi*, the *Discorso sopra l'ordinanza e milizia Fiorentina*, and the *Discursus florentinarum rerum post mortem iunioris Laurentii Medices*, in *Opere*, ed. Sergio Bertelli (Milan: Feltrinelli, 1961). See Gramsci, QC 3:13, pp. 1617-18, 3:14, pp. 1688-91. See also Pocock, *Machiavellian Moment*, where, following Gramsci, he establishes the connection between popular institutions and a popular army—a connection that explains Machiavelli's preference for infantry over other military units. On the necessity for education and discipline, see Gramsci, QC 2:10, pp. 1293-95, 2:11, pp. 1382-83; QC 2:7, pp. 861-63; QC 3:12, pp. 1532-38; QC 3:14, pp. 1706-7; *Scritti giovanili*, pp. 10-18, 80-82, 133-35, 300-302; *L'Ordine Nuovo*, pp. 11, 22-27, 34-38, 394, 466, 469-70, 481. See also Manacorda, "La formazione del pensiero pedagogico," and Borghi, "Educazione e Scuola in Gramsci," in *Gramsci e la cultura contemporanea*.

31. Gramsci, QC 2:10, p. 1255.

32. Gramsci, *L'Ordine Nuovo*; and *Antonio Gramsci: Selections from Political Writings 1910-1920*, ed. Quintin Hoare, trans. John Mathews (New York: International Publishers, 1977), p. 68, where Gramsci says: "To tell the truth, to arrive together at the truth, is a communist and revolutionary act." In the same article, Gramsci notes that "collective discussion, which sympathetically alters men's consciousness, unifies them and inspires them to industrious enthusiasm" (p. 68). See Machiavelli's letter to Vettori, 10 December 1513, no. 13, in Allan H. Gilbert, *Letters of Machiavelli*, p. 139: "to ask them the reasons for their actions." And see the *Discourses*, dedication, and Book 1, introduction.
The notion of "reasoning without force or authority," and to give reasons for one's actions, is, of course, traceable to the Socratic and original notion of *theoria*, in which the questioning and uncovering of the preexisting "truth" or reality are central. In addition, *theoria*, the process by which the given is questioned, is related to *logos*, where one of the senses of the latter is to give an account of oneself (see Barker, Sinclair, Ehrenberg). To give reasons for one's actions—Machiavelli's very demand—is the crucial, substantive meaning that may be ascribed to *logos*. But if *theoria* and *logos* are closely related, then the notion of "truth"—the very status of "truth"—is dependent upon an interactive process that is coextensive with this "truth"; that is, "truth" is now the product of a continual movement between that which "asks" and that which "responds" (the *domandare* and the *rispondere* in Machiavelli's *The Art of War*). *Domandare/rispondere* thus describe a process, which in Gramsci becomes *riforma morale e intellettuale*, or *egemonia*.
To demand an answer, a reason, from established reality or from authority, is in effect to hold that reality and that authority accountable to one's self (Gramsci's *"personalità,"* QC 3:13, p. 1601), and it is to understand that reality as one open to modification through one's own reasoned and purposive activity. As a consequence, to arrive at the truth together, to ask for reasons, is to engage in *theoria*, which is to engage in *politica*, as Gramsci understands it. For to

demand reasons is to assert one's political and moral autonomy from the preexisting socio-political (as well as moral-intellectual) order. See Gramsci, *Scritti giovanili*, pp. 260-61; and QC 2:10, pp. 1255, 1363, 2:11, pp. 1487-90.

On the relationship between reason and discourse (*logos*) and politics, see Thucydides, *The Peloponnesian War*, trans. Benjamin Jowett (New York: Bantam Books, 1960), the Mytilenean Debate, Book 3, pp. 33-52. See also Hannah Arendt, *On Revolution* (Harmondsworth: Penguin Books, 1982), and *The Human Condition* (Chicago: University of Chicago Press, 1958), where she discusses the Aristotelian notion of politics as an activity based on speech and discourse. Following Aristotle, Arendt seriously circumscribes and reduces the topos where discourse (and thus politics) is possible, limiting it to a narrow cultural and intellectual circle from which the mass of the people are excluded, and within which only the aristocratic master-citizens define the political space of discourse and reason.

33. Machiavelli, *Discourses*, Book 2, chapters 1, 2. See also Neal Wood, "Introduction" to *The Art of War*, p. iv.

34. Gramsci, QC 1:5, pp. 657-58.

35. Gramsci, QC 3:13, p. 1601.

36. Gramsci, QC 1:5, pp. 657-58. On "absolute laicism," see Eugenio Garin, "Gramsci nella cultura italiana," in *Studi gramsciani*, Proceedings of a conference held in Rome 11-13 January 1958, Istituto Gramsci (Rome: Riuniti, 1973); and Giorgio Nardone, *Il pensiero di Gramsci* (Bari: De Donato, 1971), pp. 447-57.

37. Gramsci, QC 3:13, p. 1569. See also Nardone, *Il pensiero di Gramsci*, pp. 461-80; and Gramsci, QC 2:11, pp. 1415-16.

38. See Norberto Bobbio, "Nota sulla dialettica in Gramsci," in *Studi gramsciani*, pp. 73-86; Nardone, *Il pensiero di Gramsci*, pp. 300-306, 454-57; and Alfredo Sabetti, "Il rapporto uomo-natura nel pensiero di Gramsci e la fondazione della scienza," in *Studi gramsciani*, pp. 243-52.

39. Gramsci, QC 3:13, p. 1578.

40. Machiavelli, *Discourses*, Book 1, introduction: "And although the undertaking [impresa] is difficult, yet, aided by those who have encouraged me in this attempt, I hope to carry it sufficiently far, so that but little may remain for others to carry it to its destined end" (Modern Library).

See also Book 2, introduction, and *The Art of War*, Book 7, the last words of Fabrizio.

41. Machiavelli, *Discourses*, Book 2, introduction: "But the matter being so manifest that everybody sees it, I shall boldly and openly say what I think of the former times and of the present, so as to excite in the minds of the young men who may read my writings the desire to avoid the evils of the latter, and to prepare themselves to imitate the virtues of the former, whenever fortune presents them the occasion. For it is the duty of an honest man to teach others that good which the malignity of the times and of fortune has prevented his doing himself; so that amongst the many capable ones whom he has instructed, some one perhaps, more favored by Heaven, may perform it" (Modern Library).

Compare this to the *Arte della guerra*: "And I must regret my fate, which either should not have given me knowledge of these things, or given me the power to put them into action. Nor will the occasion ever present itself to me, since I am now old. For this reason I have freely given my knowledge to you as capable young men, who, if you agree with what I have said, may help and give advice to rulers when the occasion arises. Nor should you be wary and despair of success, for this country [provincia] seems destined to revive things long since dead, as we have already seen with poetry, painting, and sculpture" (Book 7, p. 519).

42. Machiavelli, *Discourses*, Book 1, introduction: "Although the envious nature of men, so prompt to blame and so slow to praise, makes the discovery and introduction of any new principles and systems [ordini nuovi] as dangerous almost as the exploration of unknown seas and continents" (Modern Library).

198

43. Machiavelli, *The Art of War*, Book 1, p. 9 (Neal Wood edition).

44. Machiavelli, *Discourses*, Book 2, introduction; and letter to Vettori, 10 December 1513, no. 137, in Allan H. Gilbert, *Letters of Machiavelli*, pp. 139-44.

45. Machiavelli, *The Art of War*, Book 1, pp. 10-11, and Book 7, p. 212 (Neal Wood edition).

46. Ibid., Book 1, p. 12 (Neal Wood edition).

47. See Felix Gilbert, *Machiavelli and Guicciardini*, the chapters on "Guicciardini" and on "Machiavelli."

7. The Constitution of the People as a Political Force: Hegemony, Virtù Ordinata, and the Citizen Democracy

1. These opposing dyads are found throughout Machiavelli's writings, both in the major works—*The Prince*, the *Discourses*, *The Art of War*, and the *Florentine Histories*—and in his minor political writings, such as the *Parole da dirle sopra la provisione del danaio*, *Sommario delle cose della città di Lucca*, *Relazione di una visita fatta per fortificare Firenze*, and the *Discursus florentinarum rerum post mortem iunioris Laurentii Medices*.

In the *Florentine Histories*, for example, an opposition is established between the *vivere privato* (the *vivere a sètte* of *The Art of War*) and the *vivere politico* (the *vivere civile*), and between *tirannide* and *vivere libero*, as well as between the *particulare* and the *bene comune*. The argument of the *Histories* is carried forward and acquires momentum by means of the tension produced by the interplay of these opposing dyadic polarities. Indeed, the *Histories* is to be seen as the delineation of a process by which the *bene comune* is transformed into the *particulare*, the *vivere politico* into the *vivere privato*—a process that describes the progressive disintegration of the *populo*, its loss of *libertà*, and the consequent rise of *tirannide*. In effect, the *Histories* is Machiavelli's commentary on the state of Florence in the early years of the sixteenth century, a commentary that may be best understood as the mirror opposite of the argument presented in the *Discourses*; that is, the latter work describes the emergence and development of the people, and the proliferation of *virtù* among the masses, such that we see in it Machiavelli's ideal and ardent desire (he is "*ardisce*," and "*sarò animoso a dire*"), the *res publica* as the *res populi*, and the people ruling through their *virtù ordinata*.

On the other hand, the *Histories* presents Machiavelli's realistic judgment regarding the *verità effettuale* "delle cose di Firenze"—namely, the people as an active and directing force do not exist; indeed, the history of Florence shows the progressive corruption and degeneration of the people; thus, Florence is the anti-Rome, and Florentine history is a lesson in what should not be done, in the same way that Roman history is a lesson in what should be done.

See Gramsci, *Selections from the Prison Notebooks of Antonio Gramsci*, ed. and trans. Quintin Hoare and Geoffrey Nowell Smith (New York: International Publishers, 1973), henceforth cited as SPN, pp. 172-75; and Felix Gilbert, *Machiavelli and Guicciardini: Politics and History in Sixteenth Century Florence* (Princeton: Princeton University Press, 1965), chapter 6, "Between History and Politics," pp. 236-70. For a discussion of the *particulare* and the *vivere civile e politico*, see J. G. A. Pocock, *The Machiavellian Moment: Florentine Political Thought and the Atlantic Republican Tradition* (Princeton: Princeton University Press, 1975), pp. 114-22, 143-45, 208-16.

See also Francesco de Sanctis, *Storia della letteratura italiana*, ed. Benedetto Croce (Bari: Laterza, 1965), vol. 2, pp. 105-7; Luigi Russo, *Machiavelli* (Bari: Laterza, 1975), pp. 189-203, the section entitled "Il mito della libertà e del vivere libero in Machiavelli"; Eugenio Garin, *Italian Humanism: Philosophy and Civic Life in the Renaissance*, trans. Peter Munz (New York: Harper and Row, 1965); Hans Baron, *The Crisis of the Early Italian Renaissance: Civic Humanism and Republican Liberty in an Age of Classicism and Tyranny* (Princeton: Princeton University Press, 1955), pp. 97-104, and chapter 6; Nicolai Rubinstein, "Machiavelli and the World of Florentine Politics," in

Studies on Machiavelli, ed. Myron P. Gilmore (Florence: Sansoni, 1972), pp. 3-28; and J. H. Whitfield, *Machiavelli* (New York: Russell and Russell, 1965), pp. 159-60. See also Luigi Russo's introduction to his critical edition of *Il Principe e pagine dei Discorsi e delle Istorie*, ed. Luigi Russo (Florence: Sansoni, n.d.); and Franco Gaeta, "Machiavelli storico," in *Machiavelli nel V centenario della nascita* (Bologna: Boni, 1973), pp. 139-53.

See also Antonio Gramsci, *Quaderni del carcere*, critical edition, ed. Valentino Gerratana (Turin: Einaudi, 1975), henceforth cited as QC, 2:10, p. 1325; QC 1:5, p. 675, 2:6, pp. 687, 719, 729, 758-60, 760-62, 3:19, pp. 1959-60; and QC 3:13, pp. 1578-89, where Gramsci presents his notion of the "economic-corporative," which he defines as the narrow, particular interests of a given group, in opposition to more general, universal interests, which are developed and proliferated by means of hegemonic leadership and through moral and intellectual reform. The *particulare* of Machiavelli parallels the *corporativo-economico* of Gramsci. In both Gramsci and Machiavelli the problem is the movement from the *particulare* to the *bene comune*, and from the economic-corporative to hegemony, and hence to *politica*.

In addition, see QC 2:11, pp. 1481-82; QC 3:13, pp. 1560-61; QC 3:14, pp. 1665-67; QC 2:8, pp. 1053-54; QC 2:10, pp. 1315-17. See also Carmine Donzelli's comments in his edition of Gramsci's *Quaderno 13. Noterelle sulla politica di Machiavelli* (Turin: Einaudi, 1981), "Introduzione a Gramsci," chapter 2.

2. See Russo, *Machiavelli*, pp. 11-25, 38-45; Pocock, *Machiavellian Moment*, pp. 183-219; Leo Strauss, *Thoughts on Machiavelli* (Chicago: University of Chicago Press, 1978), the chapter entitled "Machiavelli's Teaching"; Harry C. Mansfield, introduction to his translation of Machiavelli's *The Prince* (Chicago: University of Chicago Press, 1985); Jerrold Seigel, *Rhetoric and Philosophy in Renaissance Humanism* (Princeton: Princeton University Press, 1968). And Ernst Cassirer, *The Myth of the State* (New Haven: Yale University Press, 1973), chapter 7, "The Religious and Metaphysical Background of the Medieval Theory of the State," chapter 9, "Nature and Grace in Medieval Philosophy," and chapter 10, "Machiavelli's New Science of Politics."

3. Machiavelli, *Discourses*, dedication; Book 1, chapters 2, 10, 11; Book 2, introduction, chapters 1, 5; and *The Prince*, dedication, chapters 15, 18, and 25.

4. See Pocock, *Machiavellian Moment*, pp. 49-80, "Vita Activa and Vivere Civile." See also Hannah Arendt, *On Revolution* (Harmondsworth: Penguin Books, 1982), and *The Human Condition* (Chicago: University of Chicago Press, 1958), her discussion of the public and the private and the relation of these two spheres to action and speech.

5. Machiavelli, *Discourses*, dedication; Book 1, introduction; Book 2, introduction; and *The Art of War*, trans. Ellis Farnesworth, ed. Neal Wood (Indianapolis: Bobbs-Merrill, 1978), Book 1, pp. 10-15.

6. On the nature and character of the polis, see Sir Ernest Barker, *The Political Thought of Plato and Aristotle* (New York: Dover, 1949); T. A. Sinclair, *A History of Greek Political Thought* (Cleveland: Meridien Books, 1968); M. I. Finley, *Politics in the Ancient World* (Cambridge: Cambridge University Press, 1983); and Arendt, *The Human Condition*. On the nature of the Roman *res publica* and its political institutions, see Frank Ezra Adcock, *Roman Political Ideas and Practice* (Ann Arbor: University of Michigan Press, 1972); Frank Frost Abbott, *A History and Description of Roman Political Institutions* (Boston: Atheneum Press, 1901); and Max Cary, *A History of Rome* (London: Macmillan, 1962). See also George H. Sabine's introduction to Cicero's *On the Commonwealth*, trans. George H. Sabine and Stanley B. Smith (Indianapolis: Bobbs-Merrill, 1970); and Tacitus, "Dialogue on Oratory," in *The Complete Works of Tacitus* (New York: Modern Library, 1950).

7. On the concepts "freedom" and "necessity" in their classical contexts, see Arendt, *On Revolution*, pp. 59-64, and Barker's analysis of the Aristotelian concept of slavery, in *Political Thought of Plato and Aristotle*, as well as M. I. Finley, *Economy and Society in Ancient Greece* (Harmondsworth: Penguin Books, 1981), especially the essays "The freedom of the citizen in the Greek world," pp. 77-96, and "Between slavery and freedom," pp. 116-32.

200   Finley presents an interesting analysis of the relation between citizenship and the possession of slaves as private property, arriving, by means of historical inquiry, at a somewhat Hegelian position, namely, that freedom emerged in the world of classical Greece in opposition to, and as a result of its tension with, its opposite, slavery. The Middle East failed to achieve a similar idea of freedom, according to Finley, because its system of domination did not possess slavery as private property, so no tension or conflict could arise between the realm of the private (domination) and the realm of the public (freedom); in the east, since everyone is subject to the domination of the king, these distinctions are meaningless.

8. See Sir Ernest Barker's introduction to *The Politics of Aristotle*, ed. and trans. Sir Ernest Barker (Oxford: Oxford University Press, 1958). On despotism, see Melvin Richter's essay "Despotism," in the *Dictionary of the History of Ideas* (New York: Charles Scribner's Sons, 1973), vol. 2, pp. 1-18, especially pp. 2-6, 15-16.

It should be noted that speech and discourse, in the sense that Machiavelli used in his letter to Vettori where the composition of *The Prince* is announced—"to ask reasons for their actions"—are necessarily excluded from the sociopolitical structure created by a *despoteia* and a *dominium*. Thus *logos* and *theoria* are antithetical to *despoteia*; and a form of rule, as well as a conception of the world that posits an antithesis between demos and *logos* (upon which such rule is based), simultaneously assert the "freezing" and the crystallization of thought and culture into unchanging and "natural" forms of institutions that embody this antithesis. *Despoteia* and *dominium* are forms of rule that to Aristotle are prepolitical and even antipolitical, but that are by their very nature necessary to the freedom of the citizen.

9. See Machiavelli, *Discourses*, Book 1, chapters 2, 3, 4, 5, 18, 34, 55, 60; and Book 2, chapters 1, 4, 6, 33.

10. See Ronald Syme, *The Roman Revolution* (Oxford: Oxford University Press, 1939); and Lily Ross Taylor, *Party Politics in the Age of Caesar* (Berkeley: University of California Press, 1961).

11. On the distinction between the *imperium domi* and the *imperium militiae*, see Abbott, *Roman Political Institutions*, pp. 160-61, and Adcock, *Roman Political Ideas and Practice*, pp. 6-7, 10-11. For a similar concept in the classical Greek polis, see Arendt, *On Revolution*. See also, Victor Ehrenberg, *From Solon to Socrates: Greek History and Civilization During the 6th and the 5th Centuries BC* (London: Methuen, 1973), chapter 6.

12. In both instances, the relation that obtains between ruler and ruled (or general and soldier, master and servant, father and child) is such that the latter terms of the dyad describe a condition in which the subject does not possess the means, nor the political-moral autonomy, to ask questions or to respond to the actions of the ruler. See Barker, *Political Thought of Plato and Aristotle*, and Tacitus, "Dialogue on Oratory," in *Complete Works*.

13. Machiavelli, *The Art of War*, Book 1, p. 19 (Neal Wood edition).

14. Ibid., p. 14.

15. Ibid., p. 15.

16. Machiavelli, *Discourses*, Book 1, chapters 3, 4, 5.

17. Tacitus, "Dialogue on Oratory," in *Complete Works*, pp. 764-69. This statement by Tacitus should be compared to the orations delivered by Diodotus in Thucydides' *Peloponnesian War*, trans. Benjamin Jowett (New York: Bantam Books, 1960), the Mytilenean Debate, Book 3, 33-52. Note the parallel between Tacitus's "supporting their opinion with ability and eloquence" and Machiavelli's "to ask reasons for their actions" and "difendere alcuna opinione con la ragione, senza usare forza o l'autorità." Moreover, there is an echo of Tacitus's brilliant formulation—"to be mute and speechless"—in Machiavelli's self-description as a *politicus*, in his letter to Francesco Vettori, 9 April 1513, no. 120: "I have to talk about the government, and I must either make a vow of silence or discuss that" (in *The Letters of Machiavelli*, ed. and trans. Allan H. Gilbert [New York: Capricorn Books, 1961], p. 104). A few scholars—beginning with the post-Machiavelli writers of the sixteenth century—have commented on the relationship be-

tween Tacitus and Machiavelli. See, for example, Baron, *Crisis of the Early Italian Renaissance*, p. 70; Giuseppe Toffanin, *Machiavelli e il "Tacitismo": la "politica storica" al tempo della Controriforma* (Padua: A. Draghi, 1921), p. 43 and passim; Strauss, *Thoughts on Machiavelli*, pp. 160-65, where Strauss asserts that Book I, chapters 19-23, possess a "Tacitean substratum"; Peter Burke, "Tacitism," in *Tacitus*, ed. T. A. Dorey (London: Routledge & Kegan Paul, 1969), pp. 149-71; Kenneth C. Schellase, *Tacitus in Renaissance Political Thought* (Chicago: University of Chicago Press, 1976), especially pp. 66-84, 196-202; and Whitfield, *Machiavelli*, pp. 117-18.

It should be noted that Tacitus's critique of oratory as it had developed under imperial rule anticipates Machiavelli's critique of the politics and culture of his own Florence: in the same way that Tacitus contrasts the oratory of the Roman republic, where public speech was not a mere literary and rhetorical exercise, but rather was necessary to the political and cultural practice of the republic, so too Machiavelli contrasts the Florence of a Bruni, where culture and politics were united in practice, to the Florence of his own day, where the latter has degenerated into the "*ambizioso ozio*" of the rulers, and where the former has become literary formulae and mere manners:

"Credevano i nostri principi italiani, prima ch'egli assaggiassero i colpi delle oltramontane guerre, che a uno principe bastasse sapere negli scrittoi pensare una acuta risposta, scrivere una bella lettera, mostrare ne' detti e nelle parole arguzia e prontezza, sapere tessere una fraude, ornarsi di gemme e d'oro, dormire e mangiare con maggiore splendore che gli altri, tenere assai lascivie intorno, governarsi co' sudditi avaramente e superbamente, marcirsi nello ozio, dare i gradi della milizia per grazia, disprezzare se alcuno avesse loro dimostro alcuna lodevole via, volere che le parole fussero responsi di oracoli" (*Arte della guerra*, Book 7, p. 518, in *Opre*).

In both Machiavelli and Tacitus, therefore, we find a relationship established between the integrity and relevance of speech and discourse, on the one hand, and the nature and character of rule, on the other: *vivere libero e politico* is a form of rule that is related to the giving of reasons, and to the defense of one's actions by the use of reason rather than force or authority; whereas *dominium* or *tirannide* is a form of rule in which "mostrare ne' detti e nelle parole una acuta risposta" and "scrivere una bella lettera"—in other words, the trivialization and corruption of speech—are the prevailing forms of speech and cultural activity.

18. Machiavelli, *Discourses*, Book I, chapter 55, emphases added. Compare this passage to that in the *Discursus florentinarum rerum post mortem iunioris Laurentii Medices*, in *Opere*, vol. 2, ed. Sergio Bertelli (Milan: Feltrinelli, 1961): "In cities where there is a general equality among citizens a principality can only be established with great difficulty; on the other hand, a republic can not be established in cities where there is great inequality. Thus, to found a republic in Milan, where there is geat inequality, requires the destruction of its nobility, reducing it to the level of the rest of the people. But among the nobility are powerful and arrogant men the laws are unable to restrain and control, and thus a royal and strong authority is required to suppress them. On the other hand, the founding of a principality in Florence, where there is a very great equality, requires first the institution of a general inequality and the creation of many nobles and lords who command castles [*nobili di castella e ville*], who can, together with the prince, oppress the city and the entire countryside with their arms and retainers. Because a prince alone cannot maintain his power without the support of the nobility. Thus it is necessary to create between the prince and the people a middle element that will help him maintain his principality. This is to be seen in all princely states, most especially in France, where the nobility lords it over the people, the princes of the realm over the nobility, and the king over the princes" (pp. 267-68).

19. *Discourses*, Book I, chapter 55. See Gramsci, QC 2:11, pp. 1366-68, 1370. On this point, one should note what Gramsci says regarding the relation between absolute monarchy and the emergence of liberal and democratic forms of rule: "Hegel asserted that servitude is

202   the cradle of liberty. For Hegel as well as for Machiavelli the 'new principality' (that is, the period of dictatorship that characterizes the origins of every new type of State), and the servitude that is connected with it, can only be justified to the extent that they provide the education and discipline |necessary| for a person |l'uomo| who is not yet free. However, B. Spaventa (*Principii di etica*, Appendix |Naples, 1904|) comments very appropriately |on this issue|: 'But the cradle is not life. There will always be some who will want us to remain in the cradle' " (QC 2:11, p. 1370).

   20. Gramsci, QC 1:5, p. 648, 3:17, pp. 1913-14; SPN, pp. 140-41; and Gramsci, *Lettere dal carcere*, ed. Sergio Caprioglio and Elsa Fubini (Turin: Einaudi, 1965), pp. 145-46 (in Lawner's translation, pp. 109-10).

   21. Machiavelli, *Discourses*, Book 1, introduction, and chapters 16, 17, 18; Book 2, introduction, chapter 2; and *The Art of War*, proemio, and Book 7, the concluding remarks of Fabrizio. See also Pocock, *Machiavellian Moment*, pp. 207-11.

   22. Machiavelli, *Discourses*, Book 1, chapter 55. And Pocock, *Machiavellian Moment*, pp. 209-11.

   23. Machiavelli, *Arte della guerra*, Book 6, p. 487. Fabrizio, discussing the elements necessary to the creation of a disciplined and competent citizen army, says that the reputation and prestige of a general are important to the unity and cohesion of his troops: "Ma quello che sopra ogni altra cosa tiene lo esercito unito, è la reputazione del capitano; la quale solamente nasce dalla virtù sua, perché né sangue né autorità la dette mai" (pp. 486-87).

   This phrase, "neither blood nor authority," aptly summarizes the relation between the attempt to teach a new form of knowledge and the attempt to introduce a new order of things; both presuppose the overcoming of traditional forms of authority and the rejection of past usage and customs. Hence the attack on the feudal nobility and on aristocratic pretenses to power. Machiavelli opposes *virtù* to "blood and authority," and the contrast underlines the moral and intellectual force of the new conception of politics.

   Compare the statement just quoted from *The Art of War* to Machiavelli's comments in the *Istorie fiorentine, Opere*, ed. Franco Gaeta (Milan: Feltrinelli, 1962): "Nor should you be dismayed by the great lineage of the noble families |antichità del sangue| with which they reproach us. Because all men have had the same beginning, they are equally ancient, and possess the same nature. Undress us and you will see us all equal; but exchange clothes with them, and we will undoubtedly look like nobles, and they like commoners" (Book 3, chapter 13, pp. 237-38). Machiavelli attributes these words to an anonymous speaker, "one of the more daring and more experienced" of the "*uomini plebei*" ("plebeian men" |3.13, pp. 236-37|), whose audience is comprised of an assembly of the *populo minuto* (3.13, p. 236). Here Machiavelli uncovers the established bases of power and rule—"blood," "authority," "age of blood," "dress"—and simultaneously presents a new form of politics based upon a doctrine of equality. It is significant that this new teaching is put in the mouth of an unknown yet "daring and experienced"—that is, *virtuoso*—man of the common people; by so doing, Machiavelli is underlying the relation between the new form of knowledge and the new political actor that bears this knowledge and will eventually introduce it.

   24. Machiavelli, *The Prince*, chapters 6, 7, and 18. On Gramsci's *dittatura* and *egemonia*, see Walter L. Adamson, *Hegemony and Revolution: A Study of Antonio Gramsci's Political and Cultural Theory* (Berkeley: University of California Press, 1980); Carl Boggs, *Gramsci's Marxism* (London: Pluto Press, 1978); and the essays in Chantal Mouffe, ed. *Gramsci and Marxist Theory* (Boston: Routledge & Kegan Paul, 1979).

   25. There is, therefore, a consistency in Machiavelli's praise of Cesare Borgia and in his condemnation of Agathocles and Caesar: the former represents a form of action necessary to the creation of a *vivere civile* in a country previously lacking it; the second represents a form of action that destroys an already existing *vivere civile* and the disintegration of a political space

defined by the action of *"cittadini virtuosi."* See *The Prince*, chapter 7, and the *Discourses*, Book I, **203** chapter 10.

On the problem regarding the relation between *The Prince* (the moment of force) and the *Discourses* (the moment of liberty or consent), see Felix Gilbert, "Machiavelli in modern historical scholarship," in *Machiavelli nel V centenario della nascita*, pp. 157-71, especially pp. 165-66; and Gennaro Sasso, *Il pensiero politico di Niccolò Machiavelli* (Turin: ERI, 1964), pp. 36-41.

26. Machiavelli, *Discourses*, Book I, chapters I, II, 17; and the *Florentine Histories*, Book 4, chapter i.

27. See Machiavelli, *Discourses*, Book 2, chapters 2, 3, 4, 6, 7, 9, 19; Pocock, *Machiavellian Moment*, pp. 181-82, 208-18; and Sheldon S. Wolin, *Politics and Vision: Continuity and Innovation in Western Political Thought* (Boston: Little, Brown and Company, 1960), pp. 220-24. In this section, Wolin presents the now famous formulation "the economy of violence." If the notion of the economy of violence is conjoined with the problem of political space (pp. 217-30), then political action depends on the generation of an economy of violence within this space, such that the concentration and mobilization of force and violence are better attained and more efficiently deployed outside the political space. Note that the very notion of an economy of violence presupposes the classical distinction between *imperium domi* and *imperium militiae*. Wolin, in linking his notion of the economy of violence to the notion of the "unescapably autonomous nature of politics" (p. 228), is following and echoing Croce's reading of Machiavelli—for now "politics" is seen as an "economy" of pure force, that is, a technique. On the other hand, Croce would find Wolin's discussion entitled "ethics: political and private" (p. 224) overly moralistic. Nevertheless, the "economy of violence" is a brilliant formulation, which, however, requires careful qualification. It should be noted that its use in Wolin is quite ambivalent. The Centaur, after all, represents both the beast and the man, force and reason, and the problem is to construct a political space in which the former is subordinated to the latter.

28. Gramsci, QC 3:13, pp. 1599-1600 (and QC 1:4, p. 431); QC 2:11, pp. 1507-9; Pocock, *Machiavellian Moment*, p. 210; Wolin, *Politics and Vision*, pp. 230-31; and Quentin Skinner, *Foundations of Modern Political Thought* (Cambridge: Cambridge University Press, 1978), vol. I, pp. 182-83.

29. Barker, *Political Thought of Plato and Aristotle*, pp. 359-72, especially pp. 361-65. See also Barker's edition of Aristotle's *Politics*.

30. On the concepts of *dittatura* and *dominio*, see Gramsci QC 3:13, pp. 1565-66; QC 1:1, pp. 40-41, 1:1, pp. 58-59; QC 2:6, p. 691; QC 3:13, pp. 1636-38; QC 3:19, pp. 2010-11; and see *Lettere dal carcere*, p. 333. See also Adamson, *Hegemony and Revolution*; Mouffe, *Gramsci and Marxist Theory*; and Giorgio Bonomi, *Partito e rivoluzione in Gramsci* (Milan: Feltrinelli, 1976), pp. 38-39, 43-50.

31. Such a conversation, in which each demands a reason from the other, is employed by Machiavelli as a means to "retranslate" and reinterpret the ancient writers and the modern humanists, in such a way that his conversation with the past and the present becomes an attempt to reform the present and to establish a new sociocultural reality. See Skinner, *Foundations*, vol. I, pp. 128-38, 158-62; and Allan H. Gilbert, *Machiavelli's "Prince" and Its Forerunners: "The Prince" as a Typical Book de regimine principium* (Durham, N.C.: Duke University Press, 1938). But see John Plamentaz, *Man and Society* (New York: McGraw-Hill, 1963), vol. 2, p. 7; and Sir Isaiah Berlin, "The Originality of Machiavelli," in his *Against the Current: Essays in the History of Ideas*, ed. and with a bibliography by Henry Hardy, intro. Roger Hausheer (Harmondsworth: Penguin Books, 1982).

32. Notwithstanding Strauss's position, "to reason without using force or authority" is certainly a construction that has its parallels in Aristotelian political thought. Machiavelli's enterprise attempts to point the way toward a political space where the *vivere civile e libero* is not a mere transient and contingent phenomenon, but one whose *virtù* is able to resist and de-

204 fend against the violence and force of *fortuna*. See Giuliano Procacci, *Studi sulla fortuna del Machiavelli* (Rome: Istituto storico italiano, 1965), pp. 45-46, and p. 45 n. 3.

33. Pocock, *Machiavellian Moment*, pp. 194-211; Wolin, *Politics and Vision*, pp. 228-35 ("the discovery of the mass"); Skinner, *Foundations*, vol. 1, pp. 158-62; and A. R. Buzzi, *La teoria politica di Gramsci* (Florence: La Nuova Italia, 1973), pp. 152-65. All these authors note the importance of the masses in Machiavelli. However, they establish a relation between the new prince and the masses, or between the "legislator-founder" and the republic, in such a way that the former is seen as the all-powerful and all-knowing artist-shaper of the *materia* of the masses. See also Russo, *Machiavelli*, p. 24, on the "artista-eroe della teorica politica." But what is more important, these authors establish a static, sterile, and artificial relation between the new knowledge of politics and the mass. Both the "artist-hero" and the technique which he employs appear in the political arena as if he were a deus ex machina descending on a stage. Such a view, of course, is but another version of the "autonomy of politics" and the *cultura/politica* antinomy presented by Croce.

34. T. A. Sinclair, *A History of Greek Political Thought*, pp. 115-42, especially pp. 130-39.

35. Barker's edition of Aristotle's *Politics*, Book 1 1252a-1253a, Book 2 1261a, Book 3 1278b, 1280.

36. Wolin, *Politics and Vision*; Finley, *Politics in the Ancient World*. See also Gramsci, QC 3:19, pp. 1959-60.

37. Taylor, *Party Politics in the Age of Caesar*; Cary, *History of Rome*; Edward A. Freeman, *A History of Federal Government in Greece and Italy*, ed. J. B. Bury (London: Macmillan, 1893); and Finley, *Politics in the Ancient World*.

38. Gramsci, QC 3:13, pp. 1559-61, 1598-1601; Wolin, *Politics and Vision*, pp. 229-34.

39. Machiavelli, *Discourses*, Book 2, chapters 55, 58.

40. Benedetto Croce, *Etica e politica* (Bari: Laterza, 1931), the section "Elementi di politica."

41. Machiavelli, *Discourses*, Book 1, chapter 58.

42. Machiavelli, *The Prince*, chapter 9. Compare the *Discourses*, Book 1, chapter 58, and *The Prince*, chapter 9, to the *Discourses*, Book 3, chapter 7.

43. Gramsci, QC 3:13, pp. 1560-61; and QC 2:11, p. 1370. See also the *Discourses*, Book 1, introduction; Book 2, introduction, chapters 1, 2, 55, 58; Book 3, chapters 1, 7.

44. Gramsci, QC 1:5, pp. 656-62, 3:14, pp. 1688-89, 3:19, p. 2015. See also Pocock, *Machiavellian Moment*, pp. 198-204.

45. Machiavelli, *The Art of War*, Book 1, p. 12.

46. Gramsci, QC 3:13, p. 1564.

47. Machiavelli, *Discourses*, Book 1, chapter 21; and *The Prince*, chapter 12.

48. Machiavelli, *The Art of War*, proemio; Pocock, *Machiavellian Moment*, pp. 200-201.

49. Gramsci, QC 3:13, p. 1573; and QC 3:19, p. 2015.

50. Machiavelli, *Discourses*, Book 1, chapter 21; and *The Prince*, chapters 12, 13, 14, 24, 25. See the *Parole da dirle sopra la provisione del danaio*, in *Opere*, vol. 2, ed. Sergio Bertelli (Milan: Feltrinelli, 1961), in which Machiavelli addresses the republican leadership of Florence, and says that "States |le città| cannot be maintained without force. . . . |and| you are unarmed |pp. 58-59|. . . . And I say that fortune will not change where the basic laws are not changed. |But the future of| your liberty rests in your hands. And I believe that you will always love and care for it in the manner of those who are born free and desire to live freely" (p. 62).

To want to live as a free people is to want to become armed, but to become armed, one must "mutar l'ordine"—that is, transform one's institutions. What this means is that the republic (or the new principality) "chiama i suoi cittadini"—that is, it must rely on its citizens to defend itself. But this, in turn, requires that the citizenship be extended, and that the *governo* be based on the *populo minuto*. Note that Machiavelli attacks the Florentine republic for its reliance on the arms of others: "Neither a principality nor a wise republic has ever wanted to be subject to another's will [che volessi tenere lo stato suo a discrezione d'altri], or, being so subject, has ever thought itself secure" (p. 58). But to become a "repubblica armata" (The Prince, chapter 12) means to transform the political space of the republic through the arming of the people. See Gramsci, QC 3:13, pp. 1572-73, and 3:19, p. 2015. See also Machiavelli's Discorso dell'ordinare lo stato di Firenze alle armi: "only by establishing a military force subject to public control, maintained by good laws" (Opere, vol. 2, p. 95).

51. See Berlin, "The Originality of Machiavelli," in Against the Current, pp. 25-79; and Anthony Parel, ed. The Political Calculus: Essays on Machiavelli's Philosophy (Toronto: University of Toronto Press, 1972), the essays by Thomas Flanagan, "The Concept of Fortuna in Machiavelli, pp. 127-56; Neal Wood, "Machiavelli's Humanism of Action," pp. 33-57; and John Plamenatz, "In Search of Machiavellian Virtù," pp. 157-78.

52. Neal Wood, "Machiavelli's Concept of Virtù Re-considered," Political Studies 15 (1967), p. 171. See also Wood's introduction to The Art of War, pp. xli, xlvii-xlix, and liv-lxiv.

53. Felix Gilbert, Machiavelli and Guicciardini: Politics and History in Sixteenth Century Florence (Princeton: Princeton University Press, 1965), p. 154.

54. Skinner, Foundations, vol. 1, p. 129 n. 2; but see pp. 130-35, where Skinner concludes, with Berlin, that the "essential contrast [regarding the question of force and power] is rather between two different moralities—two rival and incompatible accounts of what ought ultimately to be done" (p. 135).

55. Federico Chabod, Machiavelli and the Renaissance (New York: Harper Torchbooks, 1965), p. 16: "The general character of The Prince—not only its formal scheme, but the actual spirit that powers it—is clearly revealed in the chapters on the creation of a militia." This is partly correct. The problem arises in the difference in interpretation regarding the use and organization of the militia. To Machiavelli, as to Gramsci, the militia is not a mere military and technical instrument; it is a social organization directed toward a political end. It is an instrument, therefore, that acquires meaning and utility only through a political and moral structure. See also Chabod's Scritti su Machiavelli (Turin: Einaudi, 1964), pp. 322-39.

56. Chabod, Machiavelli and the Renaissance, pp. 74, 84. For an excellent discussion of the relation between politics and military affairs see C. C. Bayley, War and Society in Renaissance Florence: The "De Militia" of Leonardo Bruni (Toronto: University of Toronto Press, 1961), in which Bayley compares Bruni and Machiavelli regarding their conceptions of the relation between politics and war.

57. Chabod, Machiavelli and the Renaissance, pp. 16-17, 20, 99-100. And this is the point at issue: a citizen militia presupposes a particular sociopolitical and sociocultural environment, as well as a moral and intellectual transformation of contemporary Italian politics and society. Thus, to call for a citizen army is to call for such a transformation.

58. See Pocock, Machiavellian Moment, pp. 199-200; Felix Gilbert, Machiavelli and Guicciardini, chapters 1 and 2; and Wood, his introduction to The Art of War, pp. xlvii, liii-lxiv.

59. Pocock, Machiavellian Moment, pp. 199-200.

60. Gramsci, QC 1:5, p. 675, 2:6, pp. 687, 719, 729, 758-60, 760-62, 3:19, pp. 1959-60, 2015.

61. Machiavelli, The Art of War (Neal Wood edition), proemio, pp. 3-4.

62. Ibid., Book 1, p. 12.

63. Ibid., pp. 14-15.

64. Machiavelli, Florentine Histories, Book 2, pp. 33-37; Book 3, p. 1; Book 7, p. 1. See also the Discourses, Book 1, introduction, pp. 55, 58; Book 2, introduction, p. 2.

65. Compare Machiavelli, The Art of War (Neal Wood edition), Book 1, pp. 14-15, and the Florentine Histories, Book 1, chapter 1; Book 8, chapter 1.

66. The loss of Florentine liberty (internally as vivere civile), and the loss of Florence's freedom of movement as an actor in the balance of power (externally), are precisely the re-

206 sults against which Machiavelli was preparing and planning in the *Parole da dirle* and in the *Discorso dell'ordinare lo stato di Firenze alle armi*. See the *proemio* to *The Art of War* (Neal Wood edition), pp. 3-5, and Book 7, pp. 208-11; and *The Prince*, chapters 24 and 26.

67. Machiavelli, *The Prince*, chapter 26; *Discourses*, Book 2, chapter 28; and *The Art of War* (Neal Wood edition), Book 7, pp. 206-11.

68. Machiavelli, *The Prince*, chapter 20; *Discourses*, Book 2, chapter 24; and the *Discursus florentinarum rerum post mortem iunioris Laurentii Medices*. See also Machiavelli's letters to Francesco Guicciardini in Allan H. Gilbert's *Letters of Machiavelli*: 4 April 1526, letter no. 206 (pp. 229-31); 17 May 1526, letter no. 207 (pp. 231-33); 2 June 1526, letter no. 209 (pp. 233-34), and a second letter of the same date, no. 210 (pp. 234-35), in which Machiavelli says that "the most harmful undertaking a republic can do is to build a fortress, or something which can be quickly made into a fortress, within its boundaries."

69. Machiavelli, *Discourses*, Book 2, chapter 24.

70. Machiavelli, *The Prince*, chapter 20.

71. Ibid.

72. Machiavelli, *Discourses*, Book 1, chapters 16, 17, 18; Book 2, chapters 2, 24.

73. On the "new principality," see Machiavelli, *The Prince*, chapters 9 and 20; and the *Discourses*, Book 1, chapters 55, 58.

8. Conclusion: Hegemony and Power

1. John Merrington, "Theory and Practice in Gramsci's Marxism," *The Socialist Register* 1969 (London: The Merlin Press, 1969), p. 154.

2. Antonio Gramsci, *Quaderni del carcere*, critical edition, ed. Valentino Gerrantana (Turin: Einaudi, 1975), henceforth cited as QC, 1:5, p. 658, 3:13, p. 1676.

3. Gramsci, QC 3:19, p. 2010.

4. Gramsci, QC 2:6, pp. 810-11.

5. Gramsci, QC 3:13, p. 1638.

6. Gramsci, QC 2:8, p. 1056.

7. On *societas Romana* and *imperium*, see Hannah Arendt, *On Revolution* (Harmondsworth: Penguin Books, 1982), p. 188. See also Edward A. Freeman, A *History of Federal Government in Greece and Rome*, ed. J. B. Bury (London: Macmillan, 1893), pp. 572-76, 578-83.

8. Hegemony itself, as a term used in political and philosophical discourse, is found in the works of ancient Greek writers, such as Thucydides, Plato, Isocrates, Aristotle, and, much later, Plutarch.

Isocrates' formulation that "speech and language are the ruler and guide of all things— *logos hegemon panton*" was discussed in chapter 7. Plato transforms it into the hegemony of philosophy over all human affairs, and into the rule of the philosophic *logos* over *politike praxis*—all of which was taken up by many subsequent thinkers, and which became quite popular among the Stoics of the early Roman Empire. On this, see T. A. Sinclair, *A History of Greek Political Thought* (Cleveland: Meridien Books, 1968), p. 313, and p. 134 for the quotation.

In Aristotle, and in contemporary Greek political understanding and practice, a *hegemon* was seen as a ruler whose power is based on the interest and consent of those over whom power is exercised. If the *hegemon* is a state, the resulting political structure is a system of alliances in which the hegemonic state exercises leadership over mutually consenting states—something similar to what Machiavelli describes in *Discourses* Book 2, chapter 4, which he calls a *"lega"* (a league or confederation). In his *Politics* (1333 a 39-1334 a 5), Aristotle describes *hegemonia* as a form of rule "directed to the interest of the led, and not to the establishment of a general system of slavery." Ernest Barker, in his translation of the *Politics*, renders *hegemonia* as leadership.

In addition, see Victor Ehrenberg, *From Solon to Socrates: Greek History and Civilization During the 6th and 5th Centuries BC* (London: Methuen, 1981), where he says: "From such individual treaties [of Sparta with other Peloponnesian states] a league was gradually built up. Instead of trying to conquer the Peloponnese, Sparta became its *hegemon*" (p. 45). Also, on p. 196, Ehrenberg talks about the hegemony of Sparta and Athens over their respective alliances. And speaking of the transformation of the Delian League into the Athenian empire, he notes that "there was no longer an alliance of independent states, but there was never a unified state with, say, overseas provinces and a full central organization, nor was there ever a colonial empire in the modern sense. The Greeks spoke of 'rule' (*arche*). The earlier 'hegemony' as a free leadership of states, especially in war, turned into a system in which increasingly by various means, sometimes not without the collaboration of the local demos, the 'allies' became 'subjects' " (p. 219).

One should also compare Ehrenberg's discussion of hegemony to Gramsci's note on the "great power" in QC 3:19, p. 1598, where he says that "the great power is a hegemonic power [*potenza egemone*], the head and guide of a system of alliances and ententes."

9. See Gramsci, *Selections from the Prison Notebooks of Antonio Gramsci*, ed. and trans. Quintin Hoare and Geoffrey Nowell Smith (New York: International Publishers, 1971), p. 124. See also QC 3:13, p. 1576.

10. Gramsci, QC 2:6, pp. 763-64.

11. Gramsci, QC, 3:13, p. 1638.

12. Ibid., pp. 1572-73, 1577-78. See Luigi Russo, *Machiavelli* (Bari: Laterza, 1975), "Prolegomeni a Machiavelli," p. 54.

13. Saveria Chemotti, *Umanesimo, Rinascimento, Machiavelli nella critica gramsciana* (Rome: Bulzoni, 1975), pp. 104, 106.

14. Gramsci, QC 2:11, p. 1489.

15. Quentin Skinner has done interesting and informative work on the Ciceronian antecedents of aspects of Machiavelli's thought. Perhaps a connection may also be made between Gramsci and Cicero, using Machiavelli as the figure that bridges the two. See Skinner, "The idea of negative liberty: philosophical and historical perspectives," *Philosophy in History*, ed. Richard Rorty, J. B. Schneewind and Quentin Skinner (Cambridge: Cambridge University Press, 1990), pp. 204-17.

16. Gramsci, QC 3:13, p. 1556.

17. Sheldon S. Wolin, *Politics and Vision: Continuity and Innovation in Western Political Thought* (Boston: Little, Brown and Company, 1960), pp. 228-35.

18. Giorgio Nardone, *Il pensiero di Gramsci* (Bari: De Donato, 1971), pp. 21-22.

19. Gramsci, QC 2:11, pp. 1485-86.

20. Gramsci, QC 1:5, p. 658.

21. Gramsci, QC 3:13, pp. 1558, 1560.

22. See J. G. A. Pocock, *The Machiavellian Moment: Florentine Political Thought and the Atlantic Republican Tradition* (Princeton: Princeton University Press, 1975), pp. 162-66.

23. Federico Chabod, *Machiavelli and the Renaissance* (New York: Harper Torchbooks, 1965), pp. 142-43.

24. The suppression of the Constituent Assembly, and the reduction of the soviets to instruments of Bolshevik policy and propaganda, set the pattern for the coming despotism of the Communist party. See Leonard Schapiro, *The Communist Party of the Soviet Union*, 2d ed. (New York: Random House, 1971), pp. 164-72, 182-83, 245-48.

25. See Lucio Magri, "Problems of the Marxist Theory of the Revolutionary Party," *New Left Review* 60 (March-April 1970), pp. 98-101, 104-5, 112-16; and Leopold H. Haimson, *The Russian Marxists and the Origins of Bolshevism* (Boston: Beacon Press, 1966), pp. 133-41, 168-81, 186-97, 209-18.

Select Bibliography

Abbate, M. *La filosofia di Benedetto Croce e la crisi della società italiana*. Turin: Einaudi, 1966.

Abbott, Frank Frost. *A History and Description of Roman Political Institutions*. Boston: Atheneum Press, 1901.

Adamson, Walter L. *Hegemony and Revolution: A Study of Antonio Gramsci's Political and Cultural Theory*. Berkeley: University of California Press, 1980.

Adcock, Frank Ezra. *Roman Political Ideas and Practice*. Ann Arbor: University of Michigan Press, 1972.

Alderisio, Felice. *Machiavelli: l'arte dello stato nell'azione e negli scritti*. Bologna: Zuffi, 1950.

———. "Ripresa machiavelliana. Considerazioni critiche sulle idee di A. Gramsci, di B. Croce e di L. Russo intorno a Machiavelli," *Annali dell'Istituto universitario di Magistero di Salerno* I (1949-50), 203-66.

Anderson, Perry. "The Antinomies of Antonio Gramsci," *New Left Review* 100 (November 1976-January 1977), 5-78.

Arato, Andrew. "The Second International: A Reexamination," *Telos* 18 (Winter 1973-74), 2-52.

Arendt, Hannah. *The Human Condition*. Chicago: University of Chicago Press, 1958.

———. *On Revolution*. Harmondsworth: Penguin Books, 1982.

Avineri, Shlomo. *Hegel's Theory of the Modern State*. Cambridge: Cambridge University Press, 1974.

Barker, Sir Ernest. *The Political Thought of Plato and Aristotle*. New York: Dover, 1949.

———. *The Politics of Aristotle*. Ed. and trans. with an introduction and notes by Sir Ernest Barker. Oxford: Oxford University Press, 1958.

Baron, Hans. "Cicero and the Roman Civic Spirit in the Middle Ages and Early Renaissance," *Bulletin of the John Rylands Library* 22 (1938), 72-97.

———. *The Crisis of the Early Italian Renaissance: Civic Humanism and Republican Liberty in an Age of Classicism and Tyranny*. Princeton: Princeton University Press, 1955.

———. *From Petrarch to Leonardo Bruni: Studies in Humanistic and Political Literature*. Chicago: University of Chicago Press, 1961.

———. "Machiavelli: The Republican Citizen and the Author of 'The Prince,' " *English Historical Review* 76 (1961), 217-53.

Bayley, C. C. *War and Society in Renaissance Florence: The "De Militia" of Leonardo Bruni*. Toronto: University of Toronto Press, 1961.

Benedetti, Ulisse. *Benedetto Croce e il fascismo*. Rome: G. Volpe, 1967.

Bergami, Giancarlo. *Il giovane Gramsci e il marxismo 1911-1918*. Milan: Feltrinelli, 1977.

210   Berlin, Sir Isaiah. *Against the Current: Essays in the History of Ideas.* Ed. Henry Hardy. Intro. Roger Hausheer. Harmondsworth: Penguin Books, 1982.

_____. *Vico and Herder: Two Studies in the History of Ideas.* New York: Vintage Books, 1977.

Bobbio, Norberto. *Politica e cultura.* Turin: Einaudi, 1955.

Boggs, Carl. *Gramsci's Marxism.* London: Pluto Press, 1978.

_____. *The Two Revolutions: Gramsci and the Dilemma of Western Marxism.* Boston: South End Press, 1984.

Bonomi, Giorgio. *Partito e rivoluzione in Gramsci.* Milan: Feltrinelli, 1976.

Bottomore, T. B. *Elites and Society.* London: Watt, 1964.

Broccoli, Angelo. *Antonio Gramsci e l'educazione come egemonia.* Florence: La Nuova Italia, 1972.

Buci-Glucksman, Christine. *Gramsci et l'Etat: pour une théorie matérialiste de la philosophie.* Paris: Fayard, 1975.

Buissière, Evelyne. "Il Machiavelli di Gramsci," *Critica marxista* 29, 6 (November-December 1991), 70-83.

Burckhardt, Jacob. *The Civilization of the Renaissance in Italy: An Essay.* Trans. S. G. C. Middlemere. London: George Allen and Unwin, 1965.

Burke, Peter. "Tacitism," *Tacitus.* Ed. T. A. Dorey. London: Routledge & Kegan Paul, 1969, 149-71.

Burnham, James. *The Machiavellians: Defenders of Freedom.* Chicago: Henry Regnery Company, 1970.

Buzzi, A. R. *La teoria politica di Gramsci.* Florence: La Nuova Italia, 1973.

Cammett, John. *Antonio Gramsci and the Origins of Italian Communism.* Stanford: Stanford University Press, 1967.

Carr, Wilden. *The Philosophy of Benedetto Croce.* New York: Russell and Russell, 1969.

Cary, Max. *A History of Rome.* London: Macmillan, 1962.

Cassirer, Ernst. *The Myth of the State.* New Haven: Yale University Press, 1973.

Catalano, Franco. "Le note sul Machiavelli di Antonio Gramsci," *Quarto Stato* 4, 22-23 (1-15 December 1949), 37-40.

Chabod, Federico. "Croce storico," in *Lezioni di metodo storico: con saggi su Egidi, Croce, Meinecke.* Ed. Luigi Firpo. Bari: Laterza, 1969, 179-253.

_____. *Machiavelli and the Renaissance.* New York: Harper Torchbooks, 1965.

_____. *Scritti su Machiavelli.* Turin: Einaudi, 1964.

Chemotti, Saveria. *Umanesimo, Rinascimento, Machiavelli nella critica gramsciana.* Rome: Bulzoni, 1975.

Cicero, Marcus Tullius. *On the Commonwealth.* Trans. with notes and introduction by George H. Sabine and Stanley B. Smith. Indianapolis: Bobbs-Merrill, 1970.

Cochrane, Eric. "Machiavelli: 1940-1960," *The Journal of Modern History* 33 (1961), 113-36.

Coletti, Lucio. *From Rousseau to Lenin.* Trans. John Merrington and Judith White. New York: Monthly Review Press, 1972.

Croce, Benedetto. *Il carattere della filosofia moderna.* Bari: Laterza, 1945.

_____. *Conversazioni critiche.* Vols. 2 and 4. Bari: Laterza, 1950-51.

_____. *Etica e politica.* Bari: Laterza, 1931.

_____. *Filosofia della pratica. Economica ed etica.* Bari: Laterza, 1957.

_____. *Filosofia e storiografia.* Bari: Laterza, 1949.

_____. "Gramsci era uno dei nostri." *Quaderni della critica* 3, 8 (July 1947).

_____. *Historical Materialism and the Economics of Karl Marx.* Trans. C. M. Meredith. Intro. A. D. Lindsay. New York: Russell and Russell, 1966. In Italian, *Materialismo storico ed economia marxistica.* Bari: Laterza, 1951.

_____. *History as the Story of Liberty.* Trans. Sylvia Sprigge. Chicago: Gateway Editions, 1970.

_____. *Indagini su Hegel e schiarimenti filosofici.* Bari: Laterza, 1952.

_____. *My Philosophy: Essays on the Moral and Political Problems of Our Time.* Selected by R. Klibansky. Trans. E. F. Carritt. New York: Collier Books, 1962.

———. *Nuove pagine sparse*. Naples: Ricciardi, 1949. Vol. I.

———. *Philosophy, Poetry, History: An Anthology of Essays*. Trans. with an introduction by Cecil Sprigge. Oxford: Oxford University Press, 1966; in Italian, *Filosofia, poesia, storia*. Ed. Benedetto Croce. Milan: Ricciardi, n.d.

———. *Saggio sullo Hegel*. Bari: Laterza, 1948.

———. *Storia dell'età barocca in Italia*. Bari: Laterza, 1957.

———. *Storia dell'Europa nel secolo decimonono*. Bari: Laterza, 1932.

———. *Storia d'Italia dal 1871 al 1915*. Bari: Laterza, 1967.

———. *Terze pagine sparse*. Bari: Laterza, 1955. 2 vols.

Curcio, Carlo. *Machiavelli nel Risorgimento*. Milan: Giuffrè, 1953.

Dahl, Robert A. "A Critique of the Ruling Elite Model," *American Political Science Review* 52 (1958), 369-463.

Davidson, Alastair B. *Antonio Gramsci: Towards an Intellectual Biography*. London: Merlin Press, 1977.

———. "Gramsci and Lenin, 1917-1922," *The Socialist Register*. London: Merlin Press, 1974.

———. "Gramsci and Reading Machiavelli," *Science and Society* 37, I (Spring 1973), 56-80.

Deane, Herbert A. *The Political and Social Ideas of St. Augustine*. New York: Columbia University Press, 1963.

De Grazia, Sebastian. *Machiavelli in Hell*. Princeton: Princeton University Press, 1989.

De Ruggiero, Guido. *The History of European Liberalism*. Trans. R. G. Collingwood. Boston: Beacon Press, 1967.

De Sanctis, Francesco. "La letteratura italiana nel secolo XIX," *Opere*. Ed. Niccolò Gallo. Milan: Ricciardi, 1961.

———. "Machiavelli Conferenze," *Saggi critici*. Ed. Luigi Russo. Bari: Laterza, 1965, vol. 2, pp. 309-38.

———. "La scuola democratica," *Opere*. Ed. Niccolò Gallo. Milan: Ricciardi, 1961, pp. 1115-25.

———. *Storia della letteratura italiana*. Ed. Benedetto Croce. Bari: Laterza, 1965. 2 vols.

———. "L'uomo del Guicciardini," *Saggi critici*. Ed. Luigi Russo. Bari: Laterza, 1965, vol. 3, pp. 1-23.

Ehrenberg, Victor. *From Solon to Socrates: Greek History and Civilization During the 6th and the 5th Centuries BC*. London: Methuen, 1973.

Entwistle, Harold. *Antonio Gramsci: Conservative Schooling for Radical Politics*. London: Routledge & Kegan Paul, 1979.

Ercole, Francesco. *La politica di Machiavelli*. Rome: A. R. E., 1926.

Femia, Joseph V. *Gramsci's Political Thought: Hegemony, Consciousness, and the Revolutionary Process*. Oxford: Clarendon Press, 1981.

Figgis, J. N. *Political Thought from Gerson to Grotius: 1414-1625*. New York: Harper Torchbooks, 1960.

Finley, M. I. *Economy and Society in Ancient Greece*. Harmondsworth: Penguin Books, 1981.

———. *Politics in the Ancient World*. Cambridge: Cambridge University Press, 1983.

Finocchiaro, Maurice A. *Gramsci and the History of Dialectical Thought*. Cambridge: Cambridge University Press, 1988.

———. "Gramsci's Crocean Marxism," *Telos* 41 (Fall 1979), 17-32.

Fleisher, Martin. "A Passion for Politics: The Vital Core of the World of Machiavelli," *Machiavelli and the Nature of Political Thought*. Ed. Martin Fleisher. New York: Atheneum, 1972.

Freeman, Edward A. *A History of Federal Government in Greece and Italy*. Ed. J. B. Bury. London: Macmillan, 1893.

Garin, Eugenio. *La cultura italiana tra '800 e '900*. Bari: Laterza, 1963.

———. *Italian Humanism: Philosophy and Civic Life in the Renaissance*. Trans. Peter Munz. New York: Harper and Row, 1965.

———. *Science and Civic Life in the Italian Renaissance*. Trans. Peter Munz. New York: Anchor Books, 1969.

212 Garosci, Aldo. "Croce e la politica," *Rivista storica italiana* 95, 2 (1983), 282-313.

———. *Pensiero politico e storiografia moderna: saggi di storia contemporanea.* Pisa: Nistri-Lischi, 1954.

Germino, Dante. *Antonio Gramsci: Architect of a New Politics.* Baton Rouge: Louisiana State University Press, 1990.

Gerratana, V. "Gramsci e Machiavelli," *Il Calendario del popolo,* 25, 299-300 (September-October 1969), 2779-82.

Gilbert, Allan H. *Machiavelli's "Prince" and Its Forerunners: "The Prince" as a Typical Book de regimine principium.* Durham, N.C.: Duke University Press, 1938.

Gilbert, Felix. "Bernardo Rucellai and the Orti Oricellari: A Study on the Origins of Modern Political Thought," *The Journal of the Warburg and Courtauld Institutes* 12 (1949), 101-31.

———. "The Composition and Structure of Machiavelli's *Discorsi,*" *The Journal of the History of Ideas* 14, 1 (1953), 136-56.

———. "The Concept of Nationalism in Machiavelli's Prince," *Studies in the Renaissance* 1 (1954), 38-48.

———. "The Humanist Concept of the Prince and the 'Prince' of Machiavelli," *Journal of Modern History* 11 (1939), 449-83.

———. *Machiavelli and Guicciardini: Politics and History in Sixteenth Century Florence.* Princeton: Princeton University Press, 1965.

———. "The Venetian Constitution and Florentine Political Thought." *Florentine Studies: Politics and Society in Renaissance Florence.* Ed. Nicolai Rubenstein. Evanston, Ill.: 1968, 463-500.

Gramsci, Antonio. *La formazione dell'uomo: Scritti di pedagogia.* Ed. Giovanni Urbani. Rome: Riuniti, 1974.

———. *Lettere dal carcere.* Ed. Sergio Caprioglio and Elsa Fubini. Turin: Einaudi, 1965.

———. *Letters from Prison by Antonio Gramsci.* Selected and trans. from the Italian and intro. by Lynne Lawner. New York: Harper & Row, 1973.

———. *The Modern Prince and Other Writings.* Ed., intro. and trans. Louis Marks. New York: International Publishers, 1957.

———. *Opere di Antonio Gramsci.* Turin: Einaudi, 1947-. This collection of twelve volumes includes the following:

  Lettere dal carcere, 1947.
  Il materialismo storico e la filosofia di Benedetto Croce, 1974.
  Gli intellettuali e l'organizzazione della cultura, 1966.
  Il Risorgimento, 1966.
  Note sul Machiavelli, sulla politica e sullo Stato moderno, 1966.
  Letteratura e vita nazionale, 1966.
  Passato e presente, 1974.
  Scritti giovanili, 1914-1918, 1975.
  L'Ordine Nuovo, 1919-1920, 1955.
  Sotto la Mole, 1916-1920, 1975.
  Socialismo e fascismo, L'Ordine Nuovo, 1921-1922, 1974.
  La costruzione del Partito comunista, 1923-1926, 1972.

———. *Prison Notebooks.* Vol. 1. Ed. and trans. with introduction by Joseph A. Buttigieg. New York: Columbia University Press, 1992.

———. *Quaderni del carcere.* Critical edition of the Gramsci Institute. Ed. Valentino Gerratana. Turin: Einaudi, 1975. 4 vols.

———. *Quaderno 13. Noterelle sulla politica di Machiavelli.* Intro. and notes by Carmine Donzelli. Turin: Einaudi, 1981.

———. *Quaderno 19. Risorgimento italiano.* Intro. and notes by Corrado Vivanti. Turin: Einaudi, 1977.

———. *Antonio Gramsci: Selections from Cultural Writings*. Ed. and intro. David Forgacs and Geoffrey Nowell-Smith. Trans. William Boelhower. Cambridge, Mass.: Harvard University Press, 1985.

———. *Antonio Gramsci: Selections from Political Writings*, 1910-1920. Ed. Quintin Hoare. Trans. John Mathews. New York: International Publishers, 1977.

———. *Antonio Gramsci: Selections from Political Writings*, 1921-1926. Ed. and trans. Quintin Hoare. New York: International Publishers, 1978.

———. *Selections from the Prison Notebooks of Antonio Gramsci*. Ed. and trans. Quintin Hoare and Geoffrey Nowell-Smith. New York: International Publishers, 1973.

———. *Scritti 1913-1926*. Turin: Einaudi, 1980-87. 4 vols. This collection of Gramsci's pre-prison writings includes the following:

    Cronache torinesi 1913-1917. Ed. Sergio Caprioglio. Turin: Einaudi, 1980.

    La città futura 1917-1918. Ed. Sergio Caprioglio. Turin: Einaudi, 1982.

    Il nostro Marx 1918-1919. Ed. Sergio Caprioglio. Turin: Einaudi, 1984.

    L'Ordine Nuovo 1919-1920. Ed. Valentino Gerratana and Antonio A. Santucci. Turin: Einaudi, 1987.

Gramsci e la cultura contemporanea. Proceedings of the international conference of Gramsci studies held in Cagliari 23-27 April 1967. Ed. Pietro Rossi. Rome: Riuniti-Istituto Gramsci, 1975. See especially the essays by Norberto Bobbio, "Gramsci e la concezione della società civile," vol. 1, pp. 75-100; Lamberto Borghi, "Educazione e scuola in Gramsci," vol. 1, pp. 207-38; Eugenio Garin, "Politica e cultura in Gramsci (il problema degli intellettuali," vol. 1, pp. 37-74; Mario Alighiero Manacorda, "La formazione del pensiero pedagogico di Gramsci 1915-1926," vol. 2, pp. 227-61; and Ernesto Ragionieri, "Gramsci e il dibattito teorico nel movimento operaio internazionale," vol. 2, pp. 101-47.

Gruppi, Luciano. "Machiavelli e Gramsci," *Critica marxista* 7, 3 (May-June 1969), 81-91.

Guicciardini, Francesco. *Dialogo e Discorsi del reggimento di Firenze*. Ed. R. Palmarocchi. Bari: Laterza, 1932.

———. *Maxims and Reflections*. Trans. Mario Domandi. Intro. by Nicolai Rubinstein. Philadelphia: University of Pennsylvania Press, 1972.

———. *Ricordi*. Critical edition. Ed. R. Spongano. Florence: Sansoni, 1951.

———. *Scritti politici e Ricordi*. Ed. R. Palmarocchi. Bari: Laterza, 1932.

Haimson, Leopold H. *The Russian Marxists and the Origins of Bolshevism*. Boston: Beacon Press, 1966.

Hall, A. R. *The Scientific Revolution 1500-1800: The Formation of the Modern Scientific Attitude*. Boston: Beacon Press, 1972.

Hegel, G. W. F. *Hegel's Lectures on the History of Philosophy*. Trans. E. S. Haldane and Frances H. Simson. New York: Humanities Press, 1974. Vol. 3.

———. *The Philosophy of History*. Trans. T. M. Knox. Oxford: Oxford University Press, 1960.

———. *Political Writings*. Trans. T. M. Knox. Oxford: Oxford University Press, 1964.

Hobsbawm, Eric J. "The Great Gramsci," *New York Review of Books* (4 April 1974), 39-44.

Hook, Sidney. *From Hegel to Marx: Studies in the Intellectual Development of Karl Marx*. Ann Arbor: University of Michigan Press, 1968.

———. *Marxism and Beyond*. Totowa, N.J.: Rowman & Littlefield, 1983.

Hughes, H. Stuart. *Consciousness and Society: The Reorientation of European Social Thought 1890-1930*. New York: Vintage Books, 1961.

Hughes, Serge. *The Fall and Rise of Modern Italy*. New York: Minerva Press, 1967.

Jacobitti, Edmund E. "Labriola, Croce, and Italian Marxism 1895-1910." *Journal of the History of Ideas* 36 (April-May 1975).

Jocteau, Gian Carlo. *Leggere Gramsci*. Milan: Feltrinelli, 1975.

Kamenev, L. B. "Preface to Machiavelli," *New Left Review* 15 (May-June 1962), 39-42.

214 Labedz, Leopold, ed. *Revisionism: Essays on the History of Marxist Ideas.* New York: Praeger, 1962.

Labriola, Antonio. *Scritti di pedagogia e di politica scolastica.* Ed. D. Bertoni Jovine. Rome: Riunite, 1961.

———. *Scritti filosofici e politici.* Ed. Franco Sbarberi. Turin: Einaudi, 1973. 2 vols.

La città futura: Saggi sulla figura e sul pensiero di Antonio Gramsci. Ed. Alberto Caracciolo and Gianni Scalia. Milan: Feltrinelli, 1976. See especially the essays by Emilio Agazzi, "Filosofia della prassi e filosofia dello spirito," pp. 95-175; Carlo Cicerchia, "Il rapporto col leninismo e il problema della rivoluzione italiana," pp. 19-43; Giuseppe Tamburrano, "Fasi di sviluppo del pensiero di Gramsci," pp. 47-67; and Mario Tronti, "Tra materialismo dialettico e filosofia della prassi," pp. 71-92.

Lichtheim, George. *Marxism: An Historical and Critical Study.* New York: Praeger, 1970.

Lombardi, Franco. *Idee pedagogiche di Antonio Gramsci.* Brescia: La Scuola Editrice, 1969.

Lombardo Radice, Lucio. *Educazione e rivoluzione.* Rome: Riuniti, 1976.

Lo Piparo, Franco. *Lingua, intellettuali, egemonia in Gramsci.* Bari: Laterza, 1979.

Lukács, Georg. *The Young Hegel: Studies in the Relations between Dialectics and Economics.* Trans. Rodney Livingstone. Cambridge: MIT Press, 1976.

Macciocchi, Maria Antonietta. *Per Gramsci.* Bologna: Il Mulino, 1974.

Machiavelli, Niccolò. *The Art of War.* Trans. Ellis Farnesworth. Rev. ed. Introduction by Neal Wood. Indianapolis: Bobbs-Merrill, 1978.

———. *Chief Works and Others.* Trans. Allan Gilbert. Durham, N.C.: Duke University Press, 1965. 3 vols.

———. *The Letters of Machiavelli.* Ed. and trans. Allan H. Gilbert. New York: Capricorn Books, 1961.

———. *Opere.* Ed. Sergio Bertelli and Franco Gaeta. Milan: Feltrinelli, 1960-65. 8 vols. This edition includes the following works:

    Il Principe e Discorsi sopra la prima deca di Tito Livio. Ed. Sergio Bertelli, 1960.

    Arte della guerra e scritti politici minori. Ed. Sergio Bertelli, 1961.

    Legazioni e commissarie. Ed. Sergio Bertelli, 1964. 3 vols.

    Lettere. Ed. Franco Gaeta, 1962.

    Istorie fiorentine. Ed. Franco Gaeta, 1962.

    Il teatro e tutti gli scritti letterari. Ed. Franco Gaeta, 1965.

———. *The Prince and the Discourses.* New York: Modern Library, 1950.

———. *Il Principe e pagine dei discorsi e delle Istorie.* Critical edition. Ed. Luigi Russo. Florence: Sansoni, n.d.

Machiavelli nel V centenario della nascita. Bologna: Boni, 1973. Noteworthy are the contributions by Raymond Aron, "Machiavel et Marx," pp. 11-30; Fredi Chiappelli, "Machiavelli segretario," pp. 45-60; Luigi Firpo, "Machiavelli politico," pp. 113-36; Franco Gaeta, "Machiavelli storico," pp. 139-53; Felix Gilbert, "Machiavelli in modern historical scholarship," pp. 157-71; Emile Namer, "Machiavel et l'humanisme politique," pp. 175-89.

McInnes, Neil. "From Marx to Marcuse," *Survey* 16, 1 (1971), 147-67.

Magri, Lucio. "Problems of the Marxist Theory of the Revolutionary Party." *New Left Review* 60 (March-April 1970), 97-128.

Manacorda, Mario Alighiero. *Il principio educativo in Gramsci: Americanismo e fordismo.* Rome: Riuniti, 1974.

Mansfield, Harry C. "Introduction," in his translation of Machiavelli's *The Prince.* Chicago: University of Chicago Press, 1985.

Marcuse, Herbert. *Reason and Revolution: Hegel and the Rise of Social Theory.* Boston: Beacon Press, 1968.

———. *Studies in Critical Philosophy.* Boston: Beacon Press, 1972.

Marx, Karl. *Karl Marx: Early Writings.* Ed. T. B. Bottomore. New York: McGraw-Hill, 1964.

———. *The Eighteenth Brumaire of Louis Bonaparte*. New York: International Publishers, 1963. **215**

———. *The Poverty of Philosophy*. New York: International Publishers, 1967.

———. "Theses on Feuerbach," *The German Ideology*. Marx and Engels. New York: International Publishers, 1968.

Marx, Karl, and Frederick Engels. *Collected Works*. New York: International Publishers, 1975, vols. 3, 4.

———. *The German Ideology*. New York: International Publishers, 1968.

———. *The Marx-Engels Reader*. Ed. Robert Tucker. New York: W. W. Norton, 1972.

———. *Selected Correspondence*. Trans. I. Lasker. Ed. S. Ryazanskaya. Moscow, 1965.

Matteucci, Nicola. *Antonio Gramsci e la filosofia della prassi*. Milan: Giuffrè, 1951.

———. "Partito e Consigli di fabbrica nel pensiero di Gramsci," *Il Mulino* 4, 4 (April 1955), 350-59.

Medici, Rita. *La Metafora Machiavelli: Mosca Pareto Michels Gramsci*. Modena: Mucchi Editore, 1990.

Meinecke, Friedrich. *Machiavellism: The Doctrine of Raison d'Etat and Its Place in Modern History*. Trans. Douglas Scott. New York: Praeger, 1965.

Merrington, John. "Theory and Practice in Gramsci's Marxism," *The Socialist Register*. London: Merlin Press, 1969, 145-76.

Miller, James Edward. *From Elite to Mass Politics: Italian Socialism in the Giolittian Era 1900-1914*. Kent, Ohio: Kent State University Press, 1990.

Momigliano, Attilio. "La critica," *La rassegna d'Italia* 1 (February-March 1946).

Mondolfo, R. *Il pensiero politico nel Risorgimento italiano*. Milan: Nuova Accademia, n.d.

———. *Umanesimo di Marx: studi filosofici 1908-1966*. Turin: Einaudi, 1968.

Morpurgo-Tagliabue, Guido. "Gramsci tra Croce e Marx," *Il Ponte* 4, 5 (May 1948), 429-38.

Mosca, Gaetano. *The Ruling Class*. Ed. and rev. A. Livingston. Trans. Hannah D. Kahn. New York: McGraw-Hill, 1939.

Mouffe, Chantal, ed. *Gramsci and Marxist Theory*. Boston: Routledge & Kegan Paul, 1979. See especially the essays by Biagio de Giovanni, "Lenin and Gramsci: state, politics, and party," pp. 259-88; Chantal Mouffe, "Hegemony and ideology in Gramsci," pp. 168-204; Massimo Salvadori, "Gramsci and the PCI: Two Conceptions of Hegemony," pp. 237-58; and Jacques Texier, "Gramsci, theoretician of the superstructures," pp. 48-79.

Mullett, Michael. *Radical Religious Movements in Early Modern Europe*. Boston: George Allen and Unwin, 1980.

Naïr, Sami. *Machiavel et Marx: fétichisme du pouvoir et passion du social*. Paris: Presses Universitaires de France, 1984.

Nardone, Giorgio. *Il pensiero di Gramsci*. Bari: De Donato, 1971.

Nietzsche, Friedrich. *Beyond Good and Evil*. Trans. with notes and introduction by Walter Kaufmann. New York: Vintage Books, 1966.

———. *Human, All Too Human*. Trans. Marion Farber with Stephen Lehmann. Intro. and notes by Marion Farber. Lincoln: University of Nebraska Press, 1984.

Olschki, Leonardo. *Machiavelli the Scientist*. Berkeley: The Gillick Press, 1945.

Orfei, R. *Antonio Gramsci: coscienza critica del marxismo*. Milan: Relazioni sociali, 1965.

Ottino, Carlo L. *Concetti fondamentali nella teoria politica di Antonio Gramsci*. Milan: Feltrinelli, 1956.

Paggi, Leonardo. *Antonio Gramsci e il moderno principe*. Rome: Riuniti, 1970.

———. "Gramsci's General Theory of Marxism," *Telos* 33 (Fall 1977), 27-70.

———. "Machiavelli e Gramsci," *Studi storici* 10, 4 (1969), 856-66.

Paolucci, Henry, ed. *The Political Writings of St. Augustine*. Chicago: Gateway Editions, 1970.

Parel, Anthony, ed. *The Political Calculus: Essays on Machiavelli's Philosophy*. Toronto: University of Toronto Press, 1972. See especially the essays by Anthony Parel, "Introduction: Machiavelli's Method and His Interpreters," pp. 3-32; Thomas Flanagan, "The Concept of For-

216   *tuna* in Machiavelli," pp. 127-56; John Plamenatz, "In Search of Machiavellian *Virtù*," pp. 157-78; and Neal Wood, "Machiavelli's Humanism of Action," pp. 33-57.

Piccone, Paul. "Gramsci's Hegelian Marxism," *Political Theory* 11 (January-February 1974), 32-45.

_____. "Gramsci's Marxism: Beyond Lenin and Togliatti," *Theory and Society* 3, 4 (Winter 1976), 485-512.

_____. *Italian Marxism*. Berkeley: University of California Press, 1983.

_____. "From Spaventa to Gramsci." *Telos* 31 (Spring 1977), 35-65.

Plamenatz, John. *Man and Society*. New York: McGraw-Hill, 1963. 2 vols.

Pocock, J. G. A. *The Machiavellian Moment: Florentine Political Thought and the Atlantic Republican Tradition*. Princeton: Princeton University Press, 1975.

Procacci, Giuliano. *Studi sulla fortuna del Machiavelli*. Rome: Istituto storico italiano, 1965.

Ricci, David M. *Community Power and Democratic Theory: The Logic of Political Analysis*. New York: Random House, 1971.

Richter, Melvin. "Despotism," *Dictionary of the History of Ideas*. New York: Charles Scribner's Sons, 1973, vol. 2, 1-18.

Roberts, David D. *Benedetto Croce and the Uses of Historicism*. Berkeley: University of California Press, 1987.

Rubinstein, Nicolai, ed. *Florentine Studies: Politics and Society in Renaissance Florence*. Evanston, Ill.: Northwestern University Press, 1968.

_____. "Machiavelli and the World of Florentine Politics," *Studies on Machiavelli*. Ed. Myron P. Gilmore. Florence: Sansoni, 1972.

_____. "Politics and Constitution in Florence at the End of the Fifteenth Century," *Italian Renaissance Studies*. Ed. E. F. Jacob. London: Faber and Faber, 1960.

Russo, Luigi. *Machiavelli*. Bari: Laterza, 1975.

_____, ed. Notes and introduction to *Il Principe e pagine dei Discorsi e delle Istorie*. Florence: Sansoni, n.d.

Saitta, Giuseppe. *Il pensiero italiano nell'Umanesimo e nel Rinascimento*. Florence: Sansoni, 1961. Vol. 3.

Salamini, Leonardo. "Gramsci and Marxist Sociology of Knowledge: An Analysis of Hegemony-Ideology-Knowledge," *The Sociological Quarterly* 15 (Summer 1974), 359-80.

_____. *The Sociology of Political Praxis: An Introduction to Gramsci's Theory*. London: Routledge & Kegan Paul, 1981.

Salomone, A. William. *Italy in the Giolittian Age*. Philadelphia: University of Philadelphia Press, 1960.

Salvadori, Massimo. *Gramsci e il problema storico della democrazia*. Turin: Einaudi, 1973.

Sanguineti, Federico. *Gramsci e Machiavelli*. Rome: Laterza, 1982.

Sartori, Giovanni. *Stato e politica nel pensiero di Benedetto Croce*. Naples: Morano, 1966.

Sasso, Gennaro. "Antonio Gramsci, interprete di Machiavelli," *Lo spettatore italiano* 3, 4 (April 1950), 91-93.

_____. *Niccolò Machiavelli: storia del suo pensiero*. Naples: Nella sede dell'Istituto, 1958.

_____. *Il pensiero politico di Niccolò Machiavelli*. Turin: ERI, 1964.

Sassoon, Anne Showstack. *Gramsci's Politics*. Minneapolis: University of Minnesota Press, 1987.

Schapiro, Leonard. *The Communist Party of the Soviet Union*, 2d ed. New York: Random House, 1971.

Schellase, Kenneth C. *Tacitus in Renaissance Political Thought*. Chicago: University of Chicago Press, 1976.

Schumpeter, Joseph A. *Capitalism, Socialism and Democracy*. New York: Harper, 1942.

Seigel, Jerrold. "'Civic Humanism' or Ciceronian Rhetoric? The Culture of Petrarch and Bruni," *Past and Present* 34 (1966), 7-78.

———. *Rhetoric and Philosophy in Renaissance Humanism*. Princeton: Princeton University Press, **217** 1968.

Sinclair, T. A. *A History of Greek Political Thought*. Cleveland: Meridien Books, 1968.

Skinner, Quentin. *The Foundations of Modern Political Thought*. Cambridge: Cambridge University Press, 1978. 2 vols.

———. "The idea of negative liberty: philosophical and historical perspectives," *Philosophy in History*. Ed. Richard Rorty, J. B. Schneewind, and Quentin Skinner. Cambridge: Cambridge University Press, 1990, pp. 193-221.

———. *Machiavelli*. New York: Hill and Wang, 1981.

Spitz, Lewis W. *The Protestant Reformation*. New York: Harper and Row, 1985.

Spriano, Paolo. *Storia del Partito comunista italiano*. Vol. I, *Da Bordiga a Gramsci*. Turin: Einaudi, 1967.

Strauss, Leo. *Thoughts on Machiavelli*. Chicago: University of Chicago Press, 1978.

Studi gramsciani. Proceedings of a conference held in Rome 11-13 January 1958. Compiled by the Istituto Gramsci. Rome: Riuniti, 1973. See especially the essays by Eugenio Garin, "Antonio Gramsci nella cultura italiana," 3-14; Palmiro Togliatti, "Il leninismo nel pensiero e nell'azione di A. Gramsci," 15-36; Norberto Bobbio, "Nota sulla dialettica in Gramsci," 73-86; Salvatore Graziano, "Alcune considerazioni intorno all'umanismo di Gramsci," 149-64. Serafino Cambareri, "Il concetto di egemonia nel pensiero di A. Gramsci," 87-94; Alfredo Sabetti, "Il rapporto uomo-natura nel pensiero di Gramsci e la fondazione della scienza," 243-52; Giuseppe Tamburrano, "Gramsci e l'egemonia del proletariato," 277-86; Eugenio Garin, "Gramsci nella cultura italiana," 395-418; and Palmiro Togliatti, "Gramsci e il leninismo," 419-44.

Syme, Ronald. *The Roman Revolution*. Oxford: Oxford University Press, 1939.

Tacitus, Publius Cornelius. *The Complete Works of Tacitus*. New York: Modern Library, 1950.

Tamburrano, Giuseppe. *Antonio Gramsci: la vita, il pensiero, l'azione*. Manduria: Lacaita, 1963.

Taylor, Lily Ross. *Party Politics in the Age of Caesar*. Berkeley: University of California Press, 1961.

Thucydides. *The Peloponnesian War*. Trans. Benjamin Jowett. Introductory essays by Hanson Baldwin and Moses Hadas. New York: Bantam Books, 1960.

Toffanin, Giuseppe. *Machiavelli e il "Tacitismo": la "politica storica" al tempo della Controriforma*. Padova: A. Draghi, 1921.

Togliatti, Palmiro. *Gramsci*. Rome: Riuniti, 1967.

Vigna, Carmelo. "Gramsci e l'egemonia. Una interpretazione metapolitica." In *Antonio Gramsci: il pensiero teorico politico, la "questione leninista."* 2 vols. Ed. Virgilio Melchiorre, Carmelo Vigna, and Gabriele de Rosa. Rome: Città Nuova Editrice, 1979, vol. I, pp. 11-69.

Villari, Pasquale. *The Life and Times of Niccolò Machiavelli*. Trans. Linda Villari. London: T. F. Unwin, 1892.

Whitfield, J. H. *Machiavelli*. New York: Russell and Russell, 1965.

Williams, Gwyn A. "The Concept of 'Egemonia' in the Thought of Antonio Gramsci: Some Notes on Interpretation," *Journal of the History of Ideas* 21, 4 (October-December 1960), 586-99.

Wolin, Sheldon. S. *Politics and Vision: Continuity and Innovation in Western Political Thought*. Boston: Little, Brown and Company, 1960.

Wood, Neal. *Cicero's Social and Political Thought*. Berkeley: University of California Press, 1988.

———. "Introduction," *The Art of War* by Niccolò Machiavelli. Rev. ed. Ellis Farnesworth Translation. Indianapolis: Bobbs-Merrill, 1978.

———. "Machiavelli's Concept of Virtù Re-considered," *Political Studies* 15 (1967), 159-72.

Index

219

Benedetto Fontana teaches political science at Baruch College, the City University of New York. He is currently working on several manuscripts on the influence of classical political thought on contemporary concepts of politics.